T0406096

The Making of Identity through Rural Space

Scenarios, Experiences, and Contestations

Kulturelle und technische Werte historischer Bauten
Hg. von Klaus Rheidt und Werner Lorenz

Band 10

Vera Egbers, Özge Sezer (eds.)

The Making of Identity through Rural Space

Scenarios, Experiences, and Contestations

Birkhäuser · Basel

This publication is funded by the German Research Foundation (DFG) in the framework of the Research Training Group 1913 «Cultural and Technological Significance of Historic Buildings», Brandenburg University of Technology Cottbus–Senftenberg; Leibniz Institute for Research on Society and Space, Erkner; Department of Archaeology at Humboldt University of Berlin.

Concept: Vera Egbers, Özge Sezer
Project coordination: Albrecht Wiesener, Sophia Hörmannsdorfer
Copyediting: William Hatherell
Layout, typesetting, and editing: Sophia Hörmannsdorfer
Cover design: Jörg Denkinger
Printing and binding: Beltz Grafische Betriebe GmbH, Bad Langensalza
Cover illustration: Yeniköy village, Turkey. Street view of the part built in the Early Republican Period, 2016 (photo by Özge Sezer)

Library of Congress Control Number: 2024945034

Bibliographic information published by the German National Library
The German National Library lists this publication in the Deutsche Nationalbibliografie; detailed bibliographic data is available on the Internet at http://dnb.dnb.de.

The book is also available as an ebook (ISBN 978-3-0356-2790-9).

ISBN 978-3-0356-2788-6

© 2025 Birkhäuser Verlag GmbH, Basel
P.O. Box 44, 4009 Basel, Switzerland
Part of Walter de Gruyter GmbH, Berlin/Boston

Contents

The Making of Identity through Rural Space
Scenarios, Experiences, and Contestations

Attempts to convert and shape rural Turkey through modernization and nationalization were on the rise in various state programs starting from the late 19th century and continuing up until today. Under the imperial authority of the late Ottoman State, rural communities were designated within the scheme of a new national identity referred to as «Muslim Anatolia.» During the subsequent foundation of the republican nation-state, the economic, demographic, and socio-cultural remodeling of the country by the Kemalist regime also led towards governmental endeavors directed at the rural population, which had experienced the exhaustion of the wars, diaspora and deportations, population exchanges, and severe underdevelopment at the beginning of the 20th century. Despite different state ideologies, the main motivations behind the governing practices targeting rural communities exhibit similarities throughout the changing political periods in Turkey as well as in different nations across Europe. Particularly important were motivations and state interventions that can be described as attempts to colonize subjects living in rural areas, which often found their material expression in the creation of top-down planned settlements throughout the 20th century. Moreover, the tradition of including rural communities in governments' political agendas remained strong during the post-war period, with greater emphasis on technical and infrastructural interventions. This «spatial translation» of the state's ideological agenda on the physical environment of the inhabitants can be regarded as a method of communicating the state's «Governmentality»[1] nonverbally on the subtle stage of bodily experience.

In an attempt to further investigate the ways in which rural communities were planned and constantly re-shaped through times of political unrest and radical transformation from the late 19th century up until today, we invited an array of scholars to participate in an international symposium held online on 28 and 29 October 2021, at the DFG Research Training Group 1913 «Cultural and Technological Significance of Historic Buildings» of the Brandenburg University of Technology Cottbus-Senftenberg (Germany). This book, *The Making of Identity through Rural Space: Scenarios, Experiences, and Contestations in the Rural Built Environment*, is the outcome of this symposium of the same name (fig. 1).

1 Poster of the 2021 International Symposium that initiated this book project.

2   «Young immigrants preparing to milk their cows»: image from one of the propagandist journals of early Republican Turkey, *La Turquie Kemaliste*, promoting the agricultural productivity fostered by new rural communities that migrated to Turkey and settled in planned settlements designated by the state.

The impetus to address «identity-making through rural space» stemmed from our joint postdoctoral research on rural Turkey in the 20th century at BTU Cottbus-Senftenberg and aimed at bringing together scholars working on similar questions in different regional contexts. Though sometimes overlooked and underestimated, rural space has substantially influenced social, cultural, economic, and ideological changes. This role can be studied by looking at the (re)production of spatial agents caused by direct or indirect political interventions in rural communities. In this book, scholars looking at case studies from Turkey, Italy, Portugal, and Austria discuss the making of identity in and through rural areas, which have dramatically

changed under different political, social, and economic conditions from the turn of the 20th century up until today. By focusing on potential contestations related to such changes, the authors provide a better in-depth understanding of the complex spatial dynamics underlying the cultural and social spheres of 20th-century rurality in parts of Europe and Turkey (figs. 2 and 3).

The concept of identity plays a prominent role in cultural studies and public life, especially in connection with discourses of exclusion. We know this today, for instance, through the building of fences and the weaponizing of landscapes by nations of the so-called Global North to detain or kill migrants and refugees,[2] or through heated debates about sex and gender where the right to self-identification is threatened. In this context, research on «identity» takes place particularly within the fields of postcolonialism and feminism.[3] But negotiations of collective identities and related questions of who and what is or is not part of such a group were already highly significant in the rapidly changing political landscape of the 20th century, where former colonies fought for independence, new nation-states were formed, monarchies overthrown, with drastic, often violent or even revolutionary changes in political and social systems in countries around the world. This turbulent century still influences debates and struggles around identity today.

Another recurring theme when researching rural areas of the 19th/20th centuries can be summarized under the term of «Internal Colonization» – a term used to describe a method for governing the people, found in different ideological and political contexts and aiming to carry modernist interventions into rural areas and building new communities loyal to the authorities. «Internal Colonization» – as an actively intervening form of «Internal Colonialism» – is strongly related to the modern territoriality of emerging nation-states as well as to the political and economic dismantling of imperial states starting from the 19th century. If territoriality refers to an administrative reach over the demarcation of a specific land, whose sovereignty is claimed,[4] then colonizing the inner territories through social and economic programs promotes the legitimation of state power, and evolves into a shared approach to modernization and nationalization.

The first interpretations of Internal Colonialism and its territorial relations were introduced by Vladimir Lenin within the framework of Marxist theory, defining the concept within the capitalist system in the territorial boundaries of the Russian Empire in the 19th century. Without referring to any ethnic, cultural or demographic notions, Lenin used the term «internal colonies» to refer to some particular border areas in which the agrarian production served the world market.[5] On the other hand, Antonio Gramsci formulated the Internal

3　A view of Muratlı Village, a rural settlement built for immigrants in Tekirdağ.

Innenkolonisation und Gartenstadt

Hier eine rein landwirtschaftliche Bestrebung mit dem Ziel der Schaffung landwirtschaftlichen Kleinbesitzes, dort eine Bestrebung auf dem Gebiete der städtischen Wohnungsfrage mit dem Ziele industrieller Dezentralisation und dezentralisierten weiträumigen Wohnens. Das eine erscheint vom andern so wesensverschieden, daß man kaum an Berührungspunkte glauben sollte.

Und doch sind sie vorhanden.

Bereits die Wurzel beider Bestrebungen ist die gleiche, nämlich die ungeheure Abwanderung vom platten Lande in die Städte, die Umfänge angenommen hat, daß ihr gegenüber die ehemaligen Völkerwanderungen ein Kinderspiel sind. Diese Abwanderung droht einerseits mit einer Entvölkerung des Landes und bedingt dadurch die Innenkolonisation. Und auf der andern Seite zeitigt sie die Überfüllung unserer Großstädte mit den Folgeerscheinungen gedrängten, ungesunden und teuren Wohnens und völliger Naturentfremdung und ruft in der Gartenstadt einen Helfer gegen diese Mißstände herbei. Unser großstädtisches Wohnungsproblem würde nie so schwierige Formen angenommen haben, wenn es möglich gewesen wäre, diesen ständigen Strom vom Lande zur Stadt durch eine kräftige Bewegung der Innenkolonisa-

tion abzudämmen. In der Bekämpfung unseres großstädtischen Wohnungselends erweisen sich also Gartenstadtbewegung und Innenkolonisation als Bundesgenossen. Beide streben, wenn auch auf verschiedenen Wegen eine gleichmäßigere, volkswirtschaftlich wie individuell gesundere Bevölkerungsverteilung an.

Doch nicht nur in der Wurzel, sondern auch in der äußeren Gestaltung bestehen Berührungspunkte zwischen beiden Bewegungen. Dies gilt namentlich von dem Gartenstadtplan Howards, wie auch von der ersten englischen Gartenstadt Letchworth. Nach Howard soll die Gartenstadt aus sanitären, kulturellen und wirtschaftlichen Gründen einer Größenbeschränkung unterliegen und einen landwirtschaftlichen, der Stadt gehörigen Gürtel haben, der ein Vielfaches des Wohngebiets betragen soll. Denn nur eine große, stets der Landeskultur gewidmete, baufreie Zone sichert eine gesunde Ansiedlung und stetigen Konnex mit der Natur. Sie gewährt auch ganz neue Bedingungen für die Landwirtschaft, die in dem Markt und dem technischen Rüstzeug der Stadt neue Hilfsquellen findet. In Letchworth entfallen auf das Wohngebiet 2000 Morgen und auf den landwirtschaftlichen Gürtel der Stadt 4400 Morgen. Und dieser Gürtel wird planmäßig für landwirtschaftlichen Kleinbesitz (small holdings)

4   During the first years of the 20th century, the concept of Internal Colonization emerged as an important topic in several disciplines, including spatial planning. The discourse was carried out by architects, urban planners, and ruralists contributing to the discussion around the concept. *Gartenstadt*, the periodical promoting the German Garden City movement, also considered Internal Colonization as a planning tool to form new rural communities, offering an alternative to the centralization of the population in urban areas.

Colonialism concept within the definition of cultural and economic hegemony of a particular group dominating other groups within the territorial borders of a country. Gramsci used the example of the social differences between the northern and southern parts of Italy, where small towns in a semi-feudal agrarian structure were located in the south and the capitalist bourgeoisie arose in the north. This distinction resulted in first an

economic, then cultural, inequality between the two regions. According to Gramsci, southern Italy occurred as an «Internal Colony,» providing agrarian products and raw materials for industrial and urban mechanisms, as well as being culturally and politically dominated by the intellectuals of the capitalist cities in the northern region.[6]

Neo-Marxist sociologist Michael Hechter carried his interpretation of «Internal Colonialism» to state-power relations. According to Hechter, «Internal Colonialism,» unlike «Colonialism,» describes an exploitative system where the periphery (the rural regions) is located in the position of the colony by the core (the metropolis) within the state territoriality, owing to non-parallel economic developments that result in a «cultural division of labour» in the cities versus the rural areas. For the internal colonial model, nationalism plays a significant role in connecting the core and the periphery, which have been detached in terms of economic and/or social inequalities, and nationalism also generates the controlling power of governmental acts in the peripheral regions as a form of political organization. In this sort of organization, a «distinctive ethnic identity in the peripheral group» is dissolved and people are assimilated into politically and socially unified groups. With Internal Colonialism, the state generates

(1) the degree of administrative integration, (2) the extensiveness of citizenship in the periphery, (3) the prestige of the peripheral culture, (4) the existence of the geographical contiguity, (5) the length of the association between the periphery and the core.[7]

While Michael Hechter introduces «Internal Colonialism» as a sociological method to understand the governing of Celtic nations in the UK, Marshall Gordon points to the internationality of the concept, using the examples of African-American policies in the United States, as well as exploitative strategies towards the peasantry through «forced collectivization» in the Soviet states.[8]

Following this line of thought, as a planning strategy, «Internal Colonization» generated active enforcement in the peripheral, mostly rural, territories by implementing new settlement schemes, modern infrastructure, and progressive social programs with the great aim of modernizing and nationalizing the people within state borders – hence trying to reinforce a loyalty to the ruling elites by the invention of a modern, national identity that conceals class struggles and inequalities. The analytical aspects made the concept adaptable to various geographical, political, and socio-economic conditions. With considerable replication during the first half of the 20th century, «Internal Colonization» projects took on a global context (fig. 4).[9]

The reclamation and establishment of new agrarian towns in the Pontine Marshes in Italy during the fascist period,[10] agricultural expansions of the American «New Deal» during the 1930s (fig. 5),[11] rural housing campaigns in the Silesia region during the Weimar Republic of Germany (fig. 6),[12] the restoration of agrarian land in north-west Germany to construct new rural communities of National Socialists (fig. 7),[13] new ruralist programs to regenerate the peasantry in Romania after the First World War,[14] and the Soviet approaches to rule the rural regions in accordance with the altering perspectives of the so-called «Agrarian Question» dating from the late 19th century[15] become critical examples of «Internal Colonization» as reflected in the built environment. They help to draw a genuine comparison line with «Internal Colonization» projects in Turkey that are also repeated as spatial practices aimed at development through the economic, political, and social regulation of the rural population.

Instead of solely focusing on urban centers as motors for socio-political change, this book focuses particularly on the role of rural areas as both a political tool and a social agent of identity-making processes from the 20th century up until today. In European history, the 20th century ushered in profound shifts, marked notably by urbanization and industrialization. Agriculture and rural life were relegated to the periphery as urban centers burgeoned, and technology became the centerpiece

of societal progress. This transformation reshaped landscapes, distancing individuals from their rural heritage both spatially and cognitively.[16]

Yet, immediately after World War I, rural areas emerged as experimental pathways for social, economic, and political development by bolstering food production, safeguarding border regions, enhancing (rural) infrastructure, and integrating rural populations into «modernized» societal schemes. In many cases, local authorities, government officials, politicians, scientists, and farmers participated in the discussions about the future of rural communities, envisioning ideal rural communities and efficient agricultural sectors through planning and engineering models. Policymakers, experts, and rural residents shared a belief in the progress that drove the endeavors for advanced governance and welfare independent of

5   Diane Ghirardo's contribution examines the political systems of planned communities in New Deal America and Fascist Italy. It has sparked an eye-opening discussion on the recurring pattern of identity-making tactics through planning strategies and architectural implementations in these relatively different contexts.

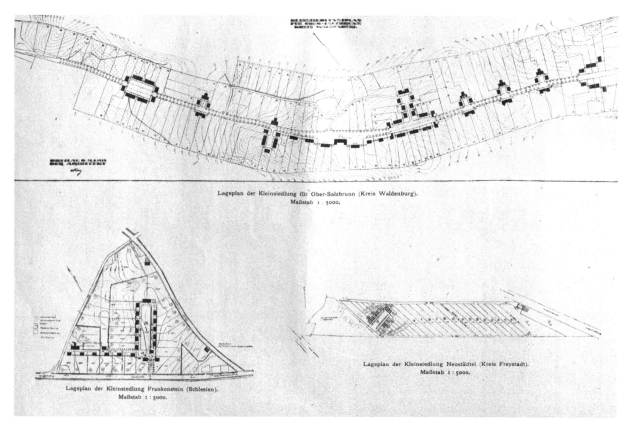

6   The Rural Housing Program of the Weimar Republic exemplifies the implementation of identity-making policies through space imme-
diately following World War I. Breslau state architect Ernst May planned settlements in the Silesian region on the western border (Ober-
Salzbrunn, Frankenstein, Freystadt) for the government to establish new German rural communities, aiming to reflect German and
Silesian identities in housing design and planning.

7   Although state forms and ideologies differed, shaping identity through rural space was a common practice. One of the most prominent propaganda campaigns of the Nazi era involved promoting rural life through the development of agricultural techniques. In the
mid-1930s, the Nazi state reclaimed several lands to implement this agenda. These two images show the settlement plan of ‹Hermann-
Göring-Koog› and a farmhouse under construction following the land reclamation in Schleswig-Holstein in 1935.

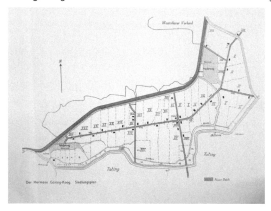

geographical location or political situation.[17] This dynamism also encouraged the shaping of demographies closely attached to the identity-making policies of the rural communities.

It goes without saying that rural space in this context is not simplistically understood as a given physical territoriality within which a simple identity-forming affiliation is given.[18] In the social sciences, an understanding of space dominates, conceptualized as a complex entity first produced by different and often conflicting interests, including built space and the natural sphere.[19]

We cannot deny that the examination of rural space sheds light on historical trajectories and fuels contemporary debates surrounding the evolution of rural societies. The connotation of «rural» did not often transcend its agricultural roots and association with rural employment until the late 20th century in Europe and its territories. However, as Fernando Collantes says, «rural is not agricultural» anymore.[20] The historical pathways leading to this paradigm shift remain largely uncharted. Agriculture became an underdeveloped sector in many countries as a substantial occupational activity compared to non-agricultural enterprises. This trend has been coupled with the consequential decline in relative living standards within rural areas. Depopulation emerged as a pivotal factor shaping the rural economic landscape, albeit at the expense of social cohesion and territorial integrity. This transition underscores the intricate interplay between economic shifts, demographic trends, and social dynamics, highlighting the multifaceted nature of rural identity-formation amidst evolving socio-economic landscapes.[21]

Our Approach

During the preparation for our symposium, and even before, as we formulated our research project, we drew inspiration from studies focusing on various aspects of reshaping rural space

8   The MODSCAPES Conference, held in 2018 in Tartu, brought together researchers from various disciplines to investigate how modernist planning strategies reshaped the rural landscape in Europe from the early 20th century.

through large-scale state projects, such as land reclamation, colonization, and agricultural development plans. Through these studies, we familiarized ourselves with the schemes, actors, and tools that were shared and created a pattern, particularly within the European cultural and historical context. Drawing from diverse disciplines including architectural history, archaeology, heritage studies, anthropology, and history, our contributors investigate key questions surrounding the production and reproduction of

9 *Governing the Rural in Interwar Europe*, edited by Liesbeth van de Grift and Amalia Forclaz, is another valuable resource that examines identity-making politics in the European context. This publication focuses on the interaction between political and social factors and rural populations in the formation of new communities during the interwar period in Europe.

rural space, the diverse array of agents involved in identity-formation, and the spatial conflicts that arise from intersecting identities and interests. By engaging in this multidisciplinary dialogue, we aim to deepen our understanding of the intricate spatial dynamics that underpin the construction of identities within rural contexts (figs. 8, 9, and 10).

Before introducing the contributions to this publication, we want to briefly mention three outstanding papers that were presented at our symposium. Although not represented with a chapter here, they gave valuable input during the conference and thereby also in the formation and conceptualization of this publication project. Hence, we decided to include a short overview over these talks as they were crucial in the discourse surrounding *The Making of Identity through Rural Space.*

Liesbeth van de Grift presented her lecture, «Reconfiguring Rural Spaces, Remaking Rural Communities,» on land reclamation and its political agendas during the interwar period.[22] To generate a discussion on identity-making policies through rural space, her research helped us to comprehend historical dynamics focused on the European landscape. Van de Grift demonstrated the different facets of the land reclamation, emphasizing the mastery of nature and societal perfectibility in 1930s Netherlands. She highlighted the ideological use of rural communities for national identity-building and agriculture's pivotal role therein. Responding to her research, we discussed evolving perspectives on land reclamation, from political structures to rural actors' concerns, such as self-conceptualization and environmental appreciation. The discourse extended the need to address shifts in governance modes and conflicts arising from conservation policies (for instance Natura 2000),[23] and contemporary challenges such as land use conflicts, biodiversity loss, rural marginalization, and the rise of political extremism.

Hollyamber Kennedy presented another path to our debate and broadened the concept of Internal Colonization within the framework of colonial studies. Through her lecture, «Wasteland of Empire: Reclamation and the Rural as Agent and Medium,»[24] she emphasized spatial infrastructures and mass population movements driven by state hegemony. Kennedy elucidated how rural modernization, integral to broader modernization efforts, unfolded through territorial, demographic, political, and economic processes. Highlighting the emergency of land reclamation as a transnational tool for state-led place-making amidst population upheavals from the late 19th century onwards, she demonstrated the contested nature of rural space, noting its historical role in state sovereignty and nation-building, and underscored the manipulation of rural landscapes for economic and cultural ends, often framing rural populations as subaltern within a settler colonial context. Drawing parallels between colonial and rural architecture, Kennedy illustrated how both were employed as tools of identity construction. This perspective helped us to better comprehend and define the structure of this project.

On the other hand, **Ian Kuijt** and **Ayşe Bursalı** enlightened another facet of the dynamics of place-making strategies by delving into the intricate relationship between people and the rural environment. They presented their research, «From Houses to Ruins to Movie Sets: Negotiating Identity through Resettlement and Architectural Change in a Turkish Village,»[25] exploring how rural landscapes shape social contacts, and hence identity. They employed a comparative approach to uncover commonalities and differences across diverse rural contexts, aiming to understand the impact of rural transformation on individuals. In doing so, they examined a village community, which relocated due to a natural disaster. Kuijt and Bursalı detailed the villagers' adaptation to their new settlement, highlighting the preservation of their cultural identity through architectural reuse and the commemoration of their old village's ruins. This case clearly illustrated the dynamic interplay between identity, space, and the resilience strategies employed by rural communities.

Within the framework of our 2021 symposium, these three additional studies helped us to design this book project as a discussion on making identity through rural space. The articles contributed to this book represent a range of studies that

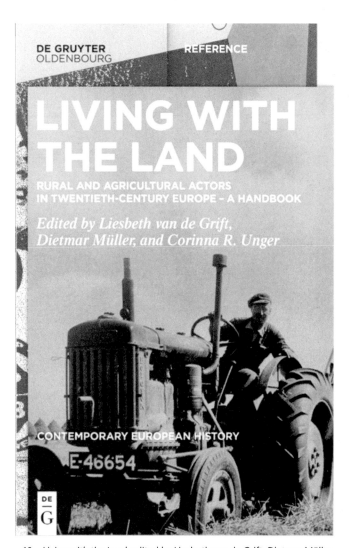

10   *Living with the Land*, edited by Liesbeth van de Grift, Dietmar Müller, and Corinna R. Unger, provides a comprehensive exploration of the formation of rural life within the historical and cultural context of 20th Century Europe.

are guided by a commitment to eschew historical closure, recognizing the enduring impact of past processes on contemporary realities. By adopting top-down and bottom-up perspectives, we seek to illuminate the complex interplay between historical legacies and present-day realities, offering fresh insights into the multifaceted nature of rural identity-formation and its enduring resonance in contemporary discourse.

Contributions

The book begins with **Paolo Gruppuso**'s exploration of «Landscape and Identity in-the-Making» within the Reclamation District of Agro Pontino, south of Rome, in fascist Italy. Gruppuso unveils the complexities of rural–urban dynamics as he navigates the transformation of the Pontine Marshes into the bustling urban center of Latina, shedding light on the blurred boundaries between rural and urban identities. Through ethnographic and historical analysis, Gruppuso unveils the layers of contested politics and identity within the reclaimed marshlands and tackles the topic of «ruralization.»

Continuing the exploration of landscape dynamics, **Cristina Pallini** and **Aleksa Korolija**'s chapter, «Embedding Apulian Landscapes of Nomadism into Rural Modernization Schemes,» delves into another large-scale reclamation project implemented under Italy's fascist regime. They illuminate the complexity of settlement planning in the Apulian Tableland, which fused planning and architecture through experimental endeavors as well as divergent modernization strategies. This chapter demonstrates the impacts of an «integral reclamation» through a case study that unveils a new field for research on this topic.

Marta Prista's contribution «Virtualities of Internal Colonization: Modernity as Heritage in-the-Making?» looks at Portuguese internal colonization within the context of the dictatorship, the Estado Novo (New State). Prista specifically examines the intersection of nationalism, colonialism and historical myth surrounding Portugal's imperial past and rural values. Using the modernity–coloniality framework, this chapter integrates political history, memory studies, and heritage studies through micro-ethnographic methods, and provides insight into rural development and cultural preservation amidst colonial legacies.

In «The Memory of Houses,» **Eva Maria Froschauer** navigates the fraught history of South Tyrolean settlements in Northern Tyrol, revealing the enduring legacies of geopolitical conflicts and forced labor in rural architecture. Through the lens of Felix Mitterer's play «Verkaufte Heimat,» Froschauer navigates the tensions between historical memory and contemporary redevelopment, shedding light on the charged narratives embedded within rural housing estates.

This examination of memory embedded within rural settlements resonates with **Ayşegül Dinççağ Kahveci**'s study, «The «Museum House» Phenomenon of Imbros,» which explores the preservation of traditional houses as repositories of collective memory within diasporic communities in Turkey. Through ethnographic research, Dinççağ Kahveci reveals the role of material culture in constructing a sense of belonging and continuity within transnational communities.

Özge Sezer and **Vera Egbers**' analysis of «Identity Policies in a Nutshell» offers insights into the top-down planning of rural settlements in Turkey, tracing the legacy of late Ottoman and early Republican interventions in the attempt to actively shape a national identity. Through the lens of postcolonial human geography, Egbers and Sezer – similar to Dinççağ Kahveci's paper – investigate the agency of marginalized rural populations in negotiating competing visions of modernity and nationhood.

Finally, **Mayowa Willoughby**'s «Thickening the Plot and Queering the Plantation» delves into the complexities of black identity formation in contemporary Turkey, tracing its roots to the manumission and resettlement of enslaved Africans in western and southwestern Anatolia. Through a nuanced analysis of historical conditions and contemporary experiences, Willoughby illuminates the enduring legacies of forced labor and freedom in shaping rural livelihoods and survival strategies. While introducing the conducted research, Willoughby invites the reader on a journey to African-descended communities today and reflects upon the roots of these particular identities created under different states through time.

Together, these chapters provide a diverse array of perspectives on the complex interplay between landscapes, identities, and historical narratives, highlighting the multifaceted process of identity-formation amidst transformative events. Employing interdisciplinary scholarship and nuanced analysis, the anthology prompts readers to reflect on the reciprocal relationship between landscapes and the intricate dynamics of politics, culture, and memory.

Acknowledgements

We express our gratitude to all participants of the 2021 International Symposium, *The Making of Identity through Rural Space: Scenarios, Experiences, and Contestations*, whose insightful contributions and discussions provided the cornerstone for this volume. The symposium was organized by the editors of this volume within the framework of the DFG Research Training Group «Cultural and Technological Significance of Historic Buildings» at Brandenburg University of Technology Cottbus-Senftenberg. We extend our heartfelt thanks to the members of the group whose collaborative efforts were instrumental in shaping the conference, and hence this book.

We also acknowledge the invaluable input of the peer reviewers, whose feedback enriched the texts and strengthened arguments. Special recognition goes to the series editors Klaus Rheidt and Werner Lorenz for their indispensable role in bringing this volume to fruition, as well as to Sophia Hörmannsdorfer for her expertise in layout, typesetting, and coordination, and William Hatherell for his meticulous copy editing.

Furthermore, we are most grateful for the unwavering support of Katja Richter, Arielle Thürmel, and Kerstin Protz from Birkhäuser Verlag. Their assistance has been invaluable in the publication process.

Berlin, July 2024
Vera Egbers, Özge Sezer

1   Foucault 1991.
2   De Léon / Wells 2015.
3   Castro Varela / Dhawan 2015, 45, 163.
4   Giddens 1987.
5   Lenin 1977; van de Grift 2015.
6   Gramsci 1971; Buci-Gluksmann 1979.
7   Hechter 1975.
8   Marshall 1993.
9   van de Grift 2015.
10 See Paolo Gruppuso's contribution in this volume.
11 Ghirardo 1989.
12 Henderson 2002.
13 Trende 2011.
14 Muşat 2015.
15 Bruisch 2018.
16 Unger et al. 2022, 4.
17 van de Grift / Ribi Forclaz 2018, xi.
18 The French Marxist human geographer Henri Lefebvre was famously one of the first scholars who characterized space as a product instead of a mere given material backdrop (Lefebvre 1991, Lefebvre 2000 [1974]).
19 Bernbeck / Egbers 2019, 60. In this context, see Bachmann-Medick 2014 on the so-called «spatial turn.»
20 Collantes 2007, 76.
21 Collantes 2007, 76–78.
22 Sümertaş 2022.
23 https://natura2000.eea.europa.eu/html/Disclaimer.html (accessed 21 June 2024).
24 Sümertaş 2022.
25 Sümertaş 2022.

Bachmann-Medick 2014
D. Bachmann-Medick: Spatial Turn, in: Cultural Turns: Neuorientierungen in den Kulturwissenschaften, 5th ed. (Reinbek bei Hamburg 2014) 284–328

Bernbeck / Egbers 2019
R. Bernbeck / V. Egbers: Subalterne Räume: Versuch einer Übersicht. Forum Kritische Archäologie 8, 2019, 59–71.

Bruisch 2018
K. Bruisch: Knowledge and Power in the Making of the Soviet Village, in: L. van de Grift, Amalia Ribi Forclaz (eds.): Governing the Rural in Interwar Europe (New York 2018) 139–163.

Buci-Gluksmann 1979
C. Buci-Gluksmann: State, Transition and Passive Revolution, in: C. Mouffe (ed.): Gramsci and Marxist Theory (London 1979).

Castro Varela / Dhawan 2015
M. Castro Varela / N. Dhawan: Postkoloniale Theorie: Eine kritische Einführung (Bielefeld 2015).

Collantes 2007
F. Collantes: The Decline of Agrarian Societies in the European Countryside: A Case Study of Spain in the Twentieth Century. The Agricultural History Society, 2007, 76–97.

De Léon / Wells 2015
J. De Léon / M. Wells: The Land of Open Graves: California Series in Public Anthropology 36 (Berkeley 2015).

Foucault 1991
M. Foucault: Governmentality, in: G. Burchell, C. Gordon, P. Miller (eds.): The Foucault Effect: Studies in Governmentality (Chicago 1991) 87–104.

Ghirardo 1989
D. Y. Ghirardo: Building New Communities: New Deal America and Fascist Italy (Princeton 1989).

Giddens 1987
A. Giddens: The Nation-State and Violence: Contemporary Critique of Historical Materialism (Berkeley 1987).

Gramsci 1971
A. Gramsci: Selection from Prison Notebooks. Q. Hoare / G. Nowell Smith (eds.) (London 1971).

Hechter 1975
M. Hechter: Internal Colonialism: The Celtic Fringe in British National Development 1536–1966 (London 1975).

Henderson 2002
S. R. Henderson: Ernst May and the Campaign to Resettle the Countryside: Rural Housing in Silesia, 1919–1925. Journal of the Society of Architectural Historians 61, no. 2, 2002, 188–211.

Lefebvre 1991
H. Lefebvre: The Production of Space (Oxford 1991).

Lefebvre 2000 [1974]
H. Lefebvre: La production de l'espace, 4th ed. (Paris 2000 [1974]).

Lenin 1977
V. I. Lenin: Collected Works, Volume 3: The Development of Capitalism in Russia, 4. Ed. (Moscow 1977).

Marshall 1993
G. Marshall: Internal Colonialism, in: A Dictionary of Sociology (Oxford 1993).

Muşat 2015
R. Muşat: Lessons for Modern Living: Planned Rural Communities in Interwar Romania, Turkey and Italy. Journal of Modern European History 13, no.4, 2015, 534–548.

Sümertaş 2022
F. M. Sümertaş: International Symposium «The Making of Identity through Rural Space: Scenarios, Experiences and Contestations in the Rural Built Environment» (Symposium Report), https://www-docs.b-tu.de/dfg-graduiertenkol-leg-1913/public/Veranstaltungen/GRK1913_RuralSpace_Report.pdf (21 June 2024).

Trende 2011
F. Trende: Neuland! War Das Zauberwort: Neue Deiche in Hitlers Namen (Heide 2011).

van de Grift 2015
L. van de Grift: Introduction: Theories and Practices of Internal Colonization, The Cultivation of Lands and People in the Age of Modern Territoriality. International Journal for History, Culture and Modernity 3, no. 2, 2015, 139–158. http://doi.org/10.18352/hcm.480.

van de Grift / Ribi Forclaz 2018
L. van de Grift / A. Ribi Forclaz (eds.): Governing the Rural in Interwar Europe. Routledge Studies in Modern European History (London, New York 2018).

Unger et al. 2022
C. Unger / L. van de Grift / D. Müller: Introduction, in: L. van de Grift, D. Müller, C. Unger (eds.): Living with the Land: Rural and Agricultural Actors in Twentieth-Century Europe – A Handbook (Berlin, Boston 2022).

Image Sources

1   BTU Cottbus-Senftenberg, 2021.
2   L'immigration en Turquie, La Turquie Kemaliste, no. 23, 1938, 16.
3   L'Immigration en Turquie, La Turquie Kemaliste, no. 23, 1938, 15.
4   Innenkolonisation und Gartenstadt. Gartenstadt 4, no. 3, 1910, 1.
5   Princeton University Press 1989.
6   Ländliche Kleinsiedlungen der Schlesischen Landgesell-schaft in der Provinz Schlesien, in: E. May: Der Städtebau, 1 February 1919, pl. 45.
7   Der Hermann-Göring-Koog: Denkschrift anläßlich der Einweihung Ende Oktober 1935, Hr. Oberpräsident u. Gauleiter v. Schleswig Holstein, Felgentreff, Berlin, 1935, 12, 14.
8   MODSCAPES 2018.
9   Routledge 2018.
10 De Gruyter Oldenburg 2022.

Landscape and Identity in-the-Making
The Reclamation District of Agro Pontino

Paolo Gruppuso

The term ‹rural› is redolent of idyllic imaginaries associated with agricultural landscapes characterized by gentle shapes, calm canals, rich pastures, and promising local, fresh, and tasty food to be bought in picturesque farmers' markets. The etymology of the term, from the Latin *rus*, evokes such imaginaries related to a healthy and peaceful lifestyle «characteristic of the countryside,» and based on the cultivation of the land.[1] This is a longstanding stereotype associated with Mediterranean countries, to such an extent that the very geographical and scholarly category of ‹Mediterranean› is grounded in this idea of the ‹rural›,[2] which corresponds with the archetypical agrarian landscapes imagined by Virgil in the *Georgics*:[3] leveled fields, drained, ordered, and productive, in opposition to marshlands and woods, envisioned as wild and dangerous spaces.[4]

Demystifying the ‹Rural›

Such a dichotomy frames historical interpretation of Mediterranean rural landscapes, which are imagined to emerge in history as the result of an age-old war of man against nature, whose ultimate goal would be the transformation of marginal and uncultivated areas into agrarian spaces. The former relate to marshlands and forests, ideologically connected with primitiveness and brigandage. The latter are identified with flat and dry land and perceived as expressions of civilization and order.[5]

Since the 18th century this binary and teleological understanding of socioenvironmental relations in the Mediterranean has become largely hegemonic. The result of this view was to turn ordinary and «symbiotic techniques»[6] of land management, such as drainage and silviculture, into carriers of civilization and symbols of human ingenuity against nature and towards progress.[7] This was an ideological interpretation because despite modernist rhetoric, woods and marshlands have historically played a key role in Mediterranean rural economies, which far from being only agrarian, have always been entangled within wider agroecosystems that also included hunting, fishing, and gathering. In fact, the rhythm of Mediterranean economies since ancient times has been characterized by the integration of marginal areas and agricultural fields, as the worlds of the farmer, the herder, and the gatherer were symbiotic, entangled, and interdependent—and this symbiosis constituted the heart of rural landscapes and economies. In this sense, if woods and marshlands were often seen as politically marginal by the modern state, their economy was nevertheless very relevant, especially for local communities.

Peregrine Horden and Nicholas Purcell highlight this aspect, and comment on the hegemonic view that has historically underestimated the economic and social values of these areas in the Mediterranean:

> The peripheral environment of marsh, mountain, forest or sea was long undervalued by historians influenced by the cultural prejudice that privileges, as being more civilised, tilling the soil over other productive activities (Fumagalli 1992, 99–101). An agrarian history which stresses the interdependence of agricultural activities with other strategies for maintaining nutritional input from the environment is to be preferred.[8]

Despite this complex interdependence, what the category of the ‹rural› brings to mind is a simplified opposition between ‹agrarian› and ‹non-agrarian› spaces—such as urban areas and uncultivated land—with their respective economies and forms of sociality. This contrastive understanding was strengthened in the early 20th century, when it assumed powerful and significant ideological connotations that materialized in political projects of «ruralization.» With the unprecedented support of heavy machineries, these projects created novel landscapes and implemented new forms of governmentality that imposed an agrarian identity on previously complex agroecosystems.

This is the case of Agro Pontino, a region 70 kilometers south of Rome on the west coast of Italy. Here, in the 1930s the fascist regime experimented with a massive process of land reclamation and social engineering that was then replicated in other regions, such as Sardinia, Apulia, and Sicily, in Italy, and in the colonies.[9] This process, named *Bonifica Integrale* (wholesome reclamation), aimed to transform the Pontine Marshes, until then one the largest forested marshlands in Italy, into a rationally productive agrarian space. Accordingly, the *Bonifica Integrale* entailed not only the drainage of the Marshes, perceived by the regime as a watery desert,[10] but also a broader project that consisted of the construction of three ‹new towns,›[11] and a massive process of colonization with settlers brought from northern Italy[12] and the removal of local people.[13] This process was managed through the *Commissariato per le Migrazioni e la Colonizzazione Interna* (Committee for Migrations and Internal Colonization), created in 1930 to replace the *Comitato Permanente per la Migrazione Interna* (Permanent Committee for Internal Migration), and under the direct control of Benito Mussolini.[14] The *Bonifica Integrale* substantially changed the environmental, economic, and sociocultural structure of Agro Pontino, turning the marshland into one of the most iconic ‹rural› landscapes in Italy.

The adjective «rural» here does not identify any complex interdependence between different productive realms, but rather suggests a political project of separation of agrarian spaces, socialities, and economies from non-agrarian ones, to the detriment of the latter. This strategy of simplification was conveyed through the implementation of three key elements: land reclamation, modernization, and colonization. These were the overarching features of Mediterranean fascist regimes:[15]

> reclamation as a material and ideological regeneration of people and places; modernity as the ideology through which fascist regimes employed science and technology to create socioecologies at the service of their goals; and colonization (internal and external) as the concrete laboratory where reclamation and modernity were experimented as forms of control, regime-building, and oppression.[16]

By epitomizing these features, the *Bonifica Integrale* of Agro Pontino exemplifies the ideology of ruralization and its implementation as constitutive of the fascist political project in Italy. This aspect has been largely discussed by a broad range of scholarship addressing the multiple facets of the *Bonifica Integrale* from different perspectives. This article contributes to that scholarship by exploring how the idea of a ‹rural› identity emerged in the Italian context of the early 20th century, first as a vector of nationalist propaganda, and later as a key element of fascist ideology. It then focuses on the *Bonifica Integrale* of Agro Pontino as a colonial project of identity making that, by implementing a process of ruralization charged with strong ideological and moral connotations, transformed a complex agroecosystem into a highly geometrical agrarian space. In the conclusion, the paper moves to the present, briefly discussing the legacy and reverberations of that process in Latina (originally named Littoria), the most iconic of the fascist new towns. Here, current projects valorizing the canal system designed during the *Bonifica Integrale* seem to challenge the fascist project of identity making, as much as the idea of reclamation as the point of origin of the current landscape.[17] These projects, instead, suggest that landscape as much as identity is always in-the-making, involving ongoing processes of negotiation between communities and the environment they live in.

From Vernacular Tradition to Rural Ideology

At the beginning of the 20th century, fifty years after its formal unification in 1861, Italy was still very much a fragmented country, with regions characterized by very different identities, languages, and traditions. Beyond this fragmentation, the country was also divided by strong socioeconomic and environmental disparities between the South, predominantly rural, and the North, whose industrialization was at the time growing. Such an imbalance was exacerbated by the migration of peasants, who, looking to improve their living condition, moved from the southern countryside to the northern industrial cities, thus altering the demographic distribution of the country and its economy.[18] This process of change was seen as endangering peasant traditions, which attracted the attention of ethnographers such as Lamberto Loria, who in 1906 established the Museum of Italian Ethnography in Florence with the idea of documenting and representing what he imagined to be a world at risk of disappearing.[19]

Based on the materials and the experience he gained while establishing this museum, Lamberto Loria was invited to supervise and stage a national ethnographic exhibit that would complement the International Exhibition of 1911. The International Exhibition was organized in Rome to commemorate the fiftieth anniversary of Italian unification, and to show to the world the progress of the Italian urban bourgeoisie. On the other hand, the Ethnographic Exhibition was meant to celebrate the Italian peasantry, and to teach Italians about the richness and the diversity of their young nation's traditions. The International Exhibition and the Ethnographic Exhibition were both functional to the construction and representation of a national community that would have brought together extremely different regional identities. Architecture played a key role in this endeavor: on the one hand, the classic buildings of high architectural traditions; on the other hand, the full-scale reconstruction of vernacular buildings from all over Italy. Within this context, juxtaposed with acknowledged masterpieces of Italian architecture, vernacular buildings appeared permeated with «monumental significance,»[20] providing a common ground from which a unifying identity emerged, weaving together regional and national traditions to reflect a national heritage.

The Ethnographic Exhibition, within the wider context of the International Exhibition, is critical to understanding the genealogy of the rural ideal and its development as a key feature of fascist ideology. On this occasion, vernacular tradition—that is, the material culture and heritage of the Italian peasantry—started to be perceived as a key element in defining the identity of the young Italian nation. It is worth noticing that Loria's exhibition aimed to provide this common identity by exploring the origins of Italian «race.» His work was in fact framed within the evolutionary perspective that was at the time hegemonic. Accordingly, the peasantry, consisting of ‹rural› people, was thought to be uncorrupted by modernity, which was identified with increasing urbanization. Thus the peasantry was closer to what Loria imagined as the original features of «Italianness»: modesty, practicality, and authenticity. In this sense, vernacular tradition «offered a repository not only of Italian identity but also of noble virtue.»[21]

The symbolic connection between vernacular tradition, national identity, and noble virtue became stronger after World War I, when it was associated with the glorification of ‹rural› people as war heroes (fig. 1), carriers of moral virtue, peace, and social order, and celebrated as a prime example of «Italianness.»[22] The association between the Italian peasantry and Italianness was then adopted by fascism, becoming the ideological ground for the politics of ruralization.[23] According to Arrigo Serpieri, the father of the concept of *Bonifica*

1   Memorial stone donated in 1933 by the city council of Treviso, in Northern Italy, to the city council of Littoria. It explicitly connects World War I to the fascist Bonifica Integrale, emphasising the heroic work of Northern «rural» people in reclaiming the Pontine Marshes.

Integrale, the values that characterized ‹rural› people, and thus Italianness, were the following: gentlemanship; sense of property, family, and religion; cult of tradition; respect for hierarchies; and a deep bond with the land and with the fatherland.[24] These values reflected a very ideological interpretation of the Roman classics. Particularly, Virgil's idealization of agriculture provided a strong historical and ideological reference for the fascist politics of ruralization as based on the colonization of the land, on its cultivation by hand of sedentary small land-owners, and on the transformation of the landscape in a geometrical sense.

These values became the main lens used to read the Italian landscape, and accordingly Italian identity. This aspect clearly emerges in the following quotation from Pietro Fedele,[25] who connected the celebration for the bi-millenary anniversary of Virgil's birth with the regime's agricultural policy:

> Virgil's voice that recalls Italians to work in the fields is nowadays sanctified by the Fatherland's religion, and it has never been so trusted; and after the glory of war, given to us by the glorious King, we strive to conquest the *divina gloria ruris*, that the Head of the Government pointed to Italian people. The most effective and solemn commemoration of Virgil is, undoubtedly, the law for land reclamation, recently approved by the Italian Parliament.[26]

This quotation emphasizes the ideological ground that links the «glory of war» with the «*divina gloria ruris*» («divine glory of the fields»). What connects battlefields with agricultural fields is the Italian peasantry, whose identity is rooted in the mythical ‹rural› ground of the Roman empire as praised by Virgil and interpreted by fascism.

Clearly, fascism created a strong connection between Italian identity and Italian landscape, in which both were understood as the outcome of a glorious ‹rural› past that fascism was going to reclaim, both from the metaphorical «swamp of parliamentarism»[27] and from the material marshland of Agro Pontino. This was emphasized by Benito Mussolini in 1926, during the initial phase of the fascist regime:

> It is imperative that we create; we, people from this epoch and this generation, because we have the duty to remake the face of the Fatherland both spiritually and materially. In ten years, comrades, Italy will be unrecognisable! This is because we will have transformed it, we will have made a new one, from the mountains which we will have covered with a green coat [of trees], to the fields which will be completely reclaimed...[28]

The spiritual «face of the Fatherland» was thus connected with its material shape, as much as Italian identity with Italian landscape. In this sense, ruralization was not only a way to redefine Italian landscape but also a means to regenerate the fascist nation,[29] by imposing a new socioecological order and an identity that disrupted and replaced the longstanding environmental relations that characterized rural landscapes like the Pontine Marshes in Agro Pontino.

The Dark Side of the ‹Rural›

As I outlined above, ‹rural› is a complex term with a long history and contrasting meanings.[30] On the one hand, there is the ideological project of totalitarian regimes, for whom ‹rural› is synonymous with agrarian, and related to forms of economy and sociality based on rational agriculture implemented through land reclamation, modernization, and colonization. On the other hand, the same term identifies complex agroecosystems, based on agriculture, hunting, fishing, and gathering, that characterized the Mediterranean region until recent times. The latter meaning is the opposite of ‹rural› as envisioned, propagandized, and implemented by the fascist regime through the *Bonifica Integrale* in Agro Pontino. It involves an «obscure economy,»[31] very varied, and often invisible to the State, as much as historiography, such as the kind that characterized the Pontine Marshes until the 1930s. The expression «obscure economy» emphasizes the fragmentation of knowledges concerning marshland livelihoods in the Mediterranean, and the modernist attitude towards these environments, which are often understood as wastelands to be improved and as «*terrae nullius*» to be colonized. The Pontine Marshes epitomize this expression, appearing in the historiography of this region as a *lagoon*, in the etymological sense of *lacuna*, which in Latin identified a gap, an empty space.

This approach is summarized in the idea that «the history of the Pontine Marshes is the history of the land reclamation processes that have been attempted in order to reclaim them,»[32] as if the region was a void in history, and would not have had its own economy and forms of sociality. It is an understanding that exemplifies the hegemonic reading of Mediterranean history from an agrarian perspective, according to which the Pontine Marshes exist only as a sequence of attempts at reclamation, culminating in the *Bonifica Integrale*, when the fascist regime tamed the region's unruly nature. This was in fact only the last and most successful manifestation of a colonial agency, which in different times and according to different socio-economical contingencies, was directed at reclaiming land from water, thus imposing agrarian order and identity over the Marshes and their inhabitants. However, despite colonial imaginaries and agencies, there are no gaps or blank spaces in the world, and attempts to impose preordained identities over landscapes and their inhabitants often clash with local interests—as has happened in different periods in Agro Pontino.

References about these clashes abound in the 18th-century technical literature, when the Agro Pontino was undergoing the last significant attempt by the Papacy, under Pope Pius VI, to reclaim the Pontine Marshes. The main concern was the management of canals in relation to traditional activities that characterized the economy of the Pontine Marshes, and that were seen as hindering the process of reclamation. According to hydraulic engineers and technicians, local people were worried about losing their livelihoods if «the marshes were transformed into cultivated fields. For this reason they destroyed the banks of rivers and channels, in order to flood again the drained fields.»[33] These were certainly conscious activities of sabotage, carried out particularly by fishermen who obstructed the flow of water for creating fishponds. However, there was also damage provoked accidentally by activities that were traditionally carried out in the marshes and that benefitted from that environment, such as logging and husbandry. The problem with logging was the transportation of wood, which was cut in the forest and then moved through the waterways of the Marshes. During transportation, one tenth of the wood sank in the channels, raising the riverbed and flooding the surrounding areas. Husbandry was also problematic because animals such as buffalo and pigs pastured along the channels where their bustling destroyed the banks.[34]

These examples make different approaches to the landscape visible: on the one hand, the efforts at rationalization implemented by engineers working on a project of land reclamation that aimed to transform the marshes «into cultivated fields;» on the other hand, local inhabitants, who by implementing different activities traced a complex tangle of socioenvironmental relations with water. The former, by thinking in terms of drained fields to be cultivated, exemplify an agrarian perspective. The latter instead emphasize the presence of different activities, thus highlighting a rural economy. Indeed, the land reclamation implemented by the Papacy was not understood as a «wholesome reclamation» like the *Bonifica Integrale*. Whereas the former was a technical project aimed at improving the productivity of the land, the latter was understood as a wider political project whose ultimate goal was the creation of a novel socioecological order grounded in the imaginary of a rural tradition. However, in both cases, the identity of a community, as it emerged in the relations with its environment, was at stake.

Reclaiming Land and Men in their Reciprocal Relations

The term ‹*bonifica*› (reclamation) comes from the Latin *bonum facere*, and literally means «turning into good.»[35] Historically, in the Mediterranean context, small-scale reclamation was a common practice of land management aimed at improving (i.e. turning into good) the quality of the land, even temporarily, and at the integration of agriculture with fishing, hunting, foraging, and gathering of materials. Thus land reclamation, *bonifica*, was embedded within a dialogic relation between agricultural fields, uncultivated areas, marshlands, and woods. It was only in the 18th century that the term assumed its current meaning as an expression of modern ideas about human mastery over nature.[36] This meaning became stronger in the 20th century with the emergence of totalitarian regimes, like fascism in Italy, when *bonifica* became associated with *integrale* (wholesome), acquiring moral, political, and social connotations as a means «to reclaim land and men in their reciprocal relations in order to create the best conditions for social life.»[37]

In the context of fascism, the moral value of the verb *bonificare* (to reclaim) was emphasized by the association with the verb *redimere* (to redeem), meaning the actual religious act to save, or redeem, the land and its inhabitants from the marshes, interpreted as a sinful landscape. This religious approach has striking similarities with the experience of the earliest Puritan colonists in North America, for whom «swamps symbolised the ultimate chaos to tame, the ultimate evil to right—both spiritually and physically.»[38] For the Puritans, as for the fascist regime, land reclamation was perceived as part of a «providential mission.»[39] The comparison with the Puritan colonists brings to attention the colonial imaginary involved in the very idea of *reclaiming*, which seems to imply «a prior ownership or entitlement to something»[40] to claim back. This idea was amplified during fascism, which propagandized the *Bonifica Integrale* in Agro Pontino as a war fought to reconquest the region in the name of progress and rural civilization.[41]

In that particular context, one of the most popular expressions used to describe the Pontine Marshes, its economy and inhabitants, was «Darkest Africa,» as first used in 1905 in the sentence, «A few miles from Rome you have the perfect illusion of the darkest Africa!»[42] In the same period, the same exotic tones were also used in reference to other marshlands, for example the Everglades in Florida, described as «unknown to the white man as the heart of Africa.»[43] Anthropologist Laura Ogden observes that these kinds of narratives are situated within the poetics of colonial encounters.[44] They constitute a substratum of a colonial agency that is manifested through the narratives of scientists,

agronomists, hydraulic engineers, geologists, and cartographers, which turned the landscape into a «smooth object,» a «matter of fact» «defined by strict laws of causality, efficacy, profitability, and truth.»[45] In Agro Pontino, these narratives had a powerful impact, because they disentangled the physical environment of the Marshes from the interdependent activities that historically shaped them as a complex rural agroecosystem. Technoscientific approaches and moral values were condensed during the fascist regime and implemented through the *Bonifica Integrale*, propagandized as a generative process that created a new inhabitable landscape where life was before unbearable.

The process of disentanglement of the Pontine Marshes, as well as the emphasis on the productive aspects of the new reclaimed landscape, emerges clearly in propagandist literature. A key example is a text by Natale Prampolini, the engineer in charge of the *Bonifica Integrale* in Agro Pontino, who described the Marshes as an «age-old problem» solved by the reclamation with the construction of a number of drainage channels, drainage pumps, streets, dikes, homesteads etc. From this approach, the Pontine Marshes, read in terms of «hydraulic disorder,»[46] emerge as a *tabula rasa*, «nothing but a malaria-infested marsh.»[47] Moreover, the *Bonifica Integrale* was imagined as a war against the nature of the Marshes, regarded as antithetical to fascist ideas of productivity and sociality, and described accordingly as a «war, with its victories and casualties [fought against] the land so evil for many years which is finally overturned, crushed, defeated by the will and the genius of man.»[48] Within these narratives the Marshes appear both as a watery wasteland to claim back for civilization through drainage, and as an unruly and evil landscape to redeem through war.

The ruralization project was framed through these narratives as a process that transformed the disorderly marshes into an iconic space of agrarian modern rationality characterized by spatial and social order. The description by German journalist Emil Ludwig, who in the 1930s flew over the reclaimed Agro Pontino, paints a clear picture of this new space:

> An area of hundreds of square miles in which, up till now, no one had been able to live [...] has at length been rendered habitable with the result that in ten years or so there will be a population of many thousands [...]. All this countryside was now spread beneath my eyes like a map. I could see the parallel lines marking the newly ploughed lands, could recognise the main canals and their feeders, dug in order to drain the marsh waters away into the sea.[49]

Ludwig's description draws attention to the process of agrarian ‹geometrization› that turned the «pestilential marshes [...] into productive fields.»[50] Here, legibility and simplification appear as key features of fascist statecraft,[51] embedded within an agrarian order aimed to re-fashion people and landscape by imposing a ‹rural› identity.

Conclusion: From Imposing Identity to *Identity-in-the-Making*

Like any totalitarian project, the *Bonifica Integrale* was conducted with colonial violence by superimposing a new identity over a pre-existing landscape that was already inhabited.[52] The result of such a superimposition is that immediately after World War II, this forced identity started to loosen, and the landscape designed during fascism, characterized by homesteads with an average area of between 17 and 21 hectares,[53] was radically transformed. Many of the northern settlers abandoned their homesteads, which were then divided in smaller properties, fragmenting the original agrarian fabric. Subsequently, already in the second half of the 1950s, the economy of the region started to turn from agriculture toward manufacturing, thus transforming the social identity of the region.[54] Moreover, the town Littoria, known as «the Duce's favorite,» was renamed Latina on April 1945, as soon as the fascist regime fell.

Despite these dramatic changes, the geometry of the landscape is still very evident in Agro Pontino, particularly in the canal system that crosses the landscape with sharp cuts.[55] Canals were dug as part of a highly engineered system designed for letting the water flow as fast as possible to the sea, according to the idea of «remaking the face of the fatherland» by re-claiming land from water. In fact, the most enduring feature of the *Bonifica Integrale* is the highly sophisticated system of channels, pumps and dykes used to manage water and to keep the region «dry.» During fascism, these constituted an inhabited waterscape, as most people in Agro Pontino were employed in agricultural activities that involved a close relation with water and channels.[56] With the fall of the fascist regime, and with the subsequent industrialization, this relation has changed and the waterscape of Agro Pontino has grown apart from the social life of its inhabitants, who have only scarce opportunities to engage with channels in their daily life.

This is particularly true in Latina, whose history exemplifies the whole parable of the *Bonifica Integrale* and paints a clear picture of its legacy in present-day Agro Pontino. The town was founded in 1932 as a service center for the community of settlers brought from northern Italy. According to the fascist policy of de-urbanization it was not supposed «to awake urban aspirations to rural masses.»[57] It was rather meant to be an infrastructure, like a channel or a pumping station,[58] functional to the project of *Bonifica Integrale* and integrated with the highly engineered landscape that at the time was still under construction. However, immediately after its foundation, Littoria changed identity, and from being an anonymous rural village, became the most iconic of the fascist new towns, promoted in 1934 as the capital of the new province of the same name. Refashioned in this way, the city grew apart from the surrounding landscape and particularly from its highly engineered system of water management (fig. 2). Such a separation is nowadays very evident, as Latina has become the second largest city in the wider region of Latium, with 130,000 inhabitants, who are disentangled from the surrounding, highly fragmented landscape.[59]

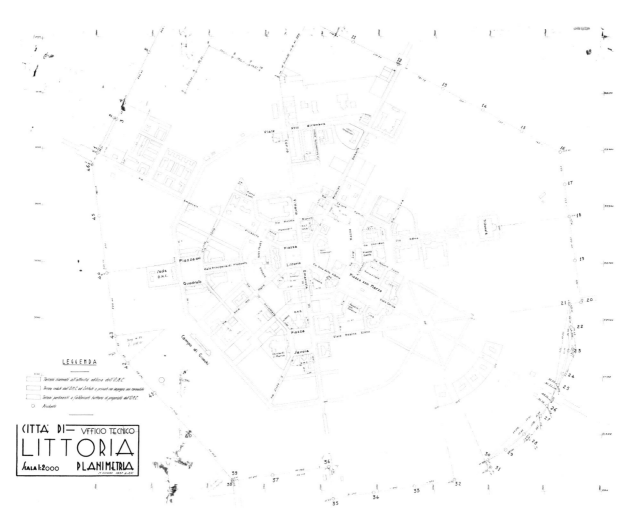

2   City plan of Littoria, 1937. It shows the slow expansion of Littoria and the change in its identity from rural village to city.

However, interest in the waterscape designed during the *Bonifica Integrale* is now growing. It has recently undergone a number of ecological restoration projects aimed at improving water quality, which has been severely affected by industrialization and intensive agriculture. A significant example of this new interest concerns one of the main channels of the reclamation network, the *Canale delle Acque Medie* (Canal of Middle Waters), which collects groundwater from the springs at the feet of the hills and carries it to the sea. This canal passes at the edge of Latina, less than two kilometers from the main square, but it has always been excluded from social life, hidden by a curtain of giant cane (Arundo donax), and considered a sewer. In the past few years, a group of local people drew attention to the canal, organizing cleaning activities along the banks that were supported by the city council. Recently, the same group of inhabitants has constituted a committee for the creation of a natural park to run along the urban tract of the canal.[60] Their aim is to strengthen the connections between the city and the surrounding landscape, improving the wider ecology of the region, and at the same time creating a green area for leisure activities such as running and walking.

This and other projects concerned with Agro Pontino's canal system teem with ambiguities and problems related to the legacy of the *Bonifica Integrale*, understood as a foundation myth, which still saturates the landscape with symbolic, ideological, and political values.[61] Despite these problems, whose description exceeds the limit and the aim of this contribution,[62] the interest shown in the canals of Agro Pontino unveils a new identity in-the-making that reflects an ongoing process of negotiation between people and the landscape they inhabit. This process is certainly affected by the ‹rural› identity imposed by the regime as much as by the fragmentation of the landscape that followed World War II. However, what this negotiation highlights is the terrain of Agro Pontino as a «process, continually made and remade, transformed by geophysical and human transformations.»[63] This aspect is important because it brings to the forefront the overlooked hydrogeology of Agro Pontino as a waterscape that has emerged in time according to—and in spite of—historical, cultural, and political contingencies.

This process has taken different shapes over time. The Pontine Marshes were a complex rural agro-ecosystem, deeply entangled in the social and economic life of its inhabitants who maintained peculiar relations with water through activities such as fishing, logging, and husbandry. The fascist *Bonifica Integrale* simplified that complexity, reading the Marshes as a wasteland. Accordingly, the regime implemented a process of agrarian transformation that involved land reclamation, colonization, and the geometrization of the landscape, which ultimately resulted in different relations with water. The second half of the 20th century was instead characterized by industrialization and the consequent marginalization of the canal system in Agro Pontino, which was forgotten and treated as a sewage system. Recently, as in the case of the Canal of Middle Waters, other patterns of relating to water have emerged, where the terrain of Agro Pontino—its hydrogeology—is read and performed as a canal, whose banks are appreciated as a site for walking and running in the urbanized landscape. When looked at from this perspective, colonial projects of imposing identity on communities and landscapes are always doomed to fail, as they always appear in-the-making, entangled in the material and ecological processes of formation.

1   Vallerani 2021, xiv.

2   Albera 2020, 275.

3   Traina 2002, 225.

4   I want to thank Roberta Cevasco, Professor of Geography at the University of Gastronomic Sciences in Pollenzo, for pointing out to me a broader and inclusive meaning of ‹rural,› beyond the agrarian perspective (personal communication, 29 June 2020).

5   Traina 2002 and 1985.

6   Horden / Purcell 2000, 188.

7   Traina 1986, 713.

8   Horden / Purcell 2000, 182.

9   See Distretti / Petti 2021 and Mariani 1976.

10   Serra 1925, 5.

11   Littoria (renamed Latina after WWII), Sabaudia, and Pontinia, established respectively in 1932, 1934, and 1935.

12   Pitkin 1990, 31–32; see also Mariani 1976 and Caprotti 2007b.

13   Vöchting 1990, 49.

14   Folchi 2000, 71.

15   Liesbeth van de Grift argues that internal colonization in interwar Europe was a common feature not only of totalitarian regimes, but of governments of all stripes (2018, 69). However, I think that ruralization as I describe it here was a specific phenomenon characterizing totalitarian regimes, such as fascist Italy, in the same period.

16   Armiero et al 2021, 9.

17   Gruppuso 2018, 398.

18 Parisella 1990, XVII.

19 Harris 2010, 50–51.

20 Harris 2010, 54.

21 Harris 2010, 60. For a wider perspective on Interwar Europe, see Patel 2018, 7.

22 Di Michele 1995, 245.

23 The reclamation and colonization of the Pontine Marshes was in fact led by the Opera Nazionale Combattenti (ONC), a veterans' organization created after World War I. One of the aims of the internal colonization in the Pontine Marshes was to give the land to veterans to reward them for their sacrifice during WWI. The fascist toponomastic of the Agro Pontino is a celebration of WWI.

24 Vallortigara 2017, 60.

25 Minister of Education from 1925 to 1928 and academic affiliated with the fascist party.

26 Quoted in Vallortigara 2017, 59.

27 Cavallo 2014, 6.

28 Quoted in Armiero/Hardenberg 2013, 284.

29 Caprotti 2007a, 652.

30 On this ambivalence, see van de Grift/Ribi Forclaz 2018, xv.

31 Zagli 2003, 160.

32 De Mandato 1933, 64–65.

33 Nicolai 1800, 140.

34 Nicolai 1800, 238.

35 Cavallo 2011, 16.

36 Archaeologist Giusto Traina (2002, 253) suggests avoiding using the term ‹bonifica› before the 18th century so as to prevent misunderstanding about different ways of land and water management.

37 Serpieri 1927, 192.

38 Vileisis 1997, 36.

39 Vileisis 1997, 36.

40 Van Dooren 2014, 77.

41 Gruppuso 2021, 60.

42 Cervesato 1922 [1905], 108–109.

43 Willoughby 1898, quoted in Ogden 2011, 103.

44 Willoughby 1898, quoted in Ogden 2011, 103.

45 Latour 2004, Politics of Nature 22, quoted in Ogden 2011, 118.

46 Prampolini [n.d.], 8.

47 Harris 1957, 311.

48 Petrucci 1932 in Gruppuso 2021, 60–61.

49 Ludwig 1933, 165.

50 Frost 1934, 584.

51 Scott 1998, 1–8.

52 Vöchting 1990, 34.

53 Vöchting 1990, 45.

54 Mangullo 2015, 9.

55 Gruppuso 2017, 145.

56 It is not unusual to find narratives about people taking baths in canals during the fascist period and even after World War II and in the 1950s.

57 Vöchting 1990, 31.

58 Folchi 2015, 70–71.

59 Cefaly 2021, 86.

60 Gruppuso 2023a.

61 Gruppuso 2018, 401.

62 Gruppuso 2023b.

63 Elden 2020, 8.

Albera 2020
D. Albera: Mediterranean Ruralities: Towards a Comparative Approach, Zeitschrift für Ethnologie / Journal of Social and Cultural Anthropology 145, 2020, 275–294.

Armiero et al. 2021
M. Armiero / R. Biasillo / P. Guimarães: Editorial: Environmental Histories of Mediterranean Fascism, Perspectivas, Journal of Political Sciences, December 2021, 9–15.

Armiero/Hardenberg 2013
M. Armiero / W. G. V. Hardenberg: Green Rhetoric in Blackshirts: Italian Fascism and the Environment, Environment and History 19, 2013, 283–311.

Caprotti 2007a
F. Caprotti: Destructive Creation: Fascist Urban Planning, Architecture and New Towns in the Pontine Marshes, Journal of Historical Geography, 33, 2007, 651–679.

Caprotti 2007b
F. Caprotti: Mussolini's Cities: Internal Colonialism in Italy, 1930–1939 (New York 2007).

Cavallo 2011
F. L. Cavallo: Terra, Acque, Macchine: Geografie della bonifica in Italia tra Ottocento e Novecento (Reggio Emilia 2011).

Cavallo 2014
F. L. Cavallo: Valori geoculturali e turisticità delle zone umide costiere italiane, in: F. L. Cavallo (ed.): Wetlandia. Tradizioni, valori, turismi nelle zone umide italiane (Lavis 2014) 1–19.

Cefaly 2021
P. Cefaly: Littoria-Latina: nascita e sviluppo della città, in: Prospettive Pontine (ed.): Contributi per una pianificazione del territorio pontino (Latina 2021) 83–93.

Cervesato 1922 [1905]
A. Cervesato: Latina tellus: La Campagna Romana, 1st ed. 1905 (Rome 1922).

De Mandato 1933
M. De Mandato: La primitività dell'abitare umano. Studi e ricerche (Turin 1933).

Di Michele 1995
A. Di Michele: I diversi volti del ruralismo fascista, Italia contemporanea, 199, 1995, 243–267.

Distretti / Petti 2021
E. Distretti / A. Petti: Borgo Rizza: Architectural Demodernization as Critical Pedagogy: Pathways for Undoing Colonial Fascist Architectural Legacies in Sicily, in: C. Oprea et al. (eds.): Architectural Dissonances (online, 2021) 119–138. https://www.internationaleonline.org/library/#architectural_dissonances.

Elden 2020
S. Elden: Terrain, Politics, History, Dialogues in Human Geography XX, 2020, 1–20.

Folchi 2000
A. Folchi: I Contadini del Duce. Agro Pontino. 1932–1941 (Rome 2000).

Folchi 2015
A. Folchi: Littoria. La pupilla del Duce. 1932–1943 (Formia 2015).

Frost 1934
R.S. Frost: The Reclamation of the Pontine Marshes, Geographical Review 24, 1934, 584–595.

Gruppuso 2017
P. Gruppuso: Reeds, in: R. Harkness (ed): An Unfinished Compendium of Materials (Aberdeen 2017) 145–153.

Gruppuso 2018
P. Gruppuso: Edenic Views in Wetland Conservation: Nature and Agriculture in the Fogliano Area, Italy, Conservation and Society 16, 2018, 397–408.

Gruppuso 2021
P. Gruppuso: In-between Solidity and Fluidity: The Reclaimed Marshlands of Agro Pontino, Theory, Culture & Society 39, 2021, 53–73.

Gruppuso 2023a
P. Gruppuso: Latina e il Canale delle Acque Medie: hydrocitizenship, idroanomia, e river literacy, in G. Osti (ed): Fiumi e città. Un amore a distanza. Volume II. Corsi d'acqua di Italia centrale e Liguria (Padova 2023) 79–90.

Gruppuso 2023b
P. Gruppuso: A chi appartiene il Canale delle Acque Medie? Lettera aperta alla comunità dei viventi, https://www.areefragili.it/?s=gruppuso (1 August 2023).

Harris 1957
L.E. Harris: Land Drainage and reclamation, in: J.C. Singer (ed.): A History of Technology (London 1957) 300–323.

Harris 2010
L.R. Harris: Picturing the «Primitive»: Photography, Architecture, and the Construction of Italian Modernism, 1911–1936, PhD Dissertation, New York University, 2010.

Horden / Purcell 2000
P. Horden / N. Purcell: The Corrupting Sea: A Study of Mediterranean History (Oxford UK, Malden USA 2000).

Ludwig 1933
E. Ludwig: Talks with Mussolini (Boston 1933).

Mangullo 2015
S. Mangullo: Il fascio e lo scudo crociato: Cassa per il mezzogiorno, politica e lotte sociali nell'Agro Pontino (1944–1961) (Milan 2015).

Mariani 1976
R. Mariani: Fascismo e «città nuove» (Milan 1976)

Nicolai 1800
N.M. Nicolai: De' bonificamenti delle terre pontine (Rome 1800).

Ogden 2011
L. Ogden: Swamplife: People, Gators, and Mangroves Entangled in the Everglades (Minneapolis 2011).

Parisella 1990
A. Parisella: Introduzione, in: Vöchting 1990, IX–XXIV.

Patel 2018
K.K. Patel: The Green Hearth of Governance: Rural Europe during the Interwar Years in a Global Perspective, in: L. van de Grift / A. Ribi Forclaz (eds.): Governing the Rural in Interwar Europe (New York 2018) 1–23.

Pitkin 1990
D.S. Pitkin: Mamma, Casa, Posto Fisso: Sermoneta Rivisitata 1951–1986 (Naples 1990).

Prampolini [n.d.]
N. Prampolini: La Bonifica Idraulica della Palude Pontina (Rome n.d.).

Scott 1998
J.C. Scott: Seeing Like a State. How Certain Schemes to Improve the Human Condition Have Failed (New Haven 1998).

Serpieri 1927
A. Serpieri: Lo stato fascista e il capitalismo agrario: La Bonifica Integrale, in: L. Villari: Il capitalismo italiano del novecento (Bari 1972) 192–208.

Serra 1925
P. Serra: La Bonifica del Pantano dei Gricilli: Mediante sollevamento meccanico e colmata (Rome 1925).

Traina 1985
G. Traina: Antico e moderno nella storia della bonifiche Italiane, Studi Storici, 26, 1985, 431–436.

Traina 1986
G. Traina: Paesaggio e ‹decadenza›. La Palude nella trasformazione del mondo antico, in: A. Giardina (ed.): Società Romana e Impero Tardoantico. Le Merci. Gli Insediamenti (Bari 1986) 711–729.

Traina 2002
G. Traina: Uso del bosco e degli incolti, in: G. Forni / A. Marcone (eds.): Storia dell'Agricoltura Italiana (Florence 2002) 225–258.

Vallerani 2021
F. Vallerani: I piaceri della villa: Vivere e raccontare la campagna tra abbandoni e ritorni (Milan 2021).

Vallortigara 2017
L. Vallortigara: «L'epos impossibile»: percorsi nella ricezione dell'Eneide nel Novecento. PhD Dissertation. Università Cà Foscari Venezia, 2017.

van de Grift/Ribi Forclaz 2018
L. van de Grift / A. Ribi Forclaz: Preface, in: L. van de Grift / A. Ribi Forclaz (eds.): Governing the Rural in Interwar Europe (New York 2018) XI–XVIII.

van de Grift 2018
L. van de Grift: Cultivating Land and People: Internal Colonization in Interwar Europe, in L. van de Grift / A. Ribi Forclaz (eds.): Governing the Rural in Interwar Europe (New York 2018) 68–92.

Van Dooren 2014
T. Van Dooren: Flightways: Life and Loss at the Edge of Extinction (New York 2014).

Vileisis 1997
A. Vileisis: Discovering the Unknown Landscape. A History of America's Wetlands (Washington 1997).

Vöchting 1990 [1942]
F. Vöchting: La bonifica della pianura pontina, 1st ed. 1942 (Rome 1990).

Zagli 2003
A. Zagli: «Oscure economie» di Palude nelle aree umide di Bientina e di Fucecchio (Secc XVI–XIX), in: A. Malvolti / G. Pinto (eds.): Incolti, fiumi, paludi Utilizzazione delle risorse naturali nella Toscana medievale e moderna (Florence 2003) 159–213.

Image Sources

1   Photograph taken by the author.
2   Courtesy of Casa dell'Architettura di Latina.

Embedding Apulian Landscapes of Nomadism into Rural Modernization Schemes
Instant Townscapes of Integral Reclamation

Cristina Pallini, Aleksa Korolija

This contribution discusses the premises and the impact of the «integral reclamation» carried out in the Apulian Tableland in Italy under the fascist regime from 1932 to 1941. It focuses on settlements conceived and built as part of subsequent reclamation schemes, which subverted a long-standing transhumance-based economy.

Through a wider historical perspective and by delving into a variety of sources—mostly pre-dating the fascist «integral reclamation» and others originated under the regime—this paper identifies the importance of rural settlement as a long-standing issue in the Apulian Tableland. Unlike the well-studied case of the Pontine Plain, the newly built settlements in Apulia bear testimony to the conflicting modernization policies that coexisted under the fascist regime, and to the experiments made to integrate planning and architecture. As engineer and urban planner Cesare Albertini[1] pointed out, roads emerged as drivers of a new urban–rural relationship, but also as key landscape features. In Apulia, where many new roads replaced old sheep tracks, this condition acquired a special significance: new rural settlements were to be seen from the road or from the railway. These settlements were designed to be compact, with a roadside square, combining «high modernism»[2] with local traditional building types with the aim of achieving a unitary visual whole that at times drifted into a picturesque composition.

The notion of «instant townscape» is proposed to define the spatial and architectural features of rural new towns that architects deployed to construct new identities.

How the Apulian Tableland Differed from the Pontine Plain

On 26 May 1928, six years after seizing power, Mussolini announced that the fascist government was to undertake rural modernization as an antidote to the negative effects of industrial urbanism. The Serpieri Law (1923) and the Mussolini Law (1928) had given way to state-supported hydraulic and road works, land redistribution, and construction of new rural settlements,[3] marking a milestone in the long debate about the «integral reclamation» of vast unproductive areas.[4] The rational exploitation of natural resources,[5] allied to an informed demographic policy favoring the reorganization of productive forces across the nation, was to gear Italian society into a productive corporatist system, associated with an array of public buildings and spaces where new behavioral patterns were to be staged in collective events and daily life.[6] Social engineering, for which the eradication of agricultural and pastoral nomadism was a prerequisite, was a common trait of totalitarian regimes, where «high modernism» made society legible and organized in a way that simplified the classic functions of taxation, conscription, and prevention of rebellion.[7]

A comprehensive territorial[8] approach involving experts from various fields (urban and landscape design, geology, agronomy, economics, sociology, and engineering) was necessary for the promotion of agriculture in a totalitarian state. Even architecture, typically associated with art, and having to cope with both technical and

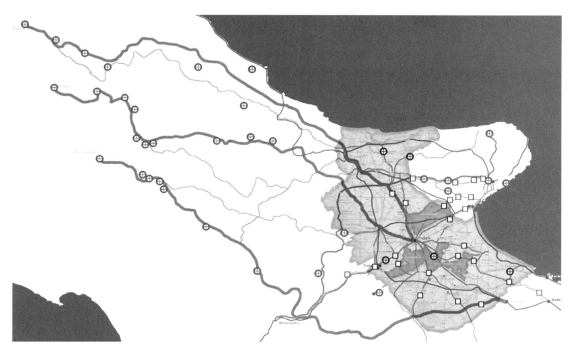

1   Map of the Capitanata region with the main sheep tracks coming from L'Aquila, Pescasseroli, and Benevento, along which were Marian shrines (cross-in-circle) and staging posts (squares).

representational factors, played a great deal in the modernization process.

This perspective prioritized the swift reclamation of the «dark Africa on the outskirts of Rome,»[9] placing the area of the Pontine Plain in the spotlight. However, the Apulian Tableland, the second largest Italian plain, and almost five times the size of the Pontine Plain, was no less critical: with its extension and untapped natural resources, the tableland could set a precedent for the whole south,[10] which Mussolini had pledged to redeem since the early 1920s. Moreover, the combination of a harsh environment and poor surface water made the Apulian region a perfect testing ground for both dry farming and tiny irrigation schemes, which primarily relied on underground water. Similar conditions were to be found elsewhere in the south, as well as in the then recently acquired (1912) colony of Libya.[11] In addition, integral reclamation in Apulia was to lead the way to the long-promised redistribution of

expropriated large estates (*latifundia*). However, a significant challenge faced southern Italy in the ratio between population growth and employment rates, exacerbated by the mechanization of cereal crops, which led to increased emigration to industrial cities in the northern Italian regions or to the United States.

In the Pontine Plain, reclamation had to cope with «virgin forest, steppe, equatorial lakes, tropical vegetation, quagmires and insect swarms,» whereas the Apulian Tableland, in spite of its dry climate, was already a rich producer of wheat and wool,[12] alternating fields, meadows and uncultivated areas along a dense network of sheep tracks lined with staging posts and grazing areas, boundary stones or route markers, rural chapels and Marian shrines guarding venerated icons. The final reclamation of the Pontine Plain capitalized on a long series of projects and vestiges of antiquity, first and foremost the Appian Way. The territorial palimpsest[13] inherited from the past also played its part in the Apulian case: the landscape of nomadism was literally embedded into the new productive countryside, which turned farmers into small landowners. The unemployed peasants from Veneto and Emilia-Romagna who settled on the Pontine Plain found there the basic state-dependent functions of modern life: a post office, a Casa del Fascio and Workers' Club, and an agrarian office run by the National Association of War Veterans (*Opera Nazionale Combattenti*, hereafter ONC). By contrast, migration in Apulia was a matter of regional demography: draining peasants from the Capitanata hillside, waged workers moved from one estate to another, including peasants evacuated from the miserable semi-rural outskirts of Foggia. For many of them, Capitanata was «America beyond the Ofanto,» a place where farmers could find abundant work cultivating vineyards and gardens on the coastal sand dunes or ploughing virgin fields. About a hundred years earlier, halfway through the transition from the *ancien régime* to unified Italy, Matteo Fraccacreta[14] wrote a colossal work on the history of the region, extolled as a piece of «historical-poetic-topographic theatre»[15] (fig. 1).

Agriculture versus Pastoralism: Historical Thresholds

The Apulian Tableland covered 3,000 square kilometers at the center of Capitanata, a region bordered by the Ofanto river to the south, the Apennine ridge to the west, and the Gargano promontory to the northeast. This windswept, steppe-like land was subject to swamping in winter: rivers flowed swiftly, forming clogged lakes and coastal marshes, causing summer outbreaks of malaria.[16] In autumn, ever since antiquity, millions of sheep moved from the Apennine to the Adriatic on long-distance drovers' paths (*tratturi*).[17] These grassy, stony, or beaten-earth routes generated over time by the trampling of herds were up to 111 meters wide, branching off

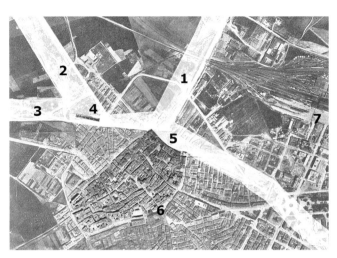

2   Sheep tracks (*tratturi*) reaching Foggia from the north: 1. Tratturo heading to the Candelaro stream (embedding Foggia-Manfredonia Road); 2. Tratturo coming from L'Aquila; 3. Tratturo Celano-Foggia; 4. Crosses; 5. Piano delle Fosse Granarie (esplanade with wheat pits); 6. Sheep Customs; 7. Railway Station.

in a complex network of smaller tracks. The main trunk lines (*tratturi reali*) from L'Aquila and Celano in Abruzzo crossed secondary sheep tracks at Foggia, a hub overseen by the Sheep Customs (1468–1806), an institution modelled on Spanish precedents to collect grazing rights and ensure a significant source of revenue for the Kingdom of Naples (fig. 2). An administrative unit since the late Middle Age, Capitanata experienced its earliest agrarian colonization scheme in 1774, when Ferdinand IV of Bourbon founded five agricultural colonies on estates expropriated from the Jesuits.[18] Two decades later, in 1798, the ploughing of grazing posts was allowed, initiating the conflict between agriculture and pastoralism. In the Papal States, the late 18th-century reformist drive resulted in the reclamation scheme of the Pontine Marshes promoted by Pope Pius VI.[19] In Apulia the late 18th century was a time of political and economic debate on independence from Naples, whose market was prone to the influence of political power, foreign merchants, and large landowners. This debate also concerned the relationship between pastoralism and agriculture.[20] Thorough investigations of the region as a whole—addressing natural resources, demographic conditions, productive structure of agriculture, arts and trade, institutions, customs and traditions[21]—opened the way to the Napoleonic reforms (1806–1811): abolition of the Sheep Customs[22] and the feudal laws, land registry and redistribution, and a «land and industrial tax» meant to foster local development.

Despite significant changes in laws and politics, multiple reports and surveys[23] conducted on Capitanata's agriculture consistently reveal a stark contrast between the poor living conditions of the rural population and the region's remarkable fertility. Historically, from the 18th century to the eve of the 20th century, Capitanata was the primary producer of cereal crops and wool for the entirety of the Bourbon reign.

The 19th century marked a major shift from pastoralism to agriculture in the region.[24] Foggia's increasing administrative role underpinned the reframing of places and footprints from the distant and recent past in a new territorial hierarchy, leaving room for agrarian experiments carried out on landed estates.[25] At the time of unification (1861), sheep from six provinces still wintered in Capitanata, which contained more than one-third (1,031 km) of Italy's 3,000 km of drovers' paths. In 1865, the Sheep Customs was permanently abolished along with grazing rights and multiple land use, with a view to strengthening cereal specialization and tree crops. The sale of over 300,000 ha of land previously subject to customs jurisdiction accelerated the transition from pastoralism to agriculture through the formation of small private properties. From 1861 to 1900, the increasing international demand for grain accelerated the transformation of the tableland into a system of mixed cereal-pastoral estates ranging from 3,700 ha to smaller farms of about 120 ha.[26] In 1907, the Italian Parliament commissioned a *Survey on the Peasants' Living Conditions in the Southern Provinces and Sicily*, written by Errico Presutti,[27] a jurist who clearly stated that a population of

shepherds had been turned into farmers. Political and economic forces contributed to the formation of a new territorial hierarchy: hilly and mountainous areas were slowly abandoned in favor of the plains, which attracted investments in reclamation schemes and agrarian experimentation.[28] At the turn of the 20th century, Italian poet Gabriele d'Annunzio immortalized the transhumant flocks descending towards the sea: «And so they walk the ancient path to the plain, almost as through a silent river of grass, following the vestiges of the forefathers.»[29] Eugenio Maury di Morancez described to the Italian Parliament the shepherds' life along a trajectory marked by staging posts:

> Sheep move at dawn into eight or ten minor flocks (*morre*). Leading the way are three mules in a row, loaded with nets, tents, blankets, net-rods, daily supplies and few utensils for making cheese. Each *morra* follows the other at a short distance, big white dogs walk along on both sides while one shepherd walks at the rear of the herd and the other ahead. [...] Each day, after six or seven hours of uninterrupted walking, the herd covers an average of 15 km. When they stop, shepherds build the nets. The campsite is already set, as mules with herders have preceded the arrival of shepherds by few hours. Sheep get milked, counted, and led into the enclosure. In the camp, men lit fires and start preparing *cacio di passo* [a dairy product belonging to the shepherds]. At sunset, the main shepherd commands to sleep [...] the other is on the night-watch. The following day, at dawn, they resume their journey: herders load their mules with crockery, tents and nets. At each stop along the way they exchange the *cacio di passo* for salt and bread. Finally, after sixteen or seventeen days, the herds descend the high mountainous slopes of Aquila reaching the Ofanto and Candelaro valleys.[30]

A few years later, in 1913, Antonio Lo Re, an expert on the agricultural problems of his time, criticized the forcibly induced modernization of Capitanata: herds still migrating from October to May were poor leftovers of a rich pastoralism. The tableland, rather than being redeemed, had disappeared due to «intransigent political Jacobinism and economic transcendentalism.» Lo Re also condemned «irrational liberalism and the suggestion of economic abstractions,» and the law of 21 February 1865 that ended southern pastoralism, leading to the misery of a large part of the mountains of Abruzzo, Sannio, and Lucania, and eventually to massive emigration.[31] He wrote:

> Where now the plough, crude and impotent, go scraping the land to better impoverish it, there were once [...] vast green meadows where, in winter and spring, myriads of beautiful lancers, mostly merino, and herds of horses and mules, oxen and cows, so beautiful and strong and numerous as no one has ever seen even in the American Pampas.[32]

Institutional Frameworks

In the aftermath of the First World War, the Civil Engineering Department (*Genio Civile*) carried out most infrastructural reconstruction works without introducing any substantial change in the rural realm. Conversely, some landowners and private companies experimented with reclamation and irrigation methods, eventually establishing the Apulian Aqueduct Authority (*Acquedotto Pugliese*) in 1919.

When the fascist state manifested itself as a «promethean engineer»[33] of a future territorial vision, large-scale interventions were discussed and planned in the Apulian Tableland, seen as an ideal field of experimentation for rural Italy and therefore attracting the best national and local experts, such as Gaetano Postiglione, an engineer from Foggia who conceived a model for transforming agriculture based on the use of groundwater and the exclusion of large cereal farms. In the 1920s, prominent agronomists such as Emanuele De Cillis from the Agricultural High School of Portici, and Enrico Pantanelli, director of the Experimental Agricultural Station of Bari, concentrated their studies on how to increase wheat production in southern Italy. Extensive drilling tests proved the presence of a rich underground aquifer whose potential, in 1925, was deemed sufficient to irrigate 20,000 ha and supply fresh water for animals and settlers. With support from the Ministry of Agriculture, the Apulian Aqueduct ran a large experimental farm near Foggia[34] showcasing the marvels of irrigation.

Limited-area irrigation made it possible to diversify dry farming beyond irrigated crops. Extensive cereal cultivation could prove less profitable than smaller farms, whose competitiveness depended on the introduction of crops with high added value (such as vineyards, olives, and vegetables) that could corner significant market segments.

In terms of social structure, this approach allowed for turning seasonal workers into smallholders, while also replacing large supra-regional migrant herds with smaller ones. Irrigated crops required specific machinery and a stable work organization providing farmers with safe, acceptable, and stable living conditions. The fascist regime equated the modernization of Apulia with a permanently inhabited countryside, where the ownership of a house and a tract land was to strengthen a sense of belonging. This implied overlapping allotment schemes on a landscape made of sheep tracks, large estates, and *masserie* (clusters of scattered buildings used by shepherds, waged workers, and nomadic rural workers) (fig. 3). Epitomizing nomadic living as well as the feudalism of landed estates, *masserie* included a main house,[35] a small chapel, and a number of shelters

3   Perspective view of a *masseria* in the upper Murgia showing areas for sheep shelter.

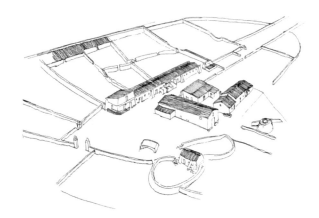

and warehouses where peasants could be accommodated. The functional buildings forming these proto-settlements were used to store agricultural tools, machinery, and animals. According to Lepre,[36] the unchanged living conditions of peasants were a consequence of the *latifundia* and of their owners' mindset; they usually consumed and did not reinvest money earned from agricultural production. With land reclamation, all this was to change dramatically. Nine reclamation districts were to cope with an array of hydrological problems, including rectification of riverbanks to prevent seasonal flooding and drainage of swampy ponds[37] for conversion into agricultural land. The first reclamation consortia appeared in 1928 at the initiative of large landowners, competing with capitalist ventures in partial contrast with the central state.[38] Some support came from the Apulian Aqueduct Authority, backed by the undersecretary of Agriculture. In 1930, reclamation and sanitation still lagged behind. Yet, as a consequence of the Mussolini Law, the coast from Margherita di Savoia to Manfredonia had changed dramatically: the geometric network of canals and the water-lifting stations at Zapponeta and Siponto allowed fast-paced drainage of Lake Salpi, which was partly integrated into the existing salt works.[39]

A milestone in the process was the 1928 competition for the master plan of Foggia, which lay at the center of the plain: it was to become a modern city of business and trade, gentrified by resettling low-income citizens in satellite villages.[40] The public works fostered by the fascist regime were also meant for this purpose.[41] In this fragmented context, decentralization required an efficient road network, a key problem ever since unification: infrastructural upgrade was to support rural development, making peasants' daily commute easier.[42] In fact, farmers migrated just like shepherds, albeit over shorter distances, during harvesting period, often sleeping in the fields, under the cart, or in animal shelters.

In 1931 a plan for the tableland's agricultural roads (*Piano delle strade d'interesse agrario del Tavoliere*) prepared by the Civil Engineering Department (*Genio Civile*) was approved. In 1932, the Central Apulian Tableland Reclamation Authority (*Comprensorio di Bonifica del Tavoliere Centrale*) called upon Emanuele De Cillis, Giuseppe Tommasi,[43] Alberto De Dominicis,[44] and engineer Giuseppe Colacicco to draw up an outline scheme project for land transformation, which, according to Gaetano Postiglione's directives, was to include four types of farms, differing in size and organization.

A Local-Level Plan Based on an Ancient Shrine: The First Project for Borgo Incoronata

The 1932 scheme by De Cillis, Tommasi, De Dominicis, and Colacicco and their pilot project for the area of Incoronata are documented in two volumes,[45] including a photographic survey, figures, maps, and drawings. The volumes include a report on climate, surface and underground hydrography, demography, anophelism, soil quality, and crop distribution. Besides Foggia, the main urban centers are Ortanova, Ordona, Carapelle and Stornara, four of the five rural villages founded by Ferdinand IV in 1774. The authors confirm that the pastoral territory of the Apulian Tableland still suffered from a lack of agrarian traditions; nevertheless, a number of passionate landowners, as documented by the photos of their farms, were pervaded by a spirit of innovation and progress. The plan envisaged twelve new rural centers, the regulation of streams, the construction of first- and second-class roads, a system of rural aqueducts, and the construction of new power lines to upgrade the existing rural electric lines.

During the fascist period, Apulia implemented rural colonization projects that included detailed plans for allotments, settlements, and farms. In this sense, the settlements were a means to improve the living conditions of peasants rather than solely to redistribute land. This urgency was noted in surveys from the Bourbon period up until just

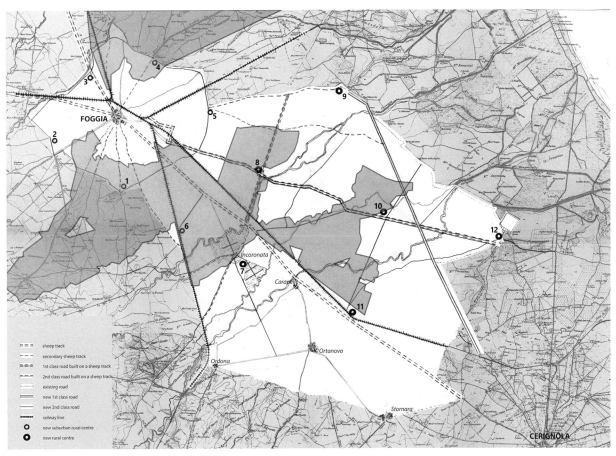

4   New roads embedding pre-existing sheep tracks, and the new settlements planned in 1932:
1. Salice, 2. Pietrafitta, 3. Lazzaretto, 4. Torre Guiducci, 5. Quadrone delle Vigne, 6. Cervaro, 7. Incoronata, 8. Fandetta, 9. Onoranza,
10. Scrofola, 11. Ortanova railway station, 12. Tressanti. In grey are the areas whose reclamation was planned by ONC in 1939
while the white boundary marks the former Central Apulian Tableland Reclamation Authority.

before WWI, which the fascist government used to portray itself as the actual modernizing force in the area. For instance, the 1884 Jacini national survey, *The Results of the Agricultural Survey* (*I Risultati della inchiesta agraria*), noted that shepherds' living and social conditions were bearable in comparison to those of farmers.[46] Presutti's 1907 survey depicted the ambivalent Apulian townscape, emphasizing the miserable conditions of peasants who lived within urban settlements and relied on seasonal work:

> The village's main street, or the crossroad, are like a stony curtain of exquisite houses that exude a small-town charm. In the back, the side streets where the peasants live are narrow and unpaved, clogged with playing children, as the roads appear to them to be a paradise in comparison to the house. Due to the soil's altimetric flow, the house is often semi-subterranean and lowland cities like Cerignola, Foggia, also follow this practice, maybe to save building expenses.[47]

One of the maps complementing De Cillis, Tommasi, De Dominicis, and Colacicco's project report shows the village locations in relation to the road network, mostly exploiting former sheep tracks across the plain. Six rural centers were to rise at a distance of about four kilometers from Foggia along the new ring road (*circumfoggiana*) (fig. 4).

5   The Incoronata Marian Shrine in the early 1930s.

The purpose of the centers was threefold: fragmenting large suburban estates; settling the rural population expelled from the city; and providing better supplies of vegetables, fruit, and milk. These centers, «connected to the roads»[48] in correspondence with pre-existing farms, were to be supplied drinking water, electricity, and basic public services. The six remaining settlements, featuring a complete urban structure, were to establish a buffer area between Foggia, the regional capital since 1912, and the tableland.[49] Ortanova, Ordona, Carapelle, and Stornara were also to serve as centers of irradiation for similar farm creations. The formation of a rural center eleven kilometers south-east of Foggia in the area of Incoronata (the name meaning «Crowned Virgin Mary»), and the planting of related farms, were considered priorities to be implemented according to the executive project included in the second volume[50] of the report.

The plan consisted in parceling two tracts of land belonging to the Foggia Municipality near the Incoronata woods in between the Cervaro and Carapelle streams, known as the Frederick II Hohenstaufen hunting ground. A convent with an infirmary and a hospice for pilgrims had been built near the oak tree where, in late April 1001, the Virgin Mary is said to have appeared to a shepherd and to the Count of Ariano Irpino, also

hunting in the woods.[51] This hermitic place amidst plains of grain and pastures had been visited by princes, cardinals, bishops, and by a host of pilgrims who travelled there inspired by a lively faith and erected temporary huts in nearby fields. Set at the crossroad of secondary tracks off the Aquila–Foggia–Ofanto sheep track,[52] the Incoronata Sanctuary, renovated in 1831 after the waves of expropriations, was a stronghold of a folkloric devotion, a destination for pilgrims and shepherds alike (fig. 5). The feast of Incoronata was celebrated at the end of the winter grazing season, with a dressing of the Madonna and a cavalcade evoking what had happened in the forest in April 1001.

De Cillis, Tommasi, De Dominicis, and Colacicco considered that the area, subject to several drilling tests, required only some technical interventions along the River Cervaro in addition to other minor works. The pre-existing church was seen as an asset, as the two reclamation areas of Bosco Incoronata and Piana Padule would only need a school and a service center (fig. 6).

These buildings were to face on opposite sides at the head of an oblong wooded area park with a drinking trough. The surrounding land was reserved for future expansion to accommodate food processing industries, dairies, and a social wine cellar. The provision of a dairy plant was a clear indication of the coexistence between agriculture and semi-nomadic livestock rearing. The project to build a school and service building testifies to a pragmatic approach to design based on functional solutions adapted from handbook prototypes. In line with the small rural schools of post-unification Italy, the size and layout of the school was dictated by the expected school population: 180 pupils on two daily shifts required two classrooms on the ground floor and two teachers' lodgings on the first floor.[53] The building was designed to offer a basic education to village children. Its symmetrical layout—drawing on the rural schools built on the Pontine Plain from 1912 to 1922[54]—was dictated by distribution criteria: a single entrance on the corridor distributing the

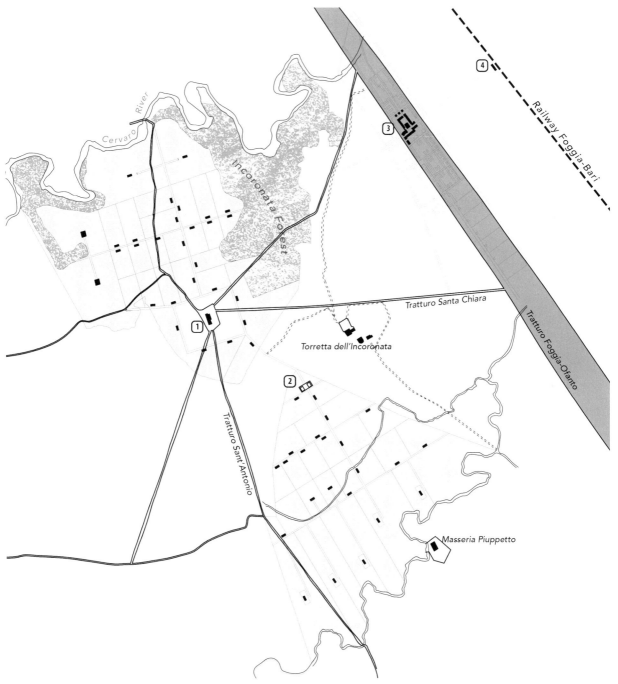

6   Map of the two reclamation areas of Bosco Incoronata to the north (previously under pasture and woodland) and Piana Padule to the south (previously cultivated with cereals). Both tracts are highlighted in light grey, whereas the Foggia-Ofanto sheep track is marked in dark grey. 1. Marian shrine, 2. Planned rural center, 3. Site of the Incoronata village built by ONC in 1938, 4. Incoronata Railway Station, unbuilt.

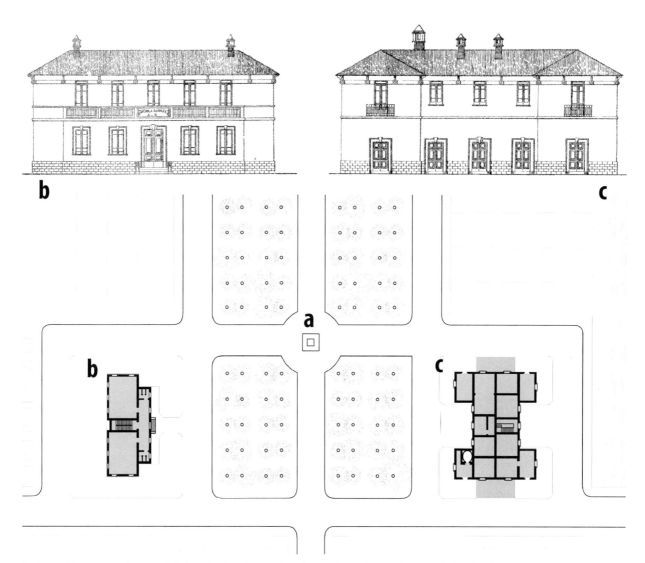

7   Plan of the new rural center with the school and general services. a. fountain/watering trough; b. school; c. general services building encompassing: mill, bakery, mechanic, kitchen, tavern, tobacconist's, municipal office, fertiliser warehouse, sanitary services, fascist workers' club, OND, seed storehouse, police station.

central staircase, the two classrooms, and the toilets on opposite sides. Following the same criteria of sobriety and economy of space, the services building featured an H-shaped plan with two axes of symmetry. The interest of this building lies in the complex program it was to accommodate, without any of these functions determining some kind of representative instance. The ground floor included a series of rooms with direct access: the town hall, the fascist party and ONC headquarters, the doctor's surgery, the mill and the oven, the machine workshop, the seed and fertilizer store, and the police station. The first floor was subdivided into four apartments: for the nurse, the midwife, the mechanic, and the innkeeper/shopkeeper. In fact, this project remained on paper as the building was not constructed nor a place selected for its construction (fig. 7).

Borgo La Serpe: A Fragment of Roberto Curato's Failed Scheme

In 1933, by royal decree, the smaller reclamation consortia merged into the Capitanata Reclamation Authority (*Consorzio generale di Bonifica e di trasformazione fondiaria della Capitanata*), a technocratic emanation of the fascist state, which concentrated knowhow accumulated over time and allowed for the simultaneous completion of works across the area.[55] In 1933, Roberto Curato, an engineer and a large landowner open to innovations, sensitive to market trends and labor relations,[56] took over the Authority's direction and drafted a plan for the tableland aimed at fighting unemployment by the fragmentation of large farms and the establishment of new rural hamlets. Curato's expertise allowed him to operate in the field of hydraulic and road works along with housing. His plan took for granted the limitation of tree crops; farms were instead to combine cereal cultivation and animal husbandry in which livestock could be fed with fodder crops, which were to change the rhythm of agricultural rotations and improve production. Based on population growth statistics, Curato proposed 103 evenly distributed settlements (one every 300 ha, to reduce the distance between the villages and the countryside) served by a homogeneous road network.[57] Five of the settlements were to act as municipal centers housing fifty families each and equipped with complete facilities. Each of the remaining 98 centers, with fewer facilities, was to host twenty families. The settlements envisaged by Curato[58] did not compare to those of the Pontine Plain. Each represented a decentralized cluster of basic services and housing units for permanent workers employed by the owners of the neighboring land. On the Pontine Plain, by contrast, the new settlements adhered to a hierarchical division of public services that designated the towns (Latina, Pontinia, and Sabaudia) as locations with institutional and administrative public activities and rural-service villages, known as *borghi*, where farmers would find activities providing basic needs for the work in the fields.[59]

VILLAGGIO BORGO MEZZANONE (Foggia) - Visto dall'alto

8   Aerial view of Borgo La Serpe (Mezzanone) in 1938.

Curato's scheme aimed at settling a nomadic population and reducing the number of day and wage workers (*sbracciantizzazione*). The prevailing socio-political intent—namely the sedentarization of the population—did not prevent Curato from experimenting with an economic-oriented approach, which included reducing natural grazing to a minimum as a cereal-livestock system relied on dry fodder; small irrigated portions fed by raising groundwater could afford a modest expansion of tree crops, whose convenience was to be checked on a case-by-case basis. Curato's scheme also envisaged an extensive development of rural roads and electrification.

The site of Borgo La Serpe (later Borgo Mezzanone) opened in July 1934 and was inaugurated by Mussolini in September 1934. It stood along the road to Barletta two kilometers east from the place where De Cillis, Tommasi, De Dominicis, and Colacicco had envisaged the rural settlement of Fandetta. Commenting on Mussolini's visit to Apulia in 1934, Friedrich Vöchting, an esteemed agrarian historian, noted that despite plans for reclamation, there were only a few kilometers of newly constructed roads and described Borgo La Serpe as an «erratic block»[60] in the tableland (fig. 8).

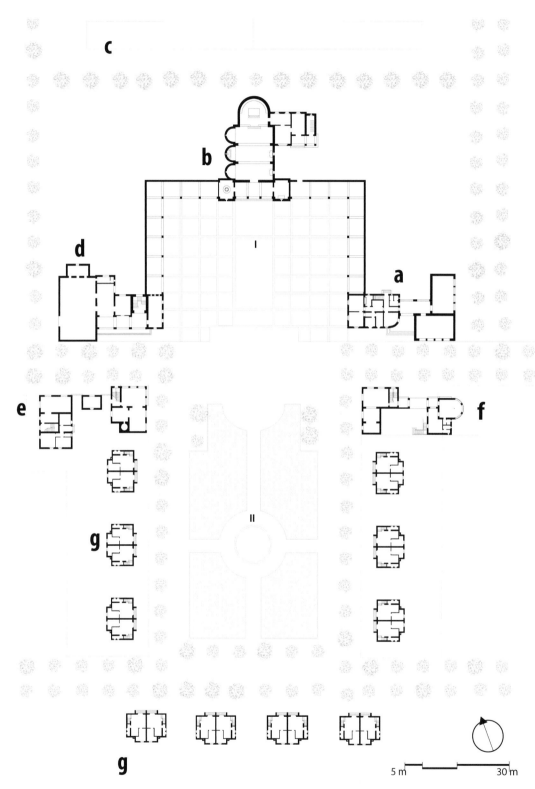

9   Plan of Borgo La Serpe (Mezzanone). I. Paved square; a. school (classroom, toilets, teacher's quarters, management, archives, museum); b. church, sacristy, office; c. sports ground; d. Casa del Fascio; e. shops (grocery, bakery, storehouse, roadhouse, craft shop, road worker's house; f. bazaar and medical post; II Park, g. semi-detached houses.

Borgo La Serpe was something in between a micro-garden city and a suburban villa.[61] The northern square clustering religious and civil functions[62] faced a wooded area surrounded by semi-detached houses and commercial activities[63] across the road connecting Foggia to Trinitapoli on the Adriatic coast. This layout reflected Mario Quaglini's standard model for a rural hamlet:[64] a large quadrangular square partly wooded and partly paved, bordered on the short side by rural roads (fig. 9).[65]

In 1934, Italian economist and politician Alberto De Stefani questioned the presence of rural squares and related hamlets, maintaining that the colonization of Apulia should be based instead on a vast system of farms supplemented by small service nuclei at convenient distances, each including a chapel, a pharmacy, a post office, and a school.[66] Agricultural technicians instead stressed the importance of rural hamlets for providing the essential conditions for civil coexistence. Italian historian and politician Gaetano Salvemini[67] argued that peasants would remain attached to the land wherever they could find a small church, a kindergarten and a school, and a weekly visit by the doctor.[68] In presenting his proposal, Curato argued that any reclamation plan should be based on an ad hoc study and declared his indebtedness to all the geologists, agrarian technicians, and hydraulic engineers of the previous decades.

Despite the initial enthusiasm and Mussolini's promises, Borgo La Serpe became an example of a failed modernization. According to a 1936 document of the Ministry of Forestry and Agriculture,[69] settlers did not manage to find a job and the three hectares of land received from the Reclamation Authority were not enough to survive: Borgo La Serpe was a head without a body, a group of houses completely unrelated to the land on which they stood (figs. 10 and 11).

With its the dense network of roads and villages, Curato's plan was bound to fail,[70] paving the way for the intervention of more centralized technocrats. In 1938, a new scheme, also never

10   Fountain at Borgo La Serpe (Mezzanone) in 1938.

completed, was drafted by Aurelio Carrante, then head of the regional agricultural inspectorate at Bari, Giuseppe Medici, and Luigi Perdisa, an expert on modern agricultural technologies. The failed experiments of Borgo Incoronata and Borgo La Serpe proved that rural modernization required adequate field allotments in a region where landed estates were hard nuts to crack. In 1939, the reclamation area was divided into three sub-units, prioritizing the central one (about 270,000 ha) from Apricena under the Gargano to the Ofanto

11   Borgo Mezzanone, December 2018.

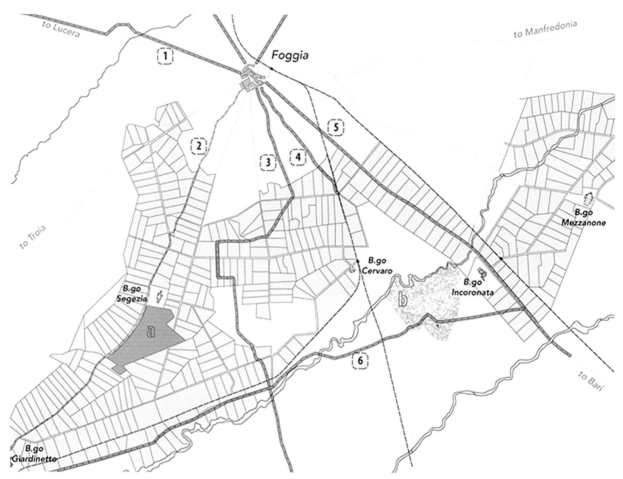

12   ONC's colonisation scheme with the four new settlements: Borgo Giardinetto, Borgo Segezia, Borgo Cervaro, Borgo Incoronata and Borgo Mezzanone. The map shows the southern area of the overall scheme, with primary and secondary sheep tracks embedded into the rural allotments or transformed into roads. 1. Tratturo Celano-Foggia; 2. Tratturello (secondary sheep track) Foggia-Carapelle converted into the road from Foggia to Borgo Segezia; 3. Tratturo Foggia-Ordona; 4. Tratturo Foggia-San Lorenzo; 5. Tratturo Foggia-Ofanto edging Borgo Incoronata, transformed into the Foggia-Bari national road; 6. Tratturo Santa Chiara reaching the Incoronata Marian Shrine. Additional highlights: a. National Sheepfold; b. Incoronata Forest and Marian Shrine.

River, which included Foggia, the world's biggest aqueduct, Europe's biggest salt works, and two Mediterranean ports. In January 1939, the ONC, which had already operated in the inner colonization of the Pontine Plain, started the construction of works in a 42,000 ha central area of Capitanata,[71] on state properties along roads and railways, before other areas could be reclaimed and allotted.

Architects on the Frontline

In 1939, the ONC president Araldo Di Crollalanza called upon Concezio Petrucci, Giorgio Calza Bini and Dagoberto Ortensi to plan three municipal centers and three rural villages within the framework of the new reclamation scheme. At a time of autarky, settlement layouts were to exploit solar and wind orientation, along with architectural simplicity, possibly using local building materials (figs. 12, 13, and 14).

The newsletter section of the first issue of *Urbanistica*,[72] mouthpiece of the National Town Planning Institute, announced that integral reclamation of the Apulian Tableland by the ONC continued at an uninterrupted pace and three rural towns were to rise in the Foggia countryside: Segezia, Incoronata, and Daunilia. A few months later, *Urbanistica*[73] informed its readers that Segezia was nearing completion while the first buildings were appearing at Incoronata.

Marcello Piacentini described Segezia a «varied and picturesque whole.»[74] According to Carlo Roccatelli, representative of the National Fascist Union of Engineers, the square was the key element, providing a common place of reference for farmers living in the surrounding area. Truly, the square was the geometric center of a cross-shaped layout at the intersection between the Benevento–Foggia state road and the rural service road. All public buildings gathered around the square: the church and rectory, the kindergarten, the primary school and adjoining sports facilities, the ONC headquarters, housing for teachers and employees, the town hall, the post and telegraph office, the ever-present Casa del Fascio with the police station, the doctor's office, the café-restaurant and shops, with a covered market at the rear. The staggered movements of the east–west and north–south roads altered the uniform continuity of the elongated square, creating continuous variations of background, which allowed public buildings to act as visual landmarks when coming from different directions. The north–south alignment was also slightly offset, enough to close off the perspective of each half-axis with the entrance gate to the schools on one side, and the Casa del Fascio on the other. On reaching the square, architecture resounded in a chorus of references, all contributing to dilate the space-time dimension. Each building was characterized by a distinguishing architectural expression, enhanced by the use of different building materials. In Petrucci's

13   Rural house type 1. Porch, 2. Silo; 3. Stable, 4. Calves; 5: Horses; 6. Kitchen; Room; 7. Storeroom.

own description, the geometric modulation of the 42 m-high bell tower was to dominate Segezia, providing a visual landmark for the peasants of the most remote farmhouses (fig. 15).

While Segezia was built on land near the Tuoro di Loreto staging post, expropriated by the ONC in 1940, Borgo Incoronata was to replace a tract of

14   Rural house type 1 near Segezia, December 2018.

and chromatic character, a warm, golden-colored stone arranged in ashlars[75]—and the whitewashed plaster of the surrounding buildings. According to Calza Bini, the compact volume of the town hall was to evoke the typical farms of the region, where the owner's residence dominated the surrounding dwellings with its dignified mass.

Dagoberto Ortensi's volume, considered a major handbook for the design of rural buildings and settlements, presented both Segezia and Borgo Incoronata with a series of urban sections where the functional program is associated with different portions of the elevations:[76] a picturesque yet unified complex summarizing the main institutions intended to regulate the life of the small community.

15   View of Segezia.

Concluding Remarks

the Foggia–Ofanto sheep track, one of the trunk lines crossing the territories of Carapelle, Orta Nova, and Stornara before reaching Cerignola. The plan for Borgo Incoronata by Giorgio Calza Bini and Roberto Nicolini was another step towards the dissolution of the pastoral landscape of Capitanata. The new settlement was built much closer to the railway and did not take into account any of the features of the plan drafted by De Cillis, De Dominicis, Tommasi, and Colacicco in 1932.

As in the case of Segezia, the road system dictated the overall arrangement of the public buildings. The staggered movement of the road connecting the Marian shrine to the (planned) railway station was to enhance the presence of the Casa del Fascio when arriving from Foggia, and of the church, whose original design drew inspiration from the Apulian Romanesque style. The central square featured an elongated rectangle hinged onto the porticoed ground floor of the town hall, forming the backdrop of the rural roads (fig. 16).

The «picturesque character» of the village depended on the contrast between the architectural quality of the town hall—due to its constructive

From 1933 to 1943, a large number of public works were completed in the Apulian Tableland: 436 km of reclamation roads, 50 km of quaysides, 59 light bridges, 35 km of electric lines. Hydraulic works included 135 km of stream canalization, 334 km of drains, three pumping machines, four new river-mouths, 600 ha of flooding gutters, five rural aqueducts covering 28 km, twelve artesian wells. Undoubtedly, the new rural settlement, built within the framework of reclamation schemes, broke new ground in terms of planning. Alberto Calza Bini, National Secretary of the Fascist Architects Union as well as founder in 1930 of the National Town Planning Institute (INU), claimed that reorganizing the productive forces in the national territory clearly proved that the term «urbanism» was not inconsistent with fascism's tendencies towards «de-urbanisation.»[77] Finally, in 1946, Amos Edallo[78] coined the neologism «rurbanism» or «ruralism»[79] to define the adoption of town planning criteria in the rural world, overcoming the commonplace of the countryside as a place of backwardness.

In a 1937 document addressed to the *Podestà* (Chief Magistrate) of Foggia, the ONC listed the

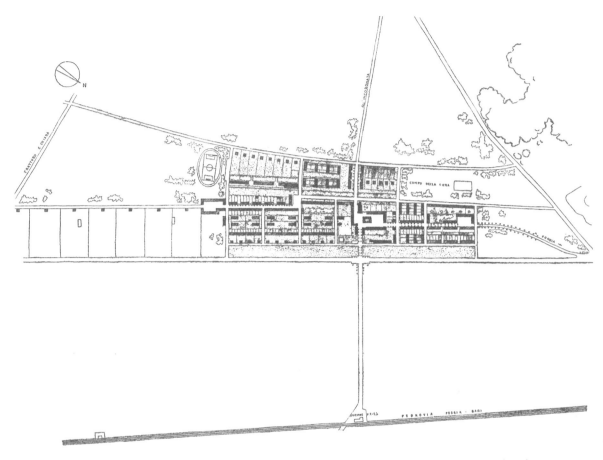

16   Plan of Borgo Incoronata.

principles to be followed when designing new rural settlements: siting was crucial and farms were to be contiguous in order to facilitate farmers' daily toil and generate new landscape features in the plain. Land parceled into holdings was to line national roads and railway lines, so as to ensure the maximum visibility of rural modernization.

As proved unequivocally by Le Corbusier's studies for the «radiant farm,»[80] designing innovative small settlements that were physically and socially coherent posed a challenge also for architects. In this respect, the Apulian case study brings to the fore a wide range of expert profiles, along with examples of buildings adapted from handbook prototypes (as in the case of the first Incoronata project) and cutting-edge proposals (as in the case of Segezia).

We may well ask to what extent different expressions of rationality, realism, and public good bore evidence to the alleged opposition between the rural and urban realms, which Michelangelo Sabatino considered «in tension.»[81] Within this tension, the new rural settlements built in the Apulian Tableland show the transition from an economy based on pastoralism to a radically new order in which Foggia—the city of institutions conforming with the fascist state—acted as a reference point for a territory undergoing an anthropological revolution. Complying with simplicity

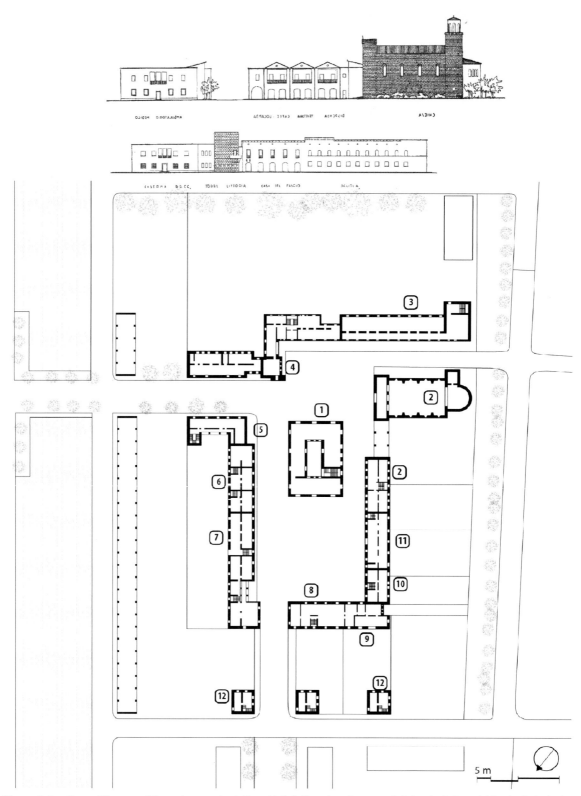

17   Plan and elevations of the core of Borgo Incoronata. 1. Town Hall; 2. Church and rectory; 3. Schools; 4. Casa del Fascio; 5. Ambulatory and doctor's house; 6. Shops; 7. Farm offices; 8. Inn; 9. Shop; 10. Dwelling; 11. Post Office; 12. Dwellings.

and modesty, settlement cores choreographed daily life, the weekly rest, and seasonal celebrations against the orderly repetition of farms.

Hovering between a particular vision—be it socio-economic or architectural—new rural settlements in Apulia bring to the fore the anomaly of «instant townscapes» aimed at the artificial creation of a rural community. Although Martinelli and Nuti in their book did not address the Apulian Tableland, they did observe that new towns were established under time, economic, and technological constraints that hindered spatial and architectural innovation.[82] Hence, the concept of the «instant townscape» is particularly fitting for the new rural towns that were constructed as part of the fascist ruralization policy. This definition aptly captures the combination of modern and traditional functions, as well as the architectural language that fused local and monumental features in both the buildings and the overall urban plan. The notion of «instant-ness» describes the need for new rural towns to evoke simultaneously in a concentrated place both familiar (regional) and distant places, mostly deriving from the Italian architectural heritage.

In this respect, the two projects for Incoronata may be seen as polar opposites. In the first project,

the new buildings are devoid of representative intents, as if the longstanding presence of the Marian shrine in the woods might well suffice as an identity feature. In the second project, conceived in the wake of Giovannoni's ideas, Calza Bini and Nicolini try to incorporate some «straightforward motifs of Apulian architectural tradition,» resulting in the juxtaposition between the self-standing iconic town hall and the surrounding elevations alternating different façade scores (fig. 17).

The pervasiveness of the picture of a self-sufficient community has affected writers, painters, politicians, and reformers. In 1934, Italian journalist and writer Corrado Alvaro wrote a memoir documenting the reclamation of the Pontine Plain, where each road reached a «clearing in the countryside» with a school, an agricultural storage and some shops, a church and a small tower: like the castle on a chess board. Before being inhabited, villages looked like «children's constructions.»[83] The case of Apulia brings to the fore different approaches to the design of the new rural settlement, as well as the contradictions generated by the efforts to erase the landscapes of nomadism through new picturesque settings associated with the overriding importance of style, loaded with references to a longer past.

1   Albertini 1935.

2   Scott 1998.

3   The Mussolini Law of 24 December 1928 summed up all the measures for land reclamation and unified reclamation plans, while also defining the necessary means for implementation. To cope with population growth and subsistence, integral reclamation was to combine hydraulic and irrigation works with agricultural transformation, all financed by the Italian State.

4   Rural development schemes implemented in Mussolini's Italy continued a process begun immediately after the unification of Italy (1861). In reality, the Serpieri Law marked a milestone in a debate dating back to the last decades of the 19th century; the very notion of «integral reclamation,» providing for the obligation to reclaim

land for agriculture upon completion of hydraulic works, emerged under Giovanni Giolitti's liberal government (1903–1914). Prior to fascism, integral reclamation was established through policies and laws that occurred following the construction of the national railway and the delays caused by malaria; generally, the idea of integral reclamation sparked awareness of the interdependence between the control of mountain water systems, the recovery of the plains, and the urgency to fight malaria as a prerequisite for permanent rural settlements.

5   Armiero et al. 2022.

6   Falasca-Zamponi 1997.

7   Scott 1998, 2.

8   Calza Bini 1941.

9   Gruppuso 2014.

10   Bevilacqua 1988.

11   The military invasion and occupation of Libya began in 1911 under Giolitti's government with the conquest of Tripolitania. It persisted after World War I until 1934, when Libya was officially declared an Italian colony.

12   Ruinas 1943.

13   Corboz 1985.

14   Matteo Fraccacreta (1772–1857) was a historian and a poet and a corresponding author for the Società Economica di Capitanata in Naples; this society published a journal between 1835 and 1847 describing the major agrarian and industrial innovations in the Capitanata region.

15   Fraccacreta 1832.

16   Dorotea 1843, 436.

17   Mascheroni 1936; Bevilacqua 1988; Russo 2015 and Russo/Bourdin 2016.

18   The five colonies of Ordona, Carapelle, Stornara, Stornarella and Ortanova still exist. Farmers who originally settled there had to undertake heavy tillage works to cultivate cereals and breed sheep, against the strain of insalubrious conditions. In spite of the initial difficulties, the five rural villages continued to grow, so much so that two of them were upgraded to the rank of municipality. The experiment of subdividing large Jesuit holdings into small plots allowed the formation of a class of small and medium-sized farmers who profoundly changed the land structure, bringing about a significant change in the agrarian landscape (Quercia 2018).

19   Rappini 1777, Folchi 2002.

20   Salvemini 1989, 88–89.

21   Apulian economist Giuseppe Palmieri had claimed that state administration, allied to economics, was to serve the happiness of citizens, thereby coping with popular education (Palmieri 1789). Giuseppe Maria Galanti, an economist close to the Neapolitan reformist Enlightenment, had advocated the overthrow of the feudal regime and agricultural progress (Nigro 2017). Claiming that investigations were to be «written in shoes,» Galanti argued that small farms should replace large estates, thus overcoming the lack of water regulation causing malaria epidemics and low population density and limiting the extent of uncultivated land feeding transhumant pastoralism.

22   In 1806, Giuseppe Bonaparte abolished the Sheep Customs and the court annexed to it, stipulating that farmers could apply for a perpetual grant of the land assigned to them for grazing, with the right to cultivate it and dispose of it freely.

23   Bronzini 1993.

24   In 1811, Joachim Murat (King of Naples from 1808 to 1815) launched a survey of the Kingdom that included a statistical report on Capitanata, which concluded that the needed reforms would foster investments in agriculture and the rise of local markets and of a local elite (Salvemini 1995, 12–14), yet undermine supra-regional

transhumant sheep farming. Economic and social aspects were part of a broader reorganization strategy, including an upgrade of the road network and integration between cereal and pastoral farms (Russo 1990, 43–44).

25   Lepre 1980.

26   Mercurio 2021, 26.

27   Presutti 1908, 16.

28   Mercurio 2021, 6.

29   D'Annunzio 1903. Authors' translation.

30   Maury 1906, 8. Authors' translation.

31   De Cesare 1859. Carlo de Cesare cites an 1852 survey stating that Capitanta had a lower population compared to other parts of the Apulia region. The survey shows that there were 321,175 inhabitants in Capitanta with a density of 136 inhabitants per square mile. In contrast, the Bari region had 497,460 inhabitants and a density of 285 inhabitants per square mile.

32   Lo Re 1913, 24–25.

33   Grassini 2012, 111.

34   Cf. Di Lonardo 1928.

35   Usually a two-storey building where either the owner, the tenant, or an appointed officer lived during sowing and harvesting. Other buildings included a built warehouse called *cafoneria* where peasants slept, with a common kitchen with a high chimney called *fucagna*; after the abolition of the Sheep Custom, an elongated porched building called *scariazzo* was the main shelter for sheep in those farms, which combined agricultural and livestock production.

36   Lepre 1980, 24.

37   Of which the Cervaro and Candelaro Reclamation Authority (1928) monitored creeks, the marshes of Siponto, and the coastal Lake Salpo.

38   D'Antone 1988.

39   Pompa 1930.

40   Caracozzi 2007.

41   Pompa 1932 b.

42   In 1865 there were a total of «600 kilometers roads for carriages connecting the main urban agglomerations and roughly 1,593 kilometers of mule tracks» (Mercurio 2021, 39).

43   Director of the Experimental Chemical-Agricultural Station of Rome.

44   From the Agricultural School of Portici like De Cillis.

45   De Cillis et al. 1932a

46   Angeloni described one of the workers' houses: «In this area, the homes of poor people mostly consist of underground rooms within the city's inner buildings or small ground-level rooms that lack proper ventilation and light. The living conditions of the *terrazzani* who rely on selling herbs and other natural resources they collect or steal from the nearby countryside, are particularly dire.» He then described the house: «A room about 2 m wide by 4 m long, no more than 3 m high. The narrowest side of the room contains a pile of wood, with an uncombined layer of reeds and wicker acting as a bed that is too small

for a person to lie down comfortably. The floor is covered in mud, soggy grass, and urine, with old tools scattered in various places.»

47 Bronzini 1993.

48 Salice, Pietrafitta, Lazzaretto, Torre Guiducci, Quadrone delle Vigne, and Cervaro.

49 In addition to Incoronata, the plan foresaw the following centers: Fandetta 12 km from Foggia at the junction of the Foggia–Barletta road (under construction) with the Palazzo d'Ascoli-Scalo S. Giovanni Rotondo road; Onoranza 14 km from Foggia on the road corresponding to the Versentino sheep track; Scrofola 20 km from Foggia along the Foggia–Barletta reclamation road; Ortanova railway station along the Foggia–Bari railway and the Foggia–Cerignola road; and Tressanti 28 km from Foggia along the Foggia–Barletta reclamation road.

50 De Cillis et al. 1932b.

51 A document from 1156 tells us that the «*monasterium Sancta Mariae Coronatae*» was under the jurisdiction of the Bishop of Troia. At the beginning of the 13th century, the Vergilians were succeeded by the Cistercians, who cultivated and reclaimed the lands of the Abbey in accordance with their rule.

52 Its route largely corresponds with the State Road, Strada Statale 16 Adriatica.

53 Each with two rooms, kitchen, hallway and a common terrace.

54 Pruneri 2018, Secchi 1923.

55 Bevilacqua 1988, 175.

56 Curato was active in promoting the use of hydropower for both agricultural and industrial purposes. Before undertaking the plan, he had clearly manifested his conviction that the purpose of rural modernization was to fight unemployment rather than to increase profits. On his own farm, from 1926, he offered stable employment to a number of families of permanent wage earners.

57 Curato's scheme only materialized in the two hamlets of Tavernola and Siponto, and the village of Borgo La Serpe (later renamed Borgo Mezzanone) along the state road from Foggia to Barletta.

58 Chiefly inspired by Arrigo Serpieri, the agronomist who drafted the Law of Integral Reclamation in 1933, establishing the role of public action in the reclamation and rural colonization of malarial and marshy areas. This law established reclamation authorities that were to be in charge of hydraulic reclamation and road construction whereas the ONC was in charge of carrying out the

colonization through the allotment of fields and the construction of settlements and farmhouses.

59 The rural service villages—*borghi*—acted as a settlement serving a catchment area of 100 farms. Each village service was equipped with an ONC office, a church, a health center with pharmaceutical cabinet, a school, a post office and some shops.

60 Vöchting 1938, 492.

61 Designed by engineer Giovanbattista Canevari and architect Domenico Sandri.

62 Namely the church, the Fascist party headquarters, the school, and the cinema.

63 The tobacconist, the post office, shops, and the Red Cross post.

64 Graduated in civil engineering from Politecnico di Milano in 1929, Mario Quaglini (1906–1964) well epitomized the technician who translated central-state policies at the local level. After designing a number of industrial plants near Bari, in Sicily, and in Lombardy, he worked as chief engineer of the Foggia Colonisation Section (Scionti 2007 and Piemontese 2010, 66). In this capacity, in the 1930s, he prepared a pilot project for a farmhouse and a rural hamlet.

65 Scionti 2007, 142.

66 De Stefani 1934.

67 Salvemini was forced into exile by Mussolini's regime and then taught History of the Italian Civilization at Harvard.

68 Salvemini 1933.

69 Cf. Mercurio 2021, 155. The author is sourcing data from a 1936 report by Arturo Maugini prepared for the Ministry of Forestry and Agriculture, General Department for Land Reclamation and Settlement (*Ministero agricoltura e foreste, Direzione generale bonifica e colonizzazione*).

70 Also due to his untimely death in 1935.

71 Ruinas 1943, 134.

72 A.A.V.V. 1941, 58–59.

73 A.A.V.V. 1941, 43.

74 Piacentini 1943.

75 Barbato 2005, 69.

76 Ortensi 1941, 494–495.

77 Calza Bini 1941.

78 Amos Edallo (1908–1965) was trained as a sculptor at Milan Fine Arts Academy of Brera and as an architect at Milan Politecnico.

79 Edallo 1946.

80 Le Corbusier 1934.

81 Sabatino 2010, 4.

82 Cfr. Nuti/Martinelli 1981.

83 Alvaro 1934, 38.

A.A.V.V 1941a
A.A.V.V: La bonifica integrale del Tavoliere e i nuovi centri rurali, Urbanistica 4–5, 1941, 43.

A.A.V.V 1941b
A.A.V.V: Le nuove borgate rurali, Urbanistica 1, 1941, 58–59.

Albertini 1934
C. Albertini: Città di strade, Le strade (Touring Club Italiano) 16 (5), 1934, 241–247.

Alvaro 1934
C. Alvaro: Terra nuova. Prima cronaca dell'agro pontino (Milan 1934).

Armiero et al. 2022
M. Armiero: Mussolini's Nature. An Environmental History of Italian Fascism (Cambridge MA 2022).

Barbato 2005
C. Barbato: La Bonifica del Tavoliere. Vicende e iconografia di un piano inconcluso, in: G. Pellegrini (ed.): Città di fondazione italiane 1928–1942 (Latina 2005) 64–70.

Bevilacqua 1988
P. Bevilacqua (ed.): Il Tavoliere di Puglia. Bonifica e trasformazione tra XIX e XX secolo (Bari 1988).

Bronzini 1993
G. B. Bronzini: Le grandi inchieste agrarie come fonti museografiche, Lares 1, 1993, 47–72.

Calza Bini 1941
A. Calza Bini: Il piano territoriale come strumento della politica fascista del disurbamento, Urbanistica 1, 1941, 3–4.

Caracozzo 2007
A. Caracozzo: L'architettura del Novecento a Foggia e in Capitanata (Foggia 2007).

Corboz 1985
A. Corboz: Il territorio come palinsesto, Casabella 516, 1985, 22–27.

Corvaglia / Scionti 1985
E. Corvaglia / M. Scionti: Il piano introvabile. Architettura e urbanistica nella Puglia fascista (Bari 1985).

D'Annunzio 1903
G. D'Annunzio: Alcyone. Sogni di terre lontane (Milan 1903).

D'Antone 1990
L. D'Antone: Scienze e governo del territorio. Medici, ingegneri, agronomi e urbanisti nel Tavoliere di Puglia (1865–1965) (Milan 1990).

Darley 2007
G. Darley: Villages of Vision (Nottingham 2007).

De Cesare 1859
C. De Cesare: Delle condizioni economiche e morali delle classi agricole nelle provincie di Puglia (Naples 1859).

De Cillis et al. 1932a
E. De Cillis / G. Tommasi / A. De Dominicis / G. Colacicco: Piano di Massima di Bonifica e di trasformazione fondiaria del Comprensorio (Bari 1932).

De Cillis et al. 1932b
E. De Cillis / G. Tommasi / A. De Dominicis / G. Colacicco: Progetto esecutivo del Centro rurale di Incoronata (Bari 1932).

De Stefani 1934
A. De Stefani: Le case dei contadini, Il Corriere della Sera, 6 April 1934, 1.

Di Lonardo 1928
G. Di Lonardo: L'ente autonomo per l'acquedotto pugliese e l'irrigazione: L'Italia Agricola, 12, 1928, 859–869.

Dorotea 1843
L. Dorotea (ed.): Terapeutica speciale delle febbri intermittenti perniciose di Francesco Corti da Modena (Naples 1843).

Edallo 1946
A. Edallo: Ruralistica (Milan 1946).

Falasca-Zamponi 1997
S. Falasca-Zamponi: Fascist Spectacle: The Aesthetic of Power in Mussolini's Italy (London 1997).

Folchi 2002
A. Folchi: Le Paludi Pontine nel Settecento (Formia 2002).

Fraccacreta 1832
M. Fraccacreta: Teatro topografico storico poetico della Capitanata e degli altri luoghi più memorabili e limitrofi della Puglia, del legale, e corrispondente della società economica di Capitanata (Naples 1832).

Grassini 2012
L. Grassini: Water resources management and territorial development: Technological changes in Apulia during the post-unification period, Plurimondi 11, 2012, 89–123.

Gruppuso 2014
P. Gruppuso: Nell'Africa tenebrosa alle porte di Roma. Viaggio nelle Paludi Pontine e nel loro immaginario (Rome 2014).

Le Corbusier 1934
Le Corbusier: La Ferme radieuse. Le village radieuse, L'Homme Réel 4 (Reorganisation agraire, edited by N. Bezard), 1934, 54–59.

Lepre 1980
A. Lepre: Azienda feudale e azienda agraria nel mezzogiorno continentale fra '500 e '800, Quaderni storici 43, 1980, 21–38.

Lo Re 1913
A. Lo Re: Capitanata. Nuovi studi economici (Foggia 1913).

Marconi 1929
P. Marconi: Il concorso per il Piano Regolatore della città di Foggia. Architettura e Arti Decorative, 2–3, 1929, 72–99.

Mascheroni 1936
E. Mascheroni: I Trattori, Italia Agricola 7, 507–515.

Maury 1906
E. Maury: Relazione sulle condizioni dell'industria pastorizia nomade, in: E. Maury: Sul regime dei tratturi (Rome 1906).

Mercurio 1990
F. Mercurio / S. Russo: L'organizzazione spaziale della grande azienda, Meridiana 10, 1990, 95–124.

Mercurio 2021
F. Mercurio: Costruire il paesaggio agrario. Le dinamiche sociali e politiche che hanno accompagnato la pianificazione territoriale dello spazio «vuoto» in età contemporanea. Il caso del

Tavoliere delle Puglie, https://www.academia.edu/51131092/Franco_Mercurio_Costruire_il_paesaggio_agrario_Le_dinamiche_sociali_e_politiche_che_hanno_accompagnato_la_pianificazione_territoriale_dello_spazio_vuoto_in_età_contemporanea_Il_caso_del_Tavoliere_delle_Puglie_EdM_2021 (23 May 2022).

Nardella 1975
T. Nardella: Serafino Gatti e la Capitanata nella statistica murattiana del 1811 (Foggia 1975).

Nigro 2017
P. Nigro: Fiumi, corsi d'acqua e costumi nel Regno di Napoli: l'Abruzzo e le sue popolazioni al tramonto del XVIII secolo, Il Capitale culturale. Studies on the Value of Cultural Heritage 16, 2017, 59–79.

Nuti / Martinelli 1981
L. Nuti / R. Martinelli: Le città di strapaese. La politica di «fondazione» nel ventennio (Milan 1981).

Ortensi 1941
D. Ortensi: Edilizia rurale urbanistica di centri comunali e di borgate rurali (Rome 1941).

Palmieri 1789
G. Palmieri: Pensieri economici relativi al Regno di Napoli (Naples 1789).

Panareo 1984
E. Panareo (ed.): Relazione sulla Puglia del '700 / Giuseppe Maria Galanti (Cavallino 1984).

Piacentini 1943
M. Piacentini: Il centro comunale di Segezia, Architetto Concezio Petrucci, Architettura 678, 1943, 174–195.

Piemontese 2010
G. Piemontese: Urbanistica ed architettura nel Tavoliere della Puglia. L'esperienza dei centri rurali 1929–1942 (Foggia 2010).

Pompa 1930
A. Pompa: La Palude sipontina (Foggia 1930).

Pompa 1932
A. Pompa: Aspetti della colonizzazione del Tavoliere (Foggia 1932).

Presutti 1909
E. Presutti: Puglie. Relazione del delegato tecnico Presutti, in: Italian Parliament: Inchiesta parlamentare sulle condizioni dei contadini nelle provincie meridionali e nella Sicilia, III, Puglie, Tomo 1 (Rome 1909).

Pruneri 2018
F. Pruneri: Pluriclassi, scuole rurali, scuole a ciclo unico dall'Unità d'Italia al 1948. In Scuola e società in Italia e Spagna tra Ottocento e Novecento, Diacronie Studi di Storia Contemporanea 32 (2), 2018, https://doi.org/10.4000/diacronie.8062.

Quercia 2018
P. Quercia: Gli small rural villages della Puglia piana. Economia e sviluppo tra Sette e Ottocento, in: Ernesto Toma (ed.): Economia, istituzioni, etica e territorio (Milan 2018).

Rappini 1983 [1777]
G. Rappini: Relazione e voto dell'ingegnere Gaetano Rappini sopra il disseccamento delle Paludi pontine alla santità di N.S. Papa Pio V (Rome 1983, reprint).

Ruinas 1943
S. Ruinas: Città di Mussolini: Segezia, Le Vie d'Italia 2, 1943, 133–138.

Russo 1989
S. Russo: Questioni di confine; la Capitanata tra Sette Ottocento, in: L. Massella / B. Salvemini (eds.): Storia d'Italia. Le regioni dall'Unità a oggi. La Puglia (Turin 1989) 271–272.

Russo 1990
S. Russo: Grano, pascolo e bosco in Capitanata tra sette e ottocento (Bari 1990).

Russo 2015
S. Russo: Tratturi di Puglia (Foggia 2015).

Russo / Bourdin 2016
S. Russo / S. Bourdin: I tratturi fra tutela e valorizzazione (Foggia 2016).

Sabatino 2010
M. Sabatino: Pride in Modesty. Modernist architecture and the vernacular tradition in Italy (Toronto 2010).

Salvemini 1989
B. Salvemini: Prima della Puglia. Terra di Bari e il sistema regionale in età moderna, in: L. Massella / B. Salvemini (eds.): Storia d'Italia. Le regioni dall'Unità a oggi. La Puglia (Turin 1989) 88–89.

Salvemini 1995
B. Salvemini: L'innovazione precaria. Spazi, mercati e società nel Mezzogiorno tra Sette e Ottocento (Catanzaro 1995).

Scionti 2007
M. Scionti: La colonizzazione in Capitanata. Dai consorzi di bonifica all'Opera Nazionale Combattenti (ONC), in: P. Culotta / G. Gresleri (eds.): Città di fondazione e plantatio ecclesiae (Bologna 2007) 138–151.

Scott 1998
J.C. Scott: Seeing like a State: How Certain Schemes to Improve the Human Condition have Failed (New Haven and London 1998).

Secchi 1923
L. Secchi: Edifici scolastici italiani primari e secondari. Norme tecnico-igieniche per lo studio dei progetti (Milan 1923).

Vöchting 1938
F. Vöchting: Problemi della Bonifica del Tavoliere di Puglia (II), Bonifica e colonizzazione 6, 1938, 490–529.

Image Sources

1   Authors' elaboration.
2   Elaboration by C. Pallini, based on Marconi 1929, 73, and Russo 2015, 12.
3   Russo 2015, 161.
4   Authors' elaboration.
5   De Cillis et al. 1932b, 11.
6, 7, 9   Drawings by A. Korolija.
8, 10   Mercurio 1990.
9   Elaboration and drawing by A. Korolija.
11   Photo by C. Pallini.
12   Drawing by A. Korolija, based on Corvaglia/Scionti 1985, 56.
13   Authors' elaboration from Ortensi 1941, 467.
14   Photo by C. Pallini.
15   Ortensi 1941, 498.
16   Ortensi 1941, 492.
17   Drawing by A. Korolija based on Ortensi 1941, 493–494.

Virtualities of Internal Colonization: Modernity as Heritage in-the-Making? A Case Study from Portugal

Marta Prista

«Internal colonization» is a term used to refer to the agricultural modernization policies and programs introduced by some European nation-states during the 20th century to counter laissez-faire capitalism and reestablish social order in a self-conscious shaping of their future.[1] Using neophysiocratic rationales, internal colonization advocated a return to the countryside as the locus of economic and social wealth. Framed by high modernism, this approach believed that order and progress were attainable through scientific and technological advancements, and the governance of material, social, and natural worlds.[2] Consequentially, land reform and the mechanization of production aimed to develop rural economies while stimulating national markets. Population resettlements were implemented to increase the availability of agricultural labor while controlling demographics and social turmoil. Modernist colonies were constructed in the countryside, spatializing the utopias and official nationalisms of these regimes through the social production of space via ideological and technological frameworks.[3] The result was the creation of modern rural landscapes, which have recently captured scholars' attention as tangible evidence of a shared 20th-century European history.[4]

Research on the agricultural modernization programs led by European regimes of different ideological backgrounds has provided compelling arguments for reevaluating methodological nationalisms within approaches to a transnational and trans-ideological historical phenomenon.[5] These programs developed within different

political contexts and their political and technical actors traveled widely, sharing ideas and practices, thereby contributing to the development of interventionist and technocratic states in Europe.[6] Moreover, internal colonization has been linked to external colonialism in the creation of modern states and their subjects through governmentality.[7] Peasants, despite discourses of authenticity, were another *other* whose backwardness was in need of modern state intervention.[8] Emplacing these knowledge/power dynamics upon rural territories, people, and imaginaries, internal colonization therefore may be approached through the lens of the *modernity–rationality–coloniality complex* that has shaped recent conceptions of a global dominant order.[9]

This chapter delves into the particularities of Portuguese internal colonization as a peripheral European experience. This process was implemented by a conservative right-wing dictatorship—the *Estado Novo* (New State), 1933–1974—that outlasted the era of fascism, and juggled nationalism and colonialism within a national myth built upon Portugal's historical imperial vocation and rural virtue.[10] In an exploratory way, the argument of the chapter draws on the modernity–coloniality framework, examining contemporary heritage processes in two Portuguese colonies as a laboratory to discuss the restructuring of the rural world under the guise of progress, and to shed light on rural communities' worldviews, given their current practices of relating, engaging, producing, and communicating the past. It thus dialogues with contributions from political history, memory and heritage studies, building upon multisite micro-ethnographic approaches.[11]

The chapter starts by introducing the program and achievements of Portuguese internal colonization within its national context in order to frame the settler's family and house as social and material technologies of rural production. The colonies of Pegões and Boalhosa are then presented in past and present terms by looking into their social production and social construction, notably through forms of heritagization. The final section resumes the argument revolving on the «virtualities» of heritage understood as sociocultural wholes exhibited by detached fragments that are hence endowed with a second life as heritage.[12] A focus on «virtualities», considering its nexus with the modernity–rationality–coloniality frame, presents a more nuanced understanding of the settlers' worldviews.

Internal Colonization in Portugal

The *Estado Novo* motto «God, Homeland and Family» is emblematic of the conservative nature of the Portuguese regime. Unlike the revolutionary nature of other European totalitarian and authoritarian regimes,[13] the Portuguese dictatorship pursued national regeneration by restoring what it saw as traditional order and values. It ruled through compromises with the interests and loyalties of Catholic, monarchist, fascist, and liberal elites.[14] Continuing debates about the fascist nature of the regime fall outside this article, but they pinpoint the particularities of a dictatorship and empire that lasted until 1974. Portugal remained predominantly rural, with limited industrialization, disparities in land-ownership structure, and enduring economic crises. The national economy, reliant on the colonial market, subordinated agricultural to commercial and industrial interests, particularly after 1940, under the super-ministry of the economy.[15] This politico-economic context tempered the transnational European drive for agricultural modernization in Portugal. Implementing its internal colonization program, Portugal embraced autarchic state intervention, aligning with international technical debates that advocated irrigated farming, agricultural experimentation, and mechanized labor. However, it drew a line at the expropriation of land in order to avoid threats to the rural status quo and manage the interests of elites to ensure their support for the regime. Some scholars argue indeed that internal colonization was more of a concession than a primary goal.

The belief in agricultural modernization as the basis for material and social progress predates *Estado Novo* and can be traced back to 19th-century agrarian reforms, which focused on addressing wastelands and rural migration issues. Modernization was later propelled by the Republican regime's (1910–1926) concerns with hygiene and infrastructure improvements, as well as by the food emergency during the First World War and its impacts on demographics, unemployment, and social unrest, which were exacerbated in 1926 by the military coup. According to Elisa Silva, the modernization of agriculture by the *Estado Novo* was a form of biopolitics aligned with autocracy, corporatism, and Catholic social doctrine,[16] aiming to counter modernity's individualism and urbanization, along with class and regional loyalties beyond the state. In other words, modernization depended on political ideas as technologies of governance, a focus that might have had more impact on labor and social control than on agricultural production. As Lourenzo Fernandez-Prieto et al. have pointed out, rurality must also be acknowledged in the study of modernist fascism to counter the urban essentialism usually associated with the ideology.[17]

To carry out the program, the *Estado Novo* established the Board for Internal Colonization (*Junta de Colonização Interna* or JCI) in 1936, under the tutelage of the Agriculture Ministry and the Ministry of Economy from 1940 onwards. The primary objectives of internal colonization, as outlined by the Corporative Chambers (1938),[18] were to increase rural population and productivity. This would redistribute population, rekindle Portuguese people's love of the land, and counteract the negative influences of urbanization. Nature and people were thus subjected to technical-scientific rationales, and wastelands were repurposed for food sufficiency and the pastoral moralization of the nation.

The program was far from homogeneous in its operation, as it had to navigate distinct decision-making spheres and accommodate different rationales within the broader context of Portuguese agrarian policies. These encompassed initiatives such as the Wheat Campaigns (1929–1938), aiming at self-sufficiency through state-controlled production and markets; the Law on Agricultural Improvements (1946), which provided technical and financial support to landlords and cooperatives; and the Plan for Irrigation and Valuation of Alentejo (1955–1964), designed to enhance productivity while improving national supply of water and electricity through dam construction. Silva's research on the contribution of internal colonization to the institutionalization of the state's power in Portugal underpins the articulations between these different politics of economic nationalism.[19] Along with Filipa Guerreiro's analysis of the resulting patterns of territorial planning and architectural production, an operational periodization of internal colonization will shed light on its development over time.[20]

During its first phase, from 1936 to 1942, the JCI tested approaches and established a methodology based on agricultural knowledge and the *Casal* as a unit of production. This was inspired by the Italian *Bonifica* and informed by the diagnosis of poverty of the Survey on Rural Housing carried out by the High Institute of Agronomy in the 1930s. A second period (1942–1946) followed the General Plan for Wastelands Use (1941) and the restructuring of the JCI (1942), broadly spanning the Second World War, and was marked by an ideological strengthening. Concentrated

settlements and «aggrandized» housing endorsed the ruralist ethos of official nationalism, while settlers' selection criteria and mechanisms of technical and social assistance reinforced the program's social engineering project. With the Law on Agricultural Improvements and the amplification of JCI functions and funding in 1946, a third period of internal colonization (1947–1953) reveals the state's modernizing efforts. Responding to the post-WW2 order, the Portuguese regime assumed a modernizing role in the construction of modernist facilities and civic centers in the colonies. Internal colonization then entered its last period with the National Development Plan of 1954. Hydraulic works and the establishment of agricultural cooperatives echoed the JCI's shift away from self-sufficiency paradigms towards emphasizing the independence of the means of production. The process was completed with the last Law on Internal Colonization in 1962, one year after the outbreak of the Anti-Colonial War (1961). After this time, the JCI only managed and concluded plans for the existing settlements.

In practice, Portugal gradually withdrew from internal colonization, constructing only seven colonies with twenty-two nuclei, only a third of the planned total. Shifting orientations and casual decisions resulted in hierarchized settlements that interconnected with traditional villages.[21] Local realities were often overlooked by decision-making authorities whose modernist rationales reproduced the idea of the traditional peasantry as backward and struggled with the communal usage of wastelands and traditional livestock economies.[22] As Silva contends, internal colonization amounted to a «history of failed modernization».[23] However, as James Scott argues in relation to Soviet collectivization, economic failure does not necessarily equate to cultural failure.[24] The question here is, thus, what internal colonization meant in Portugal in terms of the complex modernity–colonization, the emergence of new categories of culture, and new social relations of class and economics.

Technologies of Rural Production: The Settlers and their Houses

The literature on internal colonization has highlighted two key topics: social engineering and the rationalization of productivity, both referring to ideas of private property. Indeed, following the path of the Italian *Bonifica*, the Portuguese internal colonization was founded on the concept of *Casal Agrícola*—a family unit of agricultural production, legally inalienable and indivisible, and compounded of dwelling and farming, with agricultural and forestry lots and livestock facilities (fig. 1). The *Casal* was not solely an economic concept, however. It spatialized the social institution of family as the foundation of the *Estado Novo* nation-state and society,[25] functioning as a form of «banal nationalism»[26] that socialized the setters into the regime's official nationalism and values.

Internal colonization in Portugal thus emplaced the Portuguese «New Man,» who differently from other fascist or soviet equivalents, was a counterrevolutionary middle-aged godly peasant.[27] Application criteria for internal colonization complied with this image. To qualify, settlers had to be married, have children and farming experience, but not own properties, exhibit aptitude and moral behavior, and pay with one-sixth of the family's production. For Fernando Rosas, the Portuguese «New Man» was in fact «old»

1   A *Casal* in the colony of Pegões, 2017.

as a variation on the fascist genus that reflected the regime's stands, its traditional oligarchy, and the totalizing project for reeducating the Portuguese.[28] Such a purpose was fueled by other institutions, notably the National Secretariat of Propaganda (SPN/SNI) and the Foundation for Joy at Work (FNAT), with their prominent role in the objectification[29] of popular culture as a self-conscious representation of national authenticity, and its «banalization»[30] through the control of culture and leisure practices under the corporate state.

Understanding the role of *Casal Agrícola* also requires considering its materiality, as material culture embodies the cultural processes through which we give order and are ordered by the world.[31] Despite formal variations, the *Casal* was intended to be the family's technology of production. It not only encompassed housing, agricultural tool annexes, stables, and other livestock shelters, but also organized family life around a porch and kitchen / living room that led to differentiated rooms for the couple and their female and male children, as well as an inner latrine. These functional arrangements may be interpreted as modernizing efforts, incorporating technical rationalization of space and hygiene concerns. However, they also stem from economic rationales and moralizing goals related to class and gender roles within internal colonization, rural life, and the nation.

Moreover, the construction materials and techniques evoked the traditional Portuguese lifestyle. These material arrangements were consistent with the regime's emphasis on the links between family, rural home, and homeland. Compliance with *Estado Novo* housing policies was even advertised as the Portuguese people's contribution to the nation's resurgence and prosperity.[32] The *Casais* varied in design, some aligning with the conservative Portuguese House movement, others adopting a modern regionalist approach.[33] But despite variations in layout, all houses conveyed the social status of their inhabitants, especially when juxtaposed with the modernist architectures of public buildings and housing for technicians, teachers, or pastors.

In conclusion, it could be argued that the *Casal* played a role in the production of national subjects by strengthening the nexus nation–rurality–family and establishing the dispositions that structured the private, household, and work lives of the settlers.

Pegões and Boalhosa Colonies: The Laboratory and the Last Breath of Internal Colonization

As a consistent feature of Portuguese internal colonialization, the varied layouts of the *Casal Agrícola* underline the program's adjustments to national and international circumstances. Quite different are the designs of the settlements and houses of Pegões and Boalhosa, which are currently under analysis for heritage classification by the Portuguese General Directorate for Cultural Heritage. Pegões showcases houses with nationalist aesthetics in a dispersed layout, with civic centers equipped with facilities designed in experimental modernist aesthetics. Boalhosa, on the other hand, assembles semi-detached houses of regionalist inspiration in a fan-shaped urban design with scarce public services (fig. 2). The former and the latter were not just the first and the last colony built from scratch by the JCI. Their material and social engineering projects also embody the JCI's heyday and declining phases, reflecting its shifting rationales.

Pegões was the JCI's laboratory, the largest of the Portuguese colonies and the only one on the outskirts of the capital, located along the road that connected Lisbon to Spain. The rural property was bequeathed to the state by Rovisco Pais (1862–1932), who had partitioned the property into 119 plots to accommodate wage labor to his homestead.[34] In 1937, the JCI initiated an extensive topographic, socioeconomic, agrarian, hydraulic, and architectural survey and the initial project of Pegões colony was concluded in 1941. Despite the challenges posed by the Second World War, a third nucleus was added during construction, resulting

2   A *Casal* in the colony of Boalhosa, 2016.

in a total of 206 *Casais* being built. Families selected from 288 candidates moved in between 1951 and 1956.[35] The settlement offered a wide range of facilities, including single-sex schools, churches, clinics, training and technical assistance centers, a breeding station, and a cemetery along with agricultural, consumer, and cattle cooperatives. In 1957, Pegões was renamed Saint Isidro of Pegões in honor of the patron saint of farmers. In the same year, its exquisite church was inaugurated in the presence of the JCI president (fig. 3).[36]

The life story of Boalhosa is quite different. Its process goes back to the national General Plan for Wastelands Use (1941), which foresaw three colonies in Northern Portugal. In 1946 its plan comprised four concentrated nuclei with 83 semi-detached dwellings designed in a regionalist style and modern collective facilities.[37] In 1951, a reassessment scaled down the plan to 68 households, and the final 1954 project ultimately featured only 30 houses in a single nucleus—Vascões. In 1958, only fourteen families moved in and five years later only eight remained in the colony.[38] A school and a house for the teacher and a technician were constructed, but plans for a church, medical facilities, and technical buildings never materialized.

Differences between the material histories of Pegões and Boalhosa resonate in settlers' attachment to the colonies and its quotidian. Settlers explain their application to the JCI call by pointing to the physical and economic security provided by the private property of their homes and lands.[39] They «had nothing to lose» and shared a past of poverty in overcrowded and unhealthy conditions that made *Casais* look like a «farmer's homestead» in their eyes. However, the origins of the settlers differed significantly in the two colonies. In Pegões, they came from distances ranging from 80 to 200 km, nicknaming themselves according to places of origin, and brought regional traditions into the collective everyday life and festivities.[40] In contrast, settlers in Boalhosa hailed from nearby parishes and identified themselves as family by kinship or affinity, one family being actually related to two-thirds of the total households.

Settlers' lives also differed significantly in respect to social control and vigilance. Isolation and scarce adhesion in Boalhosa resulted in a circumvention of JCI selection criteria and a dearth of social and technical support.[41] In Pegões, however, settlers' labor and domestic lives socialized them

in JCI and official nationalism rhetoric. Medical assistance controlled bodies, while gendered schooling and training taught male and female settlers their roles. Technical and social assistance controlled domestic care and livestock, the «best» settlers being rewarded for productivity, hygiene, and morality. Social gatherings and leisure activities fostered community bonding, while establishing a social division of labor. The bodies and minds of the settlers were domesticated as particular subjects of the nation by sport and musical demonstrations, summer tours and camps, while having the agrarian regent as best man or arranging seating at feasts according to social status socialized settlers in their role.

Places, like people, have social lives, and Pegões and Boalhosa show how the Portuguese

3   Church of Saint Isidro in the colony of Pegões, 2017.

colonies shared features and histories but followed different paths and meanings. The life story of the two colonies is beyond the scope of this discussion, but certain events deserve attention. One concerns the agricultural cooperatives created by the JCI, which signal the *Casal*'s paradigm shift from an individual to a collective ethos.[42] In Boalhosa, the scarcity of settlers prevented the establishment of an autonomous cooperative[43] until the Farmers Society was created in 1971, and even then with limited economic outcomes. In contrast, Pegões boasted agricultural and consumption cooperatives, including the winery cooperative that, inaugurated in 1958, now holds a symbolic capital for the colony, despite the facts that it won awards and made profits only in the 21st century and that it uses grapes cultivated beyond the colony of Pegões.[44]

With the Carnation Revolution in 1974, the JCI was dissolved. Full private ownership of the *Casais*, however, had to wait until 1988. This postponement paradoxically favored the settlers when the Revolutionary Process in Course (1974–1976) called for the nationalization of property and capital. In Boalhosa, for example, conflicts with neighboring parishes over land ownership lasted for years and required police and judicial intervention. Because the colony was still under tutelage of the state, the settlers won the court case in a process that ultimately reinforced their sense of belonging.[45] When property rights were finally granted to settlers, the settlements underwent processes of material and social reconfiguration. Migration was no longer forbidden; some people left; others aged there. De-ruralization drove the adaptation of buildings to modern tastes and uses; porches were closed, kitchens were separated from living areas, latrines became bathrooms, and stables became new rooms. In Pegões, some houses were put on the property market, while new ones were built on agricultural or expansion plots; in Boalhosa, descendants of settlers moved into empty *Casais*. In both places, agriculture became primarily for family consumption while the pursuit of other livelihoods led to the former settlers' integration into local and regional economic activities.

Past Colonies in Present Tense

«The twentieth century began with utopia and ended with nostalgia,» according to Svetlana Boym.[46] In a time of presentism, memory blossomed both as an expression and a means to escape presentism.**[47]** However, neither nostalgia nor memory is just a longing for the past; they are present practices that do something. It is in this sense that heritage, as the relating, engaging, producing, and communicating of the past in present tenses,[48] may serve as a laboratorial field to question how the modernity–colonialism fix is accommodated by different actors in the re-presentation of Portuguese internal colonialism. It allows us to delve into the intertwining of official and collective memories, of cultural amnesias and nostalgic anxieties, of discourses, practices, affections, and things, which makes a *complex of memory*.[49]

Within this complex, Portuguese internal colonization has been rescued in various ways, notably in Pegões and Boalhosa. The Monument to Agriculture in Pegões, made of agricultural machinery, and the billboard explaining the new landscape of Boalhosa celebrate their entry into modernity. Exhibition rooms with memorabilia from the colonies' agricultural life can be visited at the Pegões Winery Cooperative and Boalhosa's Center for Environmental Education and Interpretation. Television coverage and the traveling press have promoted the colonies as tourist destinations due to their exceptional history and materiality.[50] A Facebook page dedicated to Pegões aims to «preserve people's memories in time» and the former colony commemorates Settler Day. People display agricultural tools in their homes as mementoes of past lives, and houses' rehabs intentionally display tangible evidence of rural traditions. There is even a children's book about conflict management in Boalhosa, published after tensions arose with settlers over nature conservation measures.[51]

Most emblematic is the classification of Corno de Bico Protected Landscape,[52] and the ongoing processes for the protection of Boalhosa and Pegões colonies, based on their historical, social and material values.[53] These actions fit Laurajane Smith's definition of an «authorized heritage discourse»[54] as a self-referenced production of experts validated in modern knowledge that shapes the way people relate to heritage. Grounded on Western elites' cultural categories, such a discourse subdues subaltern worldviews to a so-called universal rationale, aligning with theories of coloniality. Examining the two heritage processes reveals the emphasis on the material testimony of cultural and historical modernity, whose innate values often go unquestioned. These values are naturalized by technical and aesthetic categories, and discourses of progress and exceptionality, obscuring other frames of meaning and reasoning about the places and their history.

Virtualities of Heritage

The idea of heritage as a mode of cultural production delivers other layers to understand the ways internal colonization rationales are accommodated by former settlers. All heritage is plural and inherently dissonant in meaning. Its activation selects and forgets traits of the past by practices of detachment that endow it with a «second life.»[55] In other words, heritage is a fragment exhibited as the whole that is its own virtuality. What the assemblage of heritage practices in Pegões and Boalhosa suggests is that this virtuality bears upon ideas of both modernity and rurality, but often dismisses the material conditions and ideologies that shaped their imagination.

Take the conservation plans for example. In Pegões, the preservation of material heritage is the concern of intellectual and technical experts as well as former settlers. The difference is that

the latter embody their experiences and affections in space, rather than rationalizing modernity. Boalhosa's settlers, on the other hand, welcome the liveliness brought by the Interpretation Centre, but several resent the conservation plan for imposing restrictions on local agriculture, forestry, and cattle breeding. Complaints that «the wolf is now more protected than a person»[56] show that discourses of heritage and sustainability are far from consensual. In both colonies, the emotional and embodied experience of heritage by former settlers stands out. Adopting a performativity lens to explore the interaction of heritage practices and discourses thus allows for a more thorough understanding of the multiple works of heritage as cultural productions of the present.

The authorized heritage discourse framework is a useful heuristic tool here for understanding the dialectics between sanctioned and marginalized practices and knowledges. It emphasizes that people have agency, that their practices are embodied and relational, so that heritage is not just what people think and say, but how this affects their lived experience.[57] What the heritagization of internal colonization brought to the fore was the settlers' intersubjective construction of their own difference within the rural world. This difference was produced by agents of colonization through time, space, and mediated interactions, but it was also socially constructed through the lived and symbolic experience of the settlers, who now discourse it quite differently in Pegões and Boalhosa.

In Boalhosa, the settlers were enthusiastic about their *Casais*. Although they acknowledge the modernizing impulse of tractors and agricultural machinery, the features and living conditions of their houses were seen as a step forward in social mobility within the frame of a traditional social structure. The virtuality displayed by their discourses and practices is that of a pastoral rurality. Solidarity networks were built by kinship and neighborhood relations fostered by an isolated and underserved colony. The JCI is never cited, and the term «colony» is no longer used. People consider the colony to have been «of the State,» and colonization to have ended with the establishment of the Farmers Society in 1971. Their engagement with the past is nostalgic, in the longing for a happier and healthier life that contrasts with the present individualism where «everyone digs for themselves.» So, as one of the old settlers eloquently put it, «For me, it is just like any other place.»[58]

Quite differently, in Pegões, former settlers implicitly acknowledge the technologies of governance implemented by internal colonization in memories of leisure activities and celebrations, labor harshness and surveillance, health care and education. These memories reveal how structures of power produced intersubjective constructions of the colony and of its settlers as a differentiated social entity. Recently, they have been re-presented through a Facebook page as a digital community of practice, which defines people's engagement in collective knowledge processes by the sharing of interests and experiences.[59] What such online practice concedes is an affection work triggered by the sharing of historical data and old images, which, assumed to be objective, are confirmed by vivid accounts of personal experiences. This online format allows the assemblage of a wide range of actors and their social frameworks of memory, highlighting the class, gender, age, and territorial shaping of memory. It assembles «shreds of the settlers' lives» as poetically published by a former settler's daughter. But it also dictates the need to address issues of agency.

As in Boalhosa, Pegões settlers' «longing for the old times» somehow depoliticizes the JCI enterprise and neglects its coloniality. But differently here, the past seems to be re-presented by incorporation or at least repetition of the rationale of modern progress. The memorialization of internal colonization presents settlers as the «heroes» of a virtual collective that strived but succeeded in overcoming the harshness of internal colonial lifestyle, to a certain extent disregarding the colonization of their bodies and minds, even when remembering its techniques. Belonging is attested through experiences, but also in a genealogy of origins, life chronologies and *Casal* numbers, that construct biographies of people and places in terms of a rational organization of space, community, and history. Notwithstanding, events such as the Settler Day or the digital community of practice bring together generations, functioning as communicative and cultural memory. And while displaying a sense of differentiation built upon the modernity–rationality–coloniality complex, they are also places of acting and doing the collective through performativity.

The point stressed is that memory as a practice and heritage as a mode of cultural production produce the past in present terms. Internal colonization construed a cultural imaginary of social difference. Its material world is currently under heritagization according to institutional cannons. This reverberates the critique of the authorized discourse framework and the modernity–coloniality complex. However, former settlers also mobilize their colonial past and social category to construe a collective virtuality that responds to present longings and aspirations in a post-colonial and post-rural context. As Valdimar Hafstein points out, categories have a performative power, so heritage is a matter of change, not continuity.[60] The question is thus whether this change subjugates the social subjects to knowable and manageable objects or/and empowers them with a cultural difference as a resource for other political, economic, or social expediencies.[61] However, this demands a rethinking of former settlers in unbounded ways, capturing the possibilities of their meaningful assemblages through time and spatial continuums that extend beyond internal colonization's policies, spatialization, technologies, and social networks.

1   Couperus et al. 2015.
2   Scott 1998.
3   Cf. Low 1996.
4   This article results from research conducted within the projects *MODSCAPES – Modernist reinvention of the rural landscapes* (HERA 3rd JRP, HERA.15.097), *Building Salazar's people: Architecture in the making of portugueseness (1932–1945)* (FCT Portugal, 2022.03543.PTDC) and *Updating the past: modern(ist) heritage and (trans) national identities* (FCT Portugal, DL 57/2016/CP1349/CT0001).
5   van de Grift 2015, Iordachi/Bauerkämper 2014, Fernández-Prieto et al. 2014.
6   Carvalho 2018.
7   Calvert 2001, Saraiva 2009.
8   Etkind 2015, Poloni/Funari 2022.
9   Quijano 2007.
10 Rosas 2001.
11 Prista 2018, 2019.
12 Kirshenblatt-Gimblett 1998.
13 Griffin 2008.
14 Ferreira et al. 2009.
15 Freire/Lanero 2013.
16 Silva 2020.
17 Fernandez-Prieto et al. 2014.
18 Câmara Corporativa 1938
19 Silva 2020.
20 Guerreiro 2016.
21 Cardoso et al. 2020.
22 Ayán Vila/Señoran Martín 2020, Freire/Lanero 2013.
23 Silva 2020.
24 Scott 1998.
25 Portugal 1933.
26 Billig 1995.
27 Carvalho/Pinto 2018.
28 Rosas 2001.
29 Handler 1988.
30 Billig 1995.
31 Miller 1994.
32 Macedo 1942.
33 Guerreiro 2016.
34 Mestre 2009.
35 Pereira 2004.
36 Nunes 2019.
37 JCI 1946.
38 JCI 1964.
39 Interviews in Boalhosa (2017) and informal conversation in Pegões (2017; 2023); cf. Pereira 2004, Nunes 2019, Colónia Agrícola de Pegões Facebook page 2014–2023.
40 Nunes 2019.
41 JCI 1961.
42 Guerreiro 2016.
43 JCI 1961.
44 http://cooppegoes.pt/.
45 Prista 2019.
46 Boym 2007, 7.
47 Hartog 2013.
48 Smith 2006.
49 Macdonald 2013.
50 For instance https://viagens.sapo.pt/viajar/viajar-portugal/artigos/a-aldeia-moderna-de-santo-isidro-de-pegoes.
51 Cunha 2014.
52 Decree 21/99, 20 September 1999.
53 General-Directorate for Cultural Heritage, Information n.º I-2019/207901/DSBC/DRCN, 2019 (Boalhosa) and Process n.º 2009/15-07/34/CI/415, 2009 (Pegões), www.patrimoniocultural.gov.pt.
54 Smith 2006.
55 Kirshenblatt-Gimblett 1998.
56 Interview in Boalhosa 2017.
57 Smith 2021.
58 Interview in Boalhosa 2017.
59 Wenger-Trayner/Wenger-Trayner 2015.
60 Hafstein 2007.
61 Yúdice 2003.

Ayán Vila/Señorán Martín 2020
X. Ayán Vila / J. Señorán Martín: Colónias para homens novos: arqueologia da colonização agrária fascista no noroeste ibérico, in: J. Arnaud / C. Neves / A. Martins (eds.): Arqueologia em Portugal 2020 – Estado da Questão (Lisbon 2020) 2123–2134.

Billig 1995
M. Billig: Banal Nationalism (London 1995).

Boym 2007
S. Boym: Nostalgia and Its Discontents. The Hedgehog Review 9.2, 2007, 7–18.

Calvert 2001
O. Calvert: Internal Colonisation, Development and Environment. Third World Quarterly 22 (1) 2001, 51–63.

Câmara Corporativa 1938
Câmara Corporativa: Parecer referente a dois projectos de colonização interna, Diários das Sessões da Assembleia da República 10º-192º Suplemento, 29 de outubro 1938.

Cardoso et al. 2020
A. Cardoso / H. Maia / A. Trevisan: Questões da Habitação moderna no quadro da colonização interna na península ibérica: in Actas del X Congreso DOCOMOMO Ibérico. El fundamento social de la arquitectura; de lo vernáculo y lo moderno, una síntesis cargada de oportunidades (Badajoz 2020) 205–221.

Carvalho 2018
R. Carvalho: The Junta of Colonização Interna and the shaping

of the Estado Novo's peasantry: in Regionalism, Nationalism and Architecture. Conference Proceedings (Porto 2018) 54–62.

Carvalho / Pinto 2018
R. Carvalho / A. Pinto: The «Everyman» of the Portuguese New State during the fascist era, in: J Dagnino / M. Feldman / P. Stocker (eds): The «New Man» in Radical Right Ideology and Practice, 1919–45 (London 2018) 131–148.

Couperus et al. 2015
S. Couperus / V. Lagendijk / L. van de Grift: Experimental Spaces: A Decentered Approach to Planning in High Modernity, Journal of Modern European History 13 (4), 2015, 475–479.

Cunha 2014
G. Cunha: Lili e a Mediação Conflitos. Coleção Shakti 2 ([Vila Nova de Gaia] 2014).

Etkind 2015
A. Etkind: How Russia ‹Colonized Itself›. International Journal for History, Culture and Modernity 3 (2), 2015, 159–172.

Fernández-Prieto et al. 2014
L. Fernández-Prieto / J. Pan-Montojo / M. Cabo: Fascism and modernity in the European countryside: a global view, in: L. Fernández-Prieto et al.: Agriculture in the Age of Fascism: Authoritarian Technocracy and Rural Modernization, 1922–1945 (Turnhout 2014) 19–41.

Ferreira 2009
N. Ferreira / R. Carvalho / A. Pinto: Political decision-making in the Portuguese New State (1933-9): the dictator, the council of ministers and the inner-circle, in: A. Costa (eds.): Ruling elites and decision-making in fascist-era dictatorships (New York 2009) 137–164.

Freire / Lanero 2013
D. Freire / D. Lanero: The Iberian dictatorships and agricultural modernisation after the Second World War, in: P. Moser / T. Varley (ed.): Integration through Subordination: The Politics of Agricultural Modernisation in Industrial Europe (Turnhout 2013) 183–201.

Griffin 2008
R. Griffin: A Fascist Century (London 2008).

Guerreiro 2016
F. Guerreiro: Colónias Agrícolas Portuguesas construídas pela Junta de Colonização Interna entre 1936 e 1960. A casa, o assentamento, o território. Faculdade de Arquitectura da Universidade do Porto 2016.

Hafstein 2007
V. Hafstein: Claiming Culture: Intangible Heritage Inc., Folklore, Traditional Knowledge, in: D. Hemme / M. Tauschek / R. Bendix (eds.): Prädikat ‹Heritage› (Berlin, Münster 2007) 75–100.

Handler 1988
R. Handler: Nationalism and the Politics of Culture in Quebec (Wisconsin 1988).

Hartog 2013
F. Hartog: Regimes de historicidade: presentismo e experiências do tempo (Belo Horizonte 2013).

Iordachi / Bauerkämper 2014
C. Iordachi / A. Bauerkämper: The Collectivization of Agriculture in Communist Eastern Europe: Comparison and Entanglements (Budapest 2014).

JCI 1946
JCI: Núcleo da Boalhosa: Projecto de colonização (Lisbon 1946).

JCI 1961
JCI: Colónia Agrícola da Boalhosa: Relatório de 1960 (Lisbon 1961).

JCI 1964
JCI: Gestão e contabilidade agrícolas: Exercício 1962/63 (Lisbon 1964).

Kirshenblatt-Gimblett 1998
B. Kirshenblatt-Gimblett: Destination Culture: Tourism, Museums, and Heritage (California 1998).

Low 1996
S. Low: Spatializing Culture: The Social Production and Social Construction of Public Space in Costa Rica, American Ethnologist 23 (4), 1996, 861–879.

Macdonald 2013
S. Macdonald: Memorylands: Heritage and Identity in Europe (London 2013).

Macedo 1942
M. Macedo: A Casa Rural: A Habitação (Lisbon 1942).

Mestre 2009
V. Mestre: Faias e Pegões, De Terra de Acções de Bandoleiros, Guerrilheiros e Assaltantes à colonização dos anos 40 deste século 2009, http://www.vmsa-arquitectos.com/ Public_Faias-pegoes_1999.pdf (13 August 2019).

Miller 1994
D. Miller: Artefacts and the Meaning of Things; in. T. Ingold (ed.): Companion Encyclopedia of Anthropology (London 1994) 396–419.

Nunes 2019
D. Nunes: Identidade do Lugar, o caso da Colónia Agrícola de Pegões. Universidade de Évora 2019.

Pereira 2004
S. Pereira: A colonização interna durante o Estado Novo: o exemplo da colónia agrícola de Pegões. Universidade de Lisboa 2004.

Poloni / Funari 2022
J. Poloni / P. Funari: Os desertos habitados: Estado Novo, colonialismo, memória e patrimônio em perspectiva comparada, Lusotopie XXI (1), 2022, http://journals.openedition.org/lusotopie/5090 (22 September 2022).

Portugal 1933
Portugal: Constituição Política da República Portuguesa. Diário do Governo, 22 February 1933.

Prista 2019
M. Prista: The social appropriation of the Portuguese inner colonisation in Boalhosa, in: S. Bell / A. Fisher / M.H. Maia / C. Pallini / V. Capresi (eds.): Modernism, Modernisation and the Rural Landscape, Proceedings of the MODSCAPES_conference2018 & Baltic Landscape Forum, SHS Web Conferences 63, 2019, 2261–2424.

Prista 2018
M. Prista: Tradition and modernity in the Portuguese Inner Colonisation: The laboratorial case of Pegões, in: J. Pimentel / A. Trevisan / A. Cardoso (eds.): Regionalism, Nationalism & Modern Architecture Conference Proceedings (Porto 2018) 342–355.

Quijano 2007
A. Quijano: Coloniality and Modernity/Rationality. Cultural Studies 21 (2–3) 2007, 168–178.

Rosas 2001
F. Rosas: O salazarismo e o homem novo: ensaio sobre o Estado Novo e a questão do totalitarismo. Análise Social 35 (157), 2001, 1031–1054.

Saraiva 2009
T. Saraiva: Laboratories and Landscapes: the Colonization of Portugal and Mozambique and the Building of the New State. Journal of History of Science and Technology, 3 (2009), 7–39.

Scott 1998
J. Scott: Seeing like a State (Yale 1998).

Silva 2020
E. Silva: Estado, território, população: As ideias, as políticas e as técnicas de colonização interna no Estado Novo. Universidade de Lisboa 2020.

Smith 2006
L. Smith: Uses of Heritage (London 2006).

Smith 2021
L. Smith: Emotional Heritage. Visitor Engagement at Museums and Heritage Sites (London 2021).

van de Grift 2015
L. van de Grift: Introduction: Theories and Practices of Internal Colonization. The Cultivation of Lands and People in the Age of Modern Territoriality, International Journal for History, Culture and Modernity, 3 (2), 2015, 139–158.

Wenger-Trayner / Wenger Trayner 2015
E. Wenger-Trayner / B. Wenger-Trayner: Introduction to communities of practice, 2015, https://www.wenger-trayner.com/wp-content/uploads/2022/06/15-06-Brief-introduction-to-communities-of-practice.pdf (13 October 2023).

Yúdice 2003
G. Yúdice: The Expediency of Culture (Durham 2003).

Image Sources

1 © MODSCAPES/Alexandra Trevisan.
2 © MODSCAPES/Alexandra Cardoso.
3 © MODSCAPES/Helena Maia.

The Memory of Houses
Transformation Processes in Settlement Construction between North and South Tyrol 1939–2019

Eva Maria Froschauer

Two years ago, after many years of absence, I visited my birthplace in North Tyrol. I embarked on a walk to awaken memories of my childhood and youth that, instead, revealed a disturbing reality: the urban fabric that essentially shaped the village—the so-called «Südtiroler Siedlung»—had been demolished, except for one last house, and replaced by new buildings. In retrospect, I have always perceived this settlement and its spatial layout as particularly characteristic and identity-forming, an important part of my hometown experience. At that time, I did not know much about the burdened origins of the houses.[1] The so-called South Tyrolean settlements of the 1940s are among the built testimonies of a resettlement project with challenging consequences from the last century—they were part of a highly political project pursued by two dictatorships. Their disappearance leaves unsatisfactory gaps in the immaterial memory and material heritage of this region.

The following attempt at a statement, formulated in three sections, takes up some aspects of this history and is characterized by many overlaps. First of all, there is the geopolitical context as a basis for the emergence of the settlement buildings—this is well-researched and, at least locally, widely known.[2] However, the «memory of the houses» must not be forgotten, because it is connected with the difficult question of the contemporary «Wertschätzung» («appreciation») of National Socialist buildings. The second section revisits the history of the built environment in order to show the ambivalence of these houses between war-driven settlement policy and

emotional anchoring—an emotional anchoring that stands for a «re-production attempt» of homeland in times of the «völkisch» («folk culture») as well as the transnational. For a better understanding, two excursus lead beyond North Tyrol: one describes the earlier settlement planning for Fallersleben/Wolfsburg and the other describes the initiative for the South Tyrolean «Ahnenerbe» («ancestral heritage»). The concluding section is dedicated to the recently completely transformed settlement in my hometown of Zams. Hardly any case study could be better suited to explore the question of how architectural testimony requires the advocacy of remembrance.

A Bizarre Resettlement Project and the «Memory of Houses»

As a result of the political redistribution of Europe after the First World War, the former Habsburg monarchy, a so-called multi-ethnic state, was reduced to its German-speaking heartland in 1919. Parts of the country, such as South Tyrol / Trentino, fell to Italy.[3] Across these new national borders, this area became the plaything of transnational political power strategies that attempted over the decades to assimilate the German-speaking population on Italian soil with coercive measures, to marginalize this population through language bans and immigration from the south, to brutally eradicate the existing culture, and later to resettle German-speakers under the «Berlin-Rome axis» according to an ideology of «ethnic cleansing.»[4] Thus, in a notable vote at the end of 1939 (the so-called «Option» and subsequently the «Berlin Agreement»[5]), German-speaking South Tyroleans decided to migrate «Home to the Reich,» the majority to Austria (the «Ostmark») which had been «annexed» to Nazi Germany in March 1938.

About 213,000 German-speaking South Tyrolean men (women were not eligible to vote) opted for emigration, which corresponded to about 86% of those entitled to the «Option»;[6] 75,000 actually left their homeland to settle in Austria, Bohemia, Westphalia, or Luxembourg.[7] In Northern Tyrol alone and the newly created settlements there, some 38,000 people were to be accommodated.[8] The resettled were promised agricultural property as compensation in their new homelands; ultimately, the Nazi regime was interested in recruiting new workers for war-related industries, gaining a male population that could be subject to military service, and promoting ideological «Germanization.»[9] The whole process surrounding the «Option» was, up until the end of 1939, accompanied by propaganda from all sides. State threats in South Tyrol itself included the further Italianization of this part of the country or the expulsion of the German-speaking population to southern Italy.[10] The facts that in the end only about a third of the South Tyroleans who voted for emigration actually left their country, and that there was no mass resettlement in the Italian south, can be explained in several ways: on the one hand, war turmoil prevented further strategic resettlement actions and, on the other hand, with Hitler's occupation of the Italian north from 1943 onwards, a migration «Home to the Reich» no longer seemed imperative.[11]

From 1945, some of the people who had resettled in South Tyrol returned, both legally and illegally, to Italy. Their citizenship often remained unclear at first. It was not until September 1946 that the Austrian Foreign Minister Karl Gruber and the Italian Prime Minister Alcide De Gasperi signed an agreement, under which the province of South Tyrol received its first statute of autonomy (1948), and which also regulated the return of former «Optants.»[12]

The imposed resettlements from South to North Tyrol shook up the ideas of «homeland,» «identity,» and «memory» that were embedded in the buildings. The resettlements created spatial and social upheavals in both regions, especially in the north, where small, established village communities were suddenly expanded by larger settlement areas and «rewritten»[13] like palimpsests. The resettled had experiences that continue to have an effect on the following generations and that become even more bitter against the backdrop of the current demolition of the houses. This is made clear by the following passage: «We are the memory of the houses that are gradually disappearing, that are gradually being torn down. We told you what happened to us. We were not the only strangers. Strangers are everywhere, and so are false prophets. Don't listen to them.»[14]

These are the final words of Tyrolean playwright Felix Mitterer's theater piece, *Verkaufte Heimat: Das Gedächtnis der Häuser* (Sold-Off Homeland: The Memory of Houses) of 1989. In 2019—marking the 80th anniversary[15] of the «Option»—Mitterer re-enacted the story as folk theater in a poignant location, a row of houses in part of the South Tyrolean settlement of Telfs that was slated for demolition (fig. 1). Mitterer succeeded in exposing the history of the resettled sedimented in the North Tyrolean houses in an epic and haunting form. With the play set at the authentic site of memory, the human dramas involved became oppressively clear. The entanglement of the relationships between people, spaces, identities, and their political appropriations in 1939 appeared with renewed prescience at the moment of the performance.

Mitterer is not the only one who has worked with this history on the literary level; a younger generation of narrators, in particular, is working through it again. For example, Marco Balzano's novel *Resto qui (I Stay Here)*[16] was published in

1   South Tyrolean settlement Telfs. Demolition house (in 2021) and the rest of the open-air stage for the performance piece *«Verkaufte Heimat: Das Gedächtnis der Häuser»* (*«Sold-Off Homeland: The Memory of Houses»*) in 2019.

2018. The Milanese author further sharpened the historical synchronicity of the dramatic events surrounding the loss of homeland by recounting both the repressive measures against the German-speaking ethnic group and the construction of the dam on Lake Reschen, which resulted in the flooding of the village of Graun. Francesca Melandri's *Eva schläft* (*Eva sleeps*),[17] extends the fictional and the factual into the 1960s, that terror-soaked time of the South Tyrolean «liberation struggle.» How unforgotten and painful much of it is can also be heard in numerous oral history projects,[18] or more recently again in documentary film narratives.[19] In any case, it is clear that the resettlement project has left wounds and that advocacy

for remembrance will only succeed if done across borders and generations.[20]

The houses of the North Tyrolean and South Tyrolean settlements[21] are «the stone symbols of the Option.»[22] As living places of remembrance, they should definitely keep this dark phase of history alive and understandable. Renovating the aging apartments, some of which are now designated as «substandard,» in a manner appropriate to their status as monuments would presumably be less of a challenge in terms of technical construction than in terms of remembrance. Since monument protection exists only for a few ensembles as selected and representative buildings,[23] considerable parts of the old housing estates

2   South Tyrolean settlement Telfs. Comparison of an existing building (1941–44) and a replacement house (2015/16) of the «Neue Heimat Tirol», views from 2021.

have already been replaced by energy-optimized, affordable and socially acceptable housing brought up to modern standards[24]—an undoubtedly important aspiration that makes protest difficult (fig. 2).

A Re-Production Attempt of Homeland in Times of Folk Culture as Well as the Transnational

The massive resettlement project during the war years was a challenge for the National Socialists' organizational planning, which operated across borders and institutions. The construction of the settlements was designated «Sondermaßnahme S[üdtirol]» («Special Measure S[outh Tyrol]»); this classification secured more funds, materials and manpower for the project, which was under great pressure to be realized in wartime.[25] Ultimately, the South Tyrolean settlements were only one «act» within the National Socialists' housing offensive, which ranged from the construction of company dormitories to reconstruction planning.[26]

The «apparatus» of settlement construction experts from Germany, together with local architects, succeeded in planning and building over 4,500 housing units in North Tyrol alone (as part of the Gau Tirol-Vorarlberg) from 1939 to 1944.[27] The main part of the residential building program was realized by the Neue Heimat: Gemeinnützige Wohnungs- und Siedlungsgesellschaft (New Homeland: Non-Profit Apartment and Settlement Society)[28] which was founded in 1939 under the auspices of the German Labor Front (DAF) and which was also active in other Austrian regions.[29] In the second half of the year, the first planning, control, and realization processes for the «Volkswohnungen»[30] in several North Tyrolean rural communities and in Innsbruck were already underway (fig. 3).

The design of the housing estates[31] was based on urban as well as various village environments, the aim being to create an «image» of alpine homeliness or vernacular countryside in the sense of a «re-production attempt» of Heimat. The ensembles created in this way are both remarkable and questionable in terms of architectural history: they were initially part of the National Socialists' broad «social housing program.»[32] The homogeneous spatial units were designed with urban and settlement planning in mind. The houses themselves had an unusually high level of living comfort for the period in which they were built (the 1940s),[33] yet their model construction[34] followed the rationalization requirements of the war economy[35] and many of them were built by prisoners or forced laborers.[36] The latter fact alone shows the tension in these buildings between homeliness and lack of homeland. However, to find out which power structures and administrative actors were connected with these projects, it is necessary to look beyond North Tyrol.

Excursus I: The Reich-German Context

In particular, the first housing estate designs for Innsbruck must be seen in the context of the plans begun earlier for the «City of the KdF Car near Fallersleben,» today's Wolfsburg. The Austrian-German architect Peter Koller had been entrusted by General Building Inspector Albert Speer with the construction of the city around the Volkswagen factory starting in 1937/38.[37] The so-called «Koller Plan» shows how the new town was to be organized with topographical references, residential buildings in various scales as well as an unrealized «*Stadtkrone*» (an idealistic urban development).[38]

3　Newspaper clipping «Apartments for South Tyrolean *Volksgenossen* (national comrades): Huge construction program in Gau Tirol-Vorarlberg underway—Several hundred apartments completed,» from the *Innsbrucker Nachrichten: Official Party Newspaper of the NSDAP*, 18 November 1939.

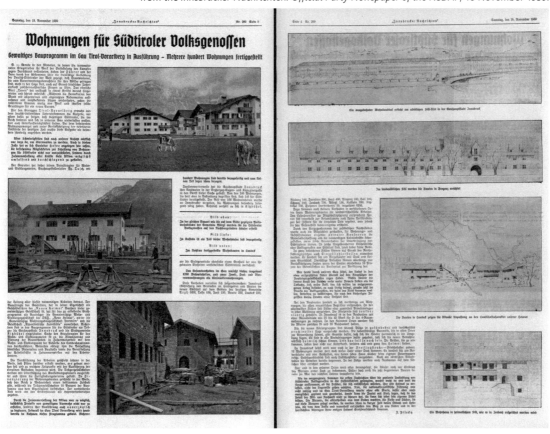

4   Comparison of a multi-story apartment building in Wolfsburg, Schillerstraße 3–5 (1939/40) and houses of the South Tyrolean settlement in Innsbruck, Langstraße 31 (1941).

First, starting in 1938/39, a housing estate for executives of the factory and the city administration was realized by Peter Koller and Titus Taeschner on Steimker Berg.[39] The terraced, semi-detached, and detached houses are set in a «picturesque» planning concept and have uniformly plastered façades and gable roofs. Dormers, wooden balconies and hinged shutters support the homely, conservative-bourgeois atmosphere of the now landmarked ensemble.[40] Subsequent buildings, such as the tenements along the Schillerstraße axis, are all based on typical floor plans,[41] like at Steimker Berg, but follow a far more urban design concept.

Why is this significant for Tyrol?[42] As mentioned, housing development in the Third Reich was a well-connected effort that brought together Reich German experts and local architects, albeit not always smoothly. For example, Neue

Heimat, a DAF enterprise in Innsbruck, was led from December 1939 by Hans Wagner, previously head of the same organization in East Prussia, while Peter Koller, with his Wolfsburg expertise, was to develop the South Tyrolean settlement areas in an urban context and the Innsbruck urban planner Jakob Albert was involved as a local actor.[43] Experiences from factory settlement and typological constructions were visibly incorporated. Titus Taeschner and Richard Dagostin, for example, justify the use of standardized houses in smaller Tyrolean towns and villages in the DAF journal, Bauen, Siedeln, Wohnen (Building, Settling, Living), with the fact that multi-family house construction typical of the locality could not be implemented here until then: «In order to avoid now bringing foreign structures into the landscape, it was necessary to develop typologies that contained six or more apartments.»[44] In addition, the authors explain the adoption of local building elements, such as those that had been traditional in the Inn Valley, which were, however, only superficial allusions. On the question of how to further develop the character of the village, especially in the urban environment, Peter Koller's views obviously clashed with those of Helmut Erdle.[45] Erdle was a representative of the Stuttgart School who had been head of the planning department in the DAF's Heimstättenamt (Office for Homesteads) in the Gau Tirol-Vorarlberg since 1939 and who criticized the unharmonious, soulless planning for Innsbruck because it did not do justice to the scale of the old town[46] (figs. 4, 5).

Many contradictions remained. On the one hand, the model construction projects, which, although offering a certain flexibility through a series of housing models,[47] were an instrument of wartime economy, and thus opposed the demand for variant-rich, landscape-friendly implementation of this special building task. In the propaganda-heavy Bauen, Siedeln, Wohnen, Hans Wagner writes: «Probably nowhere does an architect have to bear a greater responsibility than in the Gau Tirol. [...] We have a special obligation towards

5   South Tyrolean settlement Innsbruck. Façades in Gumppstraße in 2021. The motifs of the arcades, corner pylons, and bay windows were intended as particularly «South Tyrolean» elements.

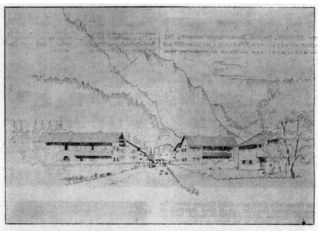

Die Bauten in Landeck zeigen die stilvolle Anpassung an den Landschaftscharakter unserer Heimat

6   South Tyrolean settlement Landeck-Perjen. Perspective drawing from the *Innsbrucker Nachrichten* of 18 November 1939 juxtaposed with a photograph from the time of construction in *Bauen, Siedeln, Wohnen*, 1940.

the returning South Tyroleans, who are leaving an architectural treasure chest of the highest order and who should not be disappointed in this respect in their new home.»[48] The desire for built homeliness was opposed to the reality that «Special Measure S» settlements followed a regional economic policy that emphasized the connection to (war-important) industries or transportation hubs. Not only were «new homes» to be created for South Tyrolean immigrants, but the shortage of labor in North Tyrol was to be counteracted. This was the case for the first completed rural settlement in Landeck-Perjen,[49] initiated by the Federal

Railroad and Reichspost, which—in association with a local textile company—all needed more living space for their workers.[50] The desire for a rural building style is clear from a 1939 statement: «The buildings in Landeck show a stylish adaptation to the landscape character of our homeland.»[51] The perspective drawing of the project published in the *Innsbrucker Nachrichten* reflects the intended homely impression. However, in a photograph from the time of construction, the uniform model character of the workers' settlement clearly comes to the fore (fig. 6).

The difference between the village idyll and the background of wartime development was even greater in Kematen, near Innsbruck.[52] The ensemble of houses, like a village within a village, is distinguished by the unique cohesiveness of its design; its spatial formation is highly convincing and it is one of the few settlements protected as a historic monument today. At the same time, the South Tyrolean settlement of Kematen stands for the Nazi armaments industry like no other: the Bavarian aircraft manufacturer, Messerschmitt AG, operated a supplier factory in the immediate vicinity of the village center. Prisoners of war were used both in the factory and for the construction of the settlement.[53]

The North Tyrolean architect Wilhelm Stigler Sr., who created a broad and respected oeuvre from the 1920s to the 1970s, worked in Kematen under the head planner of the *Heimstättenamt* in Innsbruck, the aforementioned Helmut Erdle.[54] Stiegler was ideologically committed to the planning of «Special Measure S» during the years of the Third Reich, and his contribution and the cooperation between Reich German and local architects have been meticulously researched by Juliane Mayer.[55] Despite the aura of something traditional that has evolved over time, the ensemble is based extensively on model floor plans (fig. 7). For the exterior «Tyrolization» of the buildings, Mayer suspects, based on a collection of photographs of anonymous rural buildings discovered in Stigler's estate, that various pictorial references may have been used, which would prove the dia-logic character of the houses.[56] The curious row of gapless gabled houses in Kematen, for exam-ple, is ultimately not at all typical of the locali-ty, but bears a remarkable resemblance to a row of houses in Mittenwald in Bavaria (a reconstruc-tion project of the year 1914),[57] proving that the architectural project was not about the continu-ation of verifiable local building traditions—but rather about the architectural fiction of «home-land,» about a communicative narrative that had to work for both the South Tyrolean resettled and for the receiving North Tyrolean villages (fig. 8).

In Mitterer's literary fiction, this two-faced-ness of the houses and their integrating potential is expressed in this way: «Everywhere the houses look the same, the typical Tyrolean style, so you feel right at home. Two-room apartment with a

7   South Tyrolean settlement Kematen. Plan fragment north and west view, M 1:100, from the estate of Helmut Erdle at saai Karlsruhe (Archiv für Architektur und Ingenieurbau at the KIT), here without author's details (after Mayer 2018, October 1940, comp. by Erdle/Rosenbaum/Möritz).

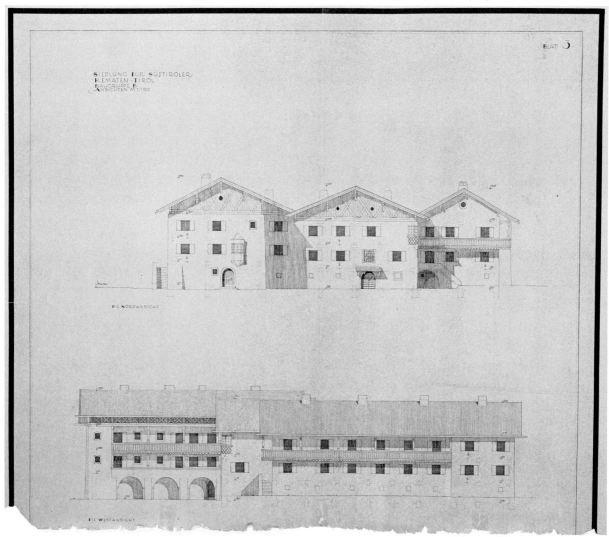

99. 1914 abgebrannte und 1915 unter Leitung des Bayrischen Landesvereins für Heimatschutz wieder aufgebaute Häuserzeile in Mittenwald, die sich als eine baukünstlerisch wie bautechnisch gleich vollkommene Lösung bewährt hat.

8   A row of houses reconstructed in 1912 in Mittenwald (Bavaria), illustrated in A. Seifert, *Das echte Haus im Gau Tirol-Vorarlberg* (1943) juxtaposed with a row of houses of the South Tyrolean settlement in Kematen.

combined kitchen-living room, bathroom and toilet, hot running water, a combination cooker that fires up the stove and heats up the oven electrically, you can grow your vegetables in the meadows between the houses.»[58]

Excursus II: Possible Origins for the Settlement Buildings and «Ancestral Heritage»

Thus, no real «South Tyrolean houses»—in the sense of indigenous building forms—were created. Rather, they are «eclectic»[59] North Tyrolean houses, composed of different elements of the local peasant heritage as if in a kind of collage of the vernacular. Moreover, the «North Tyrolean house» cannot be summarized, because its characteristics differ from valley to valley.[60] And in addition, the question of references for the overall program of the South Tyrolean settlements has sometimes been strongly ideologically veiled. Contemporary house research includes a thin booklet by Alwin Seifert published in 1943 with the unwieldy title, *Das echte Haus im Gau Tirol-Vorarlberg. Eine Untersuchung über Wesen und Herkunft des alpenländischen Flachdachhauses und die Grundsätze einer Wiedergeburt im Geiste unserer Zeit* (*The Real House in the Gau Tirol-Vorarlberg. An Investigation into the Nature and Origin of the Alpine Flat-roofed House and the Principles of a Rebirth in the Spirit of our Time*), which puts forward racial ideological arguments reflecting the Nazi view of history. Thus Seifert comes to the conclusion that the Tyrolean, Vorarlberg and Bavarian house was in no way influenced by the Mediterranean, but was clearly of Germanic origin, and that the aim must be «to participate in the further development of the house in Tyrol-Vorarlberg as a genuine and independent Nordic house.»[61] In the booklet, moreover, one finds the row of houses from Mittenwald that was possibly exemplary for Kematen.[62] «*Landschaftsgebundenheit*» («connection to landscape») seems to have been quite freely transferable for Seifert as well.

Another organization, which sought to «secure» the immobile cultural assets left behind by the resettled South Tyroleans in the homeland itself, began in 1940 with a comprehensive «overall survey of the old rural building culture in the contract area»—including language, customs and folk art. The cultural commission of the SS-«*Ahnenerbe*» (SS «ancestral heritage») in South Tyrol[63] was to record in detail, measure, draw, photograph, and typologically classify the Tyrolean peasant heritage on Italian soil, the farms still existing but threatened with abandonment. First of all, the «oldest and most primitive buildings» were selected for recording, differentiated according to regions and valleys, and special attention was paid to the «Germanic» timber construction.[64] The collected knowledge was to facilitate the reconstruction work in the new homeland. But this initiative basically came too late—fictitious Tyrolean houses had long since been built in North Tyrol by the time of this building research campaign.[65] The actual South Tyrolean building heritage thus hardly played a role as a background for reflection (fig. 9). Ultimately, it was not the intention of *Das Ahnenerbe e.V.* to build copies of South Tyrolean farms in North Tyrol; rather, the building knowledge was to be instrumentalized politically and ideologically for the future.[66] The task of this SS research and teaching community consisted, according to its statutes, essentially in «investigating and communicating the space, spirit, deed and heritage of the northern Indo-German race.»[67]

A Lost Settlement: Emergence and Transformation in the Present Day

The following discussion of the South Tyrolean settlement in Zams, which was built in direct connection with the one in Landeck-Perjen,[68] stems from the uneasiness described at the beginning of this paper. A large part of this village, which I always perceived as particularly «Tyrolean» in my childhood days, has given way to a modern residential quarter consisting of apartment buildings, which are still owned by *Neue Heimat Tirol* (NHT). Three aspects may save me from an overly sentimental testimony: the spatial qualities of the ensemble, the modification of typological buildings and their possible references, and the handling of the commemorative value of these buildings.

9   Building survey of a farmhouse in Rotwand, South Tyrol (1941) juxtaposed with an elevation drawing of the staircase entrance to the «Volkswohnung Typ 35,» published in *Bauen, Siedeln, Wohnen* 1940.

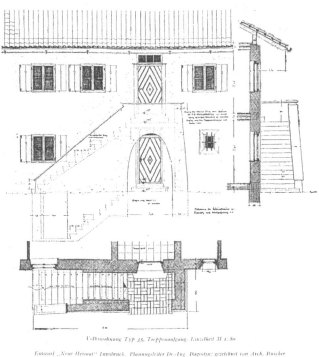

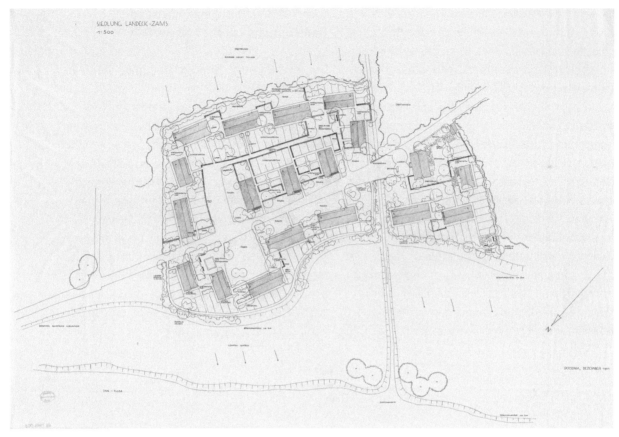

10   South Tyrolean settlement in Zams (Landeck). Site plan, M 1:500, from the estate of Herta Hammerbacher at the Architekturmuseum der TU Berlin, dated Potsdam, 1941.

The settlement in Zams was built on an open meadow plot in the immediate vicinity of the religious building of the Sisters of Mercy of St. Vincent de Paul. This would have been exchanged land, which made the considerable expansion of built fabric near the village center possible.[69] Compared to often resistant individual owners, who were sometimes threatened with the expropriation of their land, the church, monasteries and parishes were considered easier negotiating partners in the special development project, which was under enormous time pressure.[70] The *Gausiedlungsplaner* (district settlement planner) Helmut Erdle (under Peter Koller) was again responsible for the site plan of the 122 people's houses, which were ready for occupancy in May 1941.[71] In a version of the plan

from December 1939, the multi-family houses are grouped together, but are still placed on the proverbial «green field» between the banks of the Inn River, the village stream, and the monastery building without any particular reference to the topographically indistinct terrain.[72] However, there is another site plan from 1941, which is in the estate of the renowned former professor of landscape and garden design at the Technical University of Berlin, Herta Hammerbacher. This much more detailed and very differentiated plan shows house gardens and passageways, landscaped lawns and hedges, farmyards and playgrounds, overall a verdant village ensemble[73] (fig. 10).

Hammerbacher, who was married to landscape architect Hermann Mattern for some time, developed her landscape and garden planning expertise in the 1920s and 30s as part of the circle of perennial plant breeder Karl Foerster.[74] What is known about the years relevant here is that she initially planned the layout of the Reichsgartenschau in Stuttgart in 1939. Furthermore, in Jeong-Hi Go's monograph, one learns that Mattern had appreciated the advice of *Reichslandschaftsanwalt* (state landscape attorney) Alwin Seifert, who in turn advised Gauleiter Franz Hofer on planning issues[75]—the networks were thus established.[76] As a woman, Hammerbacher was excluded from larger projects surrounding the construction of the German Reichsautobahn, but she was employed for other planning tasks by the Organisation Todt (special organization of the Nazi state for construction projects, named after the founder Fritz Todt). From 1940 onwards, she worked on the South Tyrolean settlements of the Gau Tirol-Vorarlberg, designed the self-sufficient and farm gardens, and developed the open spaces around the building ensembles into the valued, village green spaces that can still be experienced today.[77]

The model buildings used in Zams were based on the neighboring settlement of Landeck-Perjen. One house type featured wood-clad gable triangles, described by Titus Taeschner and Richard Dagostin in *Bauen, Siedeln, Wohnen* (1940): «the ornamental gable formed from wooden beams [is] a characteristic of the Inn Valley, especially the Upper Inn Valley.»[78] Another house type featured recessed, suspended wooden balconies, while yet another featured exterior brick stairways on the narrow side of the houses (fig. 11). The form of such balconies, known from South and North Tyrol, became a repeated, thus supposedly «site-specific,» building element. In fact, it is a trans-temporal and trans-local motif, which can also be found in the building records of the *Ahnenerbe* (see fig. 9).

11   Photograph of «*Umsiedler-Wohnungen*» («resettler housing») in Zams-Landeck at the time of construction according to Helmut Erdle's designs, illustration published in *Das Bauen im Neuen Reich*, 1943.

12   The *Einhof* in Zams, 2024.

Ulrich Höhns, in an early assessment, described the architect Helmut Erdle as one who sought «to hang different ‹costumes› or ‹traditional folk dress›» on «*Reichsgrundrisse*» («state-sanctioned floor plans»), and not only according to the regional landscape, while Juliane Mayer also concludes that Erdle had studied the existing local building fabric in detail.[79] But for Erdle, most likely the greatest challenge was to design regionally adapted houses that could appear recognizable and familiar through traditional elements, while conforming to standard specifications and the rationalization

13   Newest residential buildings of the «*Neue Heimat Tirol*» replacing the old South Tyrolean settlement in Zams, 2021.

mandates from the «*Reichsbauformen*» and «*Landschaftsnormen*» («state-sanctioned building typologies» and «landscape norms»).[80]

Considering this work of adaptation, one wonders which architectural references were used for the design framework. After a devastating fire in Zams[81] in 1911, not much of the historical substance of the village was left. One of the prototypical buildings could be the *Einhof* (fig. 12) from the 17th century, which directly borders the settlement area and was spared from the fire. This massive masonry building with a fretted gable sits on a raised basement level and is accessed by a brick double-flight grand staircase that rises to a central landing with a balcony.[82] The characteristic double-flight staircase to the main entrance is, however, not specific to Zams. It can be found in a similarly transferred form in the South Tyrolean settlement in Reutte. There, the model was the local community house, which is also a landmarked building.[83] A second reference building in Zams could have been the so-called Old Doctor's House near the church, which was reconstructed after the village fire and points to baroque roots with its hipped roof. Another «doctor's house» is shown in the site plan within the South Tyrolean settlement, but was not executed.[84] The design from Helmut Erdle's estate dates from July 1940 and shows a building that is very similar to the Old Doctor's House, right down to the shape of the roof.[85] The two reference buildings in Zams mentioned above are still standing today and have been lovingly maintained; all the buildings in the South Tyrolean Settlement, on the other hand, have now been demolished, and the non-profit housing association NHT has built around 190 new rental apartments as replacements in seven construction phases from 2009 to 2022.[86]

For the Zams site, the only thing that can be said at this point is that the complicated, overlapping history has been wiped away, and the built context has disappeared. What has emerged is a kind of mimicry settlement that is at best vaguely reminiscent of the old development plan. Pressure to increase the density of housing has wiped out the once generous interlocking green spaces and village-like character. The idea of an architecture connected to its landscape—as fictitiously «down-to-earth» as it was—has been erased. Now, only a «*Kunst am Bau*» («Art on the Building») project takes up the task of referencing history. But this artwork appears in the new, still so-called «South Tyrolean Settlement,» strangely oblivious and historically irrelevant. It wants—according to the title of the work *YinYang-Uhr: Zeit schauen*—to «look at time».[87] Which time is the question, when architecture as a symbol of identification has disappeared, and the replacement buildings are modern, but faceless standard residential buildings without historic reference. At the same time, the NHT is more than aware of its corporate history and has dealt critically and repeatedly with its heritage in publications in the past without historic reference, most recently in the company history updated in 2013.[88]

Preliminary Summary

The South Tyrolean housing estates of the 1940s are instructive testimonies of the Nazi era, and their narrative power alone would justify their preservation. This includes, above all, the frictions and dissonances of this difficult legacy: at first glance, the houses follow regional building traditions; at second glance, one recognizes their artificial character and, at the same time, the rationalization efforts behind it. Only at third glance does the burden of history take effect.

Nevertheless, more than 60 % of the South Tyrolean housing estates in North Tyrol are to be demolished in the next few years, while about 38 % are to be renovated. To compensate for this, 5,000 new housing units will be created, an action which admittedly makes a strong argument in the tight housing market, especially since there is talk

of «contemporary and affordable housing» that is a «prime example of the careful design of new living space with the involvement of existing tenants,» according to the NHT customer magazine in 2020[98] (fig. 13). Even if the current demolition and new construction[90]—intended to raise the standard of living and the economic efficiency of the aging buildings[91]—is understandable from the perspective of both the housing industry and tenants,[92] the history and thus the memory of the buildings is being marginalized more and more.

But is the commitment to partial preservation and renovation and the few protected buildings sufficient as spaces of memory and history? Do these exemplars make up for the considerable losses of the building fabric? How can the burdened and yet insightful ambiguity of Nazi architecture continue to be experienced here?[93] It should remain a stumbling block to find the houses «beautiful,» because buildings alone do not possess morality, regardless of the immorality of the actors of the time. One would like to raise the demand for a new cultural topography, one that at least maps, surveys, and records the South Tyrolean settlements that are threatened to disappear. However, this would have to happen quickly, because the loss is already bordering on irretrievable.

Postscript I: After the manuscript was finished, a model apartment showing the interior of the 1940s has been reconstructed and made accessible in the partially landmarked settlement in Reutte through the efforts of the local museum association.[94]

Postscript II: In the meantime, the NHT has built a new residential complex in Kematen, which will be available to tenants of the Südtiroler Siedlung during the planned renovation measures from fall 2024. This measure is described as a «flagship Project» and the company writes that it is in «constructive contact» with the residents.[95]

The German text by the author was translated by John King. The German version of the text will be published in *Tiroler Heimatblätter. Zeitschrift für regionale Kultur* 99, no. 2, 2024, 50–61.

1   Cf. similar «sentimental» approach in Federer 2021, 3.

2   Höhns 1992, a comprehensive architectural-historical assessment of South Tyrolean settlements that is still valid today; Harlander 1995 discusses housing policy under the Nazi regime with studies on the history of time and/or architecture of individual settlements in North Tyrol e.g., Mayr 2002 (Landeck-Perjen, Zams); Rief 2012 (Reutte); Mayer 2018 (Kematen); Pitscheider 2019 (Kematen); Federer 2021 (Innsbruck, Hall, Reutte); comprehensive bibliography «Option und Erinnerung» 2014, among others on settlement buildings.

3   For an overview of the eventful history of South Tyrol, see Mazohl/Steininger 2020, 225–31.

4   Mazohl/Steininger 2020, 233–39.

5   Alexander et al. 1993, 22–23; the «Berlin Agreement» of 23 June 1939 was intended to resolve the «South Tyrol Question» between Nazi Germany and Fascist Italy.

6   Alexander et al. 1993, 25.

7   Alexander et al. 1993, 99; this resettlement process was only one of many under Nazi rule, see the chapter *Das Dritte Reich und seine Auslandsdeutschen*, 15–21.

8   Mayr 2002, 27.

9   Mayr 2002, 23–24.

10   Abstract in Lackner/Mader 2006, 6–7.

11   Alexander et al. 1993, 98.

12   Alexander et al. 1993, 199–204.

13   City as «repository of collected memories» after B. Bogdanovic, in Assmann 2012, 76–77.

14   Quote in dialect, transcribed from the film version of the play Mitterer 2019, ORF III, https://www.youtube.com/watch?v=hrZBdpVyR7A (March 2022): «Mir sein des Gedächtnis von di Häuser, die nach und nach verschwinden, die nach und nach abgrissen wern. Mir ham enk derzählt, wie alls kemmen isch mit ins. Mir waren net die onzigen Fremden. Fremde gibt's überall, und falsche Propheten a. Horchts net auf sie.»

15   Cf. contemporary historical waves of memory in Pfanzelter 2013, 13–40.

16   Balzano 2018; for previous literary treatments of the «Option» and South Tyrolean history, see Pfanzelter 2013, 29.

17   Melandri 2011.

18   «Option und Erinnerung» 2014.

19   Documentaries Lembergh 2018 and Hollaus 2019.

20   Cf. various commemorative narratives in South Tyrol in Pfanzelter 2013, 13–40.

21   A list of the 21 North Tyrolean municipalities with the number of dwellings and reference dates built for occupants in North Tyrol as of 1940 can be found in Mayr 2002, 91–92; Alexander et al. 1993, 121, speaks of 22 municipalities in North Tyrol and nine in Vorarlberg.

22   Pfanzelter 2013, 23; after 1945, so-called «resettler» settlements were established in Bolzano.

23   (Partial) protection of the South Tyrolean settlement in Reutte 2007 and Kematen 2010/11; Art Cadastre Tyrol, https://www.tirol.gv.at/kunst-kultur/kunstkataster/ (March 2022); culture reports from Tirol 2012, 24–28; cf. attitude of the Federal Monuments Office, Department Tyrol, written interview with the provincial conservator Michaela Frick, in Federer 2021, 114–117, where the attitude of «selected» protection is emphasized.

24   Schlosser 2019.

25   Alexander 2013, 14–20.

26   Harlander 1995.

27   Alexander et al. 1993, 128.

28   Social Contract of 1939, cf. Alexander 2013, 15, 177.

29   Alexander 2013, 14–15.

30   Alexander 2013, 17. In this context, the term «Volkswohnungen» denotes residences for the German population, with «German» being defined according to the racist doctrine of the time. For the significance of «Volk» in the context of Third Reich terminology see e.g. Meyers Lexikon 1937 «Volksgemeinschaft» or the Wikipedia article «Volksgemeinschaft»: https://en.wikipedia.org/wiki/Volksgemeinschaft.

31   Höhns 1992, 283; the author's assessment that during World War II the Germans implemented the «social housing» invented during the Nazi era in their annexed neighboring countries, including «good» houses that were above the bounds of what was possible and usual, still holds today.

32   Höhns 1992, 287–288, offers a detailed account of National Socialist settlement buildings in the «Ostmark» and «Westmark.»

33   Albrich 2013 also partially incorporates oral history sources.

34   Federer 2021, 47–48.

35   Höhns 1992, 283–284.

36   Cf. individual study on the Kematen settlement, Pitscheider 2019, 103.

37   See Fallersleben/Wolfsburg or Peter Koller, cf. Federer 2021, 7, 39–41, 78–86.

38   Schneider 1997, 68–70.

39   Koller 1940; Kautt 1997, 99–100; Federer 2021, 79.

40   The *Denkmalatlas Niedersachsen* (*Lower Saxony Monument Atlas*) states the following as justification for protection: «There is a public interest in the preservation of the housing estate due to its historical and urban development significance.» https://denkmalatlas.niedersachsen.de/viewer/piresolver?id=34201448 (March 2022).

41   Feder 1939; the comprehensive standardization efforts of the Nazi planners can be traced, for example, in «*Die neue Stadt*» for individual building uses on the basis of numerous model specification sheets.

42   For the possible connection of planning ideas from Wolfsburg to Innsbruck, see Federer 2021, 52.

43   Höhns 1992, 286–287 for a description of the personnel networks and frictions that arose with the different urban planning ideas.

44 Taeschner / Dagostin 1940, 580. Original quotation in German: «Um nun nicht fremde Baukörper in die Landschaft zu bringen, war es erforderlich, Typen zu entwickeln, die sechs oder mehr Wohnungen enthielten.»

45 For details on Helmut Erdle's career and architectural outlook, Federer 2021, 31–33.

46 Helmut Erdle, in the words of Paul Schmitthenner, here quoted from Höhns 1992, 287.

47 Taeschner / Dagostin 1940, 580, mention eight different types alone.

48 Wagner 1940, 553. Original quotation in German: «Wohl nirgendswo hat ein Architekt eine größere Verantwortung zu tragen als im Gau Tirol. [...] Ganz besonders besteht diese Verpflichtung für uns gegenüber den heimkehrenden Südtirolern, die ein architektonisches Schmuckkästchen sondergleichen verlassen und auch in dieser Hinsicht in ihrer neuen Heimat nicht enttäuscht werden sollen.»

49 Alexander et al. 1993, 121; Mayr 2002, 5, 45.

50 Mayr 2002, 52–58, on the administrative history of this settlement.

51 Innsbrucker Nachrichten 1939, 4, caption. Original quotation in German: «Die Bauten in Landeck zeigen die stilvolle Anpassung an den Landschaftscharakter unserer Heimat.»

52 Pitscheider 2019, 69–84.

53 Pitscheider 2019, comprehensive on the history of Kematen «from a farming village to an industrial community» during the Nazi period; on forced labor, 84–98; on the South Tyrolean settlement, 98–107.

54 Comprehensive in Mayer 2018, 2 vols.

55 Regarding the «Messerschmitt-Siedlung Kematen 1940–1942,» Mayer 2018, vol. 1, 282–307 provides a reconstruction of available plan versions, detailed design history with reference to standardization and typological classification, stakeholder history, and historic preservation assessment.

56 Mayer 2018, vol. 1, 278–281; Federer 2021, 44–45, speaks of an exemplary collection of photographs from the estate of the architect Heinz Möritz that was used for other settlements.

57 Mayer 2018, vol. 1, 296–301.

58 Transcript from the 2019 film adaptation of Mitterer's play, ORF III, https://www.youtube.com/watch?v=hrZBdpVyR7A (March 2022). Original quotation in German: «Überall schauen die Hauser gleich aus, Typ Tirol, damit ihr euch so richtig zu Hause fühlt. Zweizimmerwohnung mit Wohnküche, Bad und WC, fließend Warmwasser, Kombiherd, zum Anfeuern und elektrisch mit Backrohr, zwischen den Häusern auf den Wiesen könnt ihr euer Gemüse anbauen.»

59 Federer 2021, 43.

60 Markovits 2018.

61 Seifert 1943, 6. Original quotation in German: «[...] an der weiteren Entwicklung des Hauses in Tirol-Vorarlberg als eines echten und eigenständigen nordischen Hauses mitzuschaffen.»

62 Seifert 1943, 68. A friendly hint by Juliane Mayer: Wilhelm Stigler Sr. was a student of Alwin Seifert at the TH Munich; the topic of the reconstruction of Mittenwald had been omnipresent there.

63 Wedekind 2017, 1866–1878.

64 Stampfer 1990, 5–6; the first volume of 1940s construction photographs was published in book form starting in 1990.

65 Mayer 2018, vol. 1, 278–281; comprehensive assessment in the context of the Kemater settlement and W. Stigler's photo collection and the question of whether a «cultural topography» should have been created here as well; cf. Höhns 1997, 289.

66 Wedekind 2017, 1867.

67 Wedekind 2017, 1866. Original quotation in German: «Raum, Geist, Tat und Erbe des nordrassigen Indogermanentums [...]».

68 Mayr 2002 deals with both settlements, which were administratively related and were occupied in 1940/41 by the South Tyrolean resettled, among others.

69 Mayr 2002, 61–62.

70 Alexander et al. 1993, 122–123; Mayr 2002, 30.

71 Settlement in Landeck-Zams, drawn by Gausiedlungsplaner Erdle, Innsbruck, November 1939. M 1:500. Estate of Herta Hammbacher, Architekturmuseum der TU Berlin, Inv.-Nr. HH 0417,001.

72 On general aspects of settlement planning in Helmut Erdle, see Mayer 2018, vol. 1, 304.

73 Settlement Landeck-Zams [drawn by Herta Hammerbacher?], Potsdam, December 1941. M 1:500. Estate of Herta Hammbacher, Architekturmuseum der TU Berlin, Inv.-Nr. HH 0417,003.

74 Go 2006, 25–28.

75 Mayer 2018, Bd. 1, 304.

76 Go 2006, 30–33.

77 Go 2006, 32.

78 Taeschner / Dagostin 1940, 580. Original quotation in German: «[...] der aus Holzgebälk gebildete Ziergiebel [ist] ein Charakteristikum des Inntales, besonders des Oberinntales.»

79 Recent Assessment of Erdle's Achievements, Mayer, 2018, vol. 1, 304–306.

80 Höhns 1992, 293; Rief 2012, 79–80.

81 Steinwender 2011.

82 Markovits 2018, 162–163; Monument Register of the BDA. Bundesdenkmalamt, Austria. State of Tyrol 2021, https://bda.gv.at/denkmalverzeichnis/ (March 2022).

83 Rief 2012, 100; Federer 2021, 74, the author describes the house as a special type VT 2.

84 Site plan Hammerbacher 1941, Architekturmuseum TU Berlin.

85 Settlement Landeck-Zams. The doctor's house. Erdle, Rosenbaum, Gausiedlungsplaner Innsbruck, July 1940. M 1:100. Works archive Helmut Erdle, saai. Southwest German Archive for Architecture and Engineering Karlsruhe.

86   Neue Heimat Tirol, overview of construction projects, https://www.neueheimat.tirol/projekte (March 2022).
87   Art project by Christine S. Prantauer and Manfred Moser, Zams 2020, https://www.neueheimat.tirol/projekte/kunst-am-bau/zams-christine-s-prantauer (March 2022); on the fig leaf function of art in construction, see Federer 2021, 98.
88   Neue Heimat Tirol 2013, therein Alexander/Albrich 2013.
89   Neue Heim.at 2020, 4–5.
90   Hinterwaldner 2018, on demolitions in Innsbruck; Reichle 2019, on demolitions in Landeck-Perjen.
91   Cf. Schlosser 2019.
92   Points of conflict with tenants in the case of Kematen: Fritz 2020, Schnöll 2020.
93   Cf. historic preservation assessment in Mayer 2018, vol. 1, 306–307.
94   Tiroler Tageszeitung 2021.
95   Neue Heimat Tirol 2024.

Albrich 2013
S. Albrich: Schöne neue Wohnwelt – Erlebte und erzählte Geschichte, in: Neue Heimat Tirol (ed.): Die Geschichte der «Neuen Heimat Tirol» 1939–2014 (Innsbruck 2013) 99–142.

Alexander 2013
H. Alexander: Wegmarken und Weichenstellungen – Geschichte der Wohnungs- und Siedlungsgesellschaft «Neue Heimat Tirol» in Innsbruck, in: Neue Heimat Tirol (ed.): Die Geschichte der «Neuen Heimat Tirol» 1939–2014 (Innsbruck 2013) 11–80, 177–184.

Alexander et al. 1993
H. Alexander / S. Lechner / A. Leidlmair: Heimatlos. Die Umsiedlung der Südtiroler (Vienna 1993).

Assmann 2012
A. Assmann: Der Kampf um die Stadt als Identitätsverankerung und Geschichtsspeicher, in: F. Eigler / J. Kugele (ed.): Heimat. At the Intersection of Memory and Space (Berlin, Boston 2012) 71–92.

Balzano 2018
M. Balzano: Resto qui (Turin 2018). German translation «Ich bleibe hier» (Zürich 2020).

Erhard 1989
B. Erhard (ed.): Option. Heimat. Opzioni. Eine Geschichte Südtirols / Una storia dell' Alto Adige (Vienna 1989).

Feder 1939
G. Feder: Die neue Stadt. Versuch der Begründung einer neuen Stadtplanungskunst aus der sozialen Struktur der Bevölkerung (Berlin 1939).

Federer 2021
R. Federer: Die Südtiroler Siedlungen in Tirol. Ihre historische und architektonische Bedeutung als gemeinsames Erbe (shared heritage). Diplomarbeit Universität Innsbruck 2021.

Fritz 2020
K. Fritz: Aufgeheizte Stimmung in Kematen, Rundschau online, 10 March 2020, https://www.rundschau.at/telfs/chronik/aufgeheizte-stimmung-in-kematen (March 2022).

Go 2006
J.-H. Go: Herta Hammerbacher (1900–1985). Virtuosin der Neuen Landschaftlichkeit. Der Garten als Paradigma. Diss. TU Berlin 2006.

Harlander 1995
T. Harlander: Zwischen Heimstätte und Wohnmaschine. Wohnungsbau und Wohnungspolitik in der Zeit des Nationalsozialismus (Basel 1995).

Hinterwaldner 2018
K. Hinterwaldner: Operation Abriss. Innsbruck sucht Platz für moderne Häuserblocks, ff. Das Südtiroler Wochenmagazin 40, 2018, 36–39.

Höhns 1992
U. Höhns: Grenzenloser Heimatschutz 1941. Neues, altes Bauen in der «Ostmark» und der «Westmark», in: V.M. Lampugnani / R. Schneider (ed.): Moderne Architektur in Deutschland 1900 bis 1950. Reform und Tradition (Stuttgart 1992) 283–301.

Hollaus 2019
M. Hollaus: Risse. Dokumentarfilm unter Mitarbeit von A. Sommerauer. Documentary film, Austria, 2019.

Innsbrucker Nachrichten 1939
Wohnungen für Südtiroler Volksgenossen. Gewaltiges Bauprogramm im Gau Tirol-Vorarlberg in Ausführung – Mehrere hundert Wohnungen fertiggestellt: Innsbrucker Nachrichten. Parteiamtliches Organ der NSdAP, 18 November 1939, 3–4.

Kautt 1997
D. Kautt: Wolfsburg im Wandel städtebaulicher Leitbilder, in: R. Beier (ed.): aufbau west aufbau ost. Die Planstädte Wolfsburg und Eisenhüttenstadt in der Nachkriegszeit (Ostfildern-Ruit 1997) 99–109.

Kienzl 2018
P. Kienzl: Alltags-Geschichte. Die Telfer Südtiroler Siedlung (Telfs 2018).

Koller 1940
P. Koller: Die Siedlung Steimkerberg im Rahmen der Stadtplanung, Bauen, Siedeln, Wohnen 20, 1940, 656–661.

Kulturberichte aus Tirol 2012
Kulturberichte aus Tirol / 63. Denkmalbericht Denkmalpflege in Tirol / Jahresbericht des Bundesdenkmalamtes 2010/11 / Jahresbericht des Landes Tirol 2010/11 (Innsbruck 2012).

Lackner/Mader 2006
A. Lackner / G. Mader: Heimat verloren – Heimat gewonnen?

Spurensuche zur Option der Südtiroler 1939. Medienbegleitheft des Bundesministeriums für Unterricht, Kunst und Kultur (Vienna 2006).

Lembergh 2018
G. Lembergh: Das versunkene Dorf. Documentary film, Italy, 2018.

Markovits 2018
K. Markovits: Tiroler Bauernhöfe. Bäuerliche Architektur im Außerfern, Oberland, Mittleren Inntal, Unterland und in Osttirol (Innsbruck 2018).

Mayer 2018
J. Mayer: Der Architekt Wilhelm Stigler sen. 1903–1976. Neue Studien zur Architektur der Tiroler Moderne. 2 vols. (Innsbruck 2018).

Mayr 2002
S. Mayr: Das Entstehen von Volkswohnungen durch die «Neue Heimat» für Südtiroler Umsiedler im Bezirk Landeck. Diplomarbeit Universität Innsbruck 2002.

Mazohl / Steininger 2020
B. Mazohl / R. Steininger: Geschichte Südtirols (Munich 2020).

Melandri 2011
F. Melandri: Eva schläft (Munich 2011).

Mitterer 1989
F. Mitterer: Verkaufte Heimat. Eine Südtiroler Familiensage von 1938 bis 1945 (Innsbruck 1989).

Mitterer 2019
F. Mitterer: «Verkaufte Heimat – Das Gedächtnis der Häuser». Theaterstück nach Adaption des Drehbuchs von 1989, uraufgeführt an den Tiroler Volksschauspielen Telfs 2019, https://www.youtube.com/watch?v=hrZBdpVyR7A (March 2022).

Neue Heimat Tirol 2013
Neue Heimat Tirol (ed.): Die Geschichte der «Neuen Heimat Tirol» 1939–2014 (Innsbruck 2013).

Neue Heimat Tirol 2024
Neue Heimat Tirol: Schlüsselübergabe in Kematen, 17. May 2024, https://www.neueheimat.tirol/aktuelles/detail/schl%C3%BCssel%C3%BCbergabe-kematen (July 2024).

Neue Heim.at 2020
Neue Heim.at. Kundenmagazin der Neuen Heimat Tirol (Innsbruck 2020).

Option und Erinnerung 2014
Research project «Die Erinnerung an die Südtiroler Option 1939». Bibliography by Universität Innsbruck about the topic «Südtiroler Siedlungen», http://www.optionunderinnerung.org/wp-content/uploads/2014/11/S%C3%BCdtirolersiedlung.pdf (March 2022). About «Gedächtnis», http://www.optionunderinnerung.org/wp-content/uploads/2014/11/Literaturliste-Option-und-Erinnerung.pdf (March 2022).

Pfanzelter 2013
E. Pfanzelter: Die (un)verdaute Erinnerung an die Option 1939, Geschichte und Region/Storia e regione 22, 2013, 13–40.

Pitscheider 2019
S. Pitscheider: Kematen in Tirol in der NS-Zeit. Vom Bauerndorf zur Industriegemeinde. 4th ed. (Innsbruck 2019).

Reichle 2019
M. Reichle: Ende der alten Südtiroler Siedlung im Bezirk Landeck absehbar: Tiroler Tageszeitung online, 17 January 2019, https://www.tt.com/artikel/15224767/ende-der-alten-suedtiroler-siedlung-im-bezirk-landeck-absehbar (March 2022).

Rief 2012
F. Rief: Die Südtiroler Siedlung in Reutte. Die Entstehung eines Reuttener Ortsteiles im Zuge des «NS-Volkswohnungsbaus» für Südtiroler Umsiedler im Gau Tiro-Vorarlberg, ergänzt durch ein Oral History-Untersuchung. Masterarbeit Universität Innsbruck 2012.

Schlosser 2019
H. Schlosser: Gemischte Gefühle, Wohnenplus 2, 2019, 24–26.

Schneider 1997
C. Schneider: Wolfsburg unter anderen. Städtebaupolitik im Dritten Reich, in: R. Beier (ed.): aufbau west aufbau ost. Die Planstädte Wolfsburg und Eisenhüttenstadt in der Nachkriegszeit (Ostfildern-Ruit 1997) 65–73.

Schnöll 2020
G.G. Schnöll: «NHT» stellt Mieterinitiative Rute ins Fenster: Rundschau online, 30 November 2020, https://www.rundschau.at/telfs/chronik/nht-stellt-mieterinitiative-rute-ins-fenster (March 2022).

Seifert 1943
A. Seifert: Das echte Haus im Gau Tirol-Vorarlberg. Eine Untersuchung über Wesen und Herkunft des alpenländischen Flachdachhauses und die Grundsätze einer Wiedergeburt im Geiste unserer Zeit (Innsbruck 1943).

Stampfer 1990
H. Stampfer (ed.): Bauernhöfe in Südtirol: Bestandsaufnahmen 1940–1943, vol. 1: Ritten (Bozen 1990).

Steinwender 2011
E. Steinwender: Großbrand in Zams, Zammer Gemeindenachrichten 1, 2011, 8–10.

Taeschner / Dagostin 1940
T. Taeschner / R. Dagostin: Über die Bauten der «Neuen Heimat», Bauen, Siedeln, Wohnen 17, 1940, 580–581.

Tiroler Tageszeitung 2021
Einen Erinnerungsort geschaffen. Die Schauwohnung in der Reuttener Südtiroler Siedlung wurde offiziell eröffnet, Tiroler Tageszeitung, 27 September 2021.

Troost 1943
G. Troost (ed.): Das Bauen im Neuen Reich, vol. 2 (Bayreuth 1943).

Wagner 1940
H. Wagner: Neue Heimat für Südtiroler: Über die Bauten der «Neuen Heimat», Bauen, Siedeln, Wohnen 17, 1940, 552–579.

Wedekind 2017
M. Wedekind: Kulturkommission des SS-«Ahnenerbes» in Südtirol, in: M. Fahlbusch / I. Haar / A. Pinwinkler (eds.): Handbuch der völkischen Wissenschaften. Akteure, Netzwerke, Forschungsprogramme. 2nd ed. (Berlin 2017) 1866–1878.

Wittig 1993
W. Wittig: Wohnungsbau der 40er Jahre in Wolfsburg. Stadtdenkmalpflege Wolfsburg (Braunschweig 1993).

Image Sources

1, 2, 5, 8b, 12, 13   Photos: Eva Maria Froschauer, 2021.
3   Innsbrucker Nachrichten 1939, 3–4.
4a   Wittig 1993, 12.
4b   Erhard 1989, 231.
6   Innsbrucker Nachrichten 1939, 4; Bauen, Siedeln, Wohnen 17, 1940, 565.
7   saai | Archiv für Architektur und Ingenieurbau, KIT Karlsruhe, Werkarchiv Helmut Erdle.
8a   Seifert 1943, 68.
9a   Stampfer 1990, 467.
9b   Bauen, Siedeln, Wohnen 17, 1940, 581.
10   Architekturmuseum TU Berlin, Inv. Nr. HH 0417,003.
11   Troost 1943, 158.

The «Museum House» Phenomenon of Imbros
Unofficial Heritage Practices of Seasonal Returnees in Imbros/Gökçeada

Ayşegül Dinççağ Kahveci

The following paper is an excerpt from my ongoing doctoral dissertation entitled «Reclaiming Localities,» which focuses on the heritage practices of seasonal returnees from the Imbrian community to the island of Gökçeada (Imbros) in Turkey.[1] First, I will provide a historical overview of the state-initiated measures and regulations that led to the «Turkification» of the ancient Aegean island of Imbros and consequently forced thousands of Imbrian people to leave their homeland. Against this backdrop, I will then present the preliminary findings of my 2018 fieldwork, which is based on home visits and provides insights into the heritage practices of the community's seasonal returnees in inherited family houses, which they now use as summer houses. Drawing on people-centered conceptions of heritage in critical heritage studies,[2] the paper explores the social practices of «collecting,» «staging,» «exhibiting,» and «recycling» as processes of heritage-making by the Imbrian returnees and introduces the so-called «museum house» phenomenon in Imbros.

A Brief Historical Overview

Imbros and the neighboring islands of Tenedos, Thasos, Lemnos, and Samothrace form the unit of the Northeastern Aegean Islands called the Thracian Sporades (fig. 1). With its proximity to the entrance of the Dardanelles, Imbros is part of a well-connected network of cultural, social, and material exchange within the region and has

played a strategic geo-political role throughout its history.[3]

After World War I, the 1923 Treaty of Lausanne recognized the borders of the Turkish Republic and placed the two Aegean islands of Imbros and Tenedos under Turkish sovereignty, with the islands still recognized as Turkish territory today. Articles 14 and 40 of the Treaty of Lausanne required Turkey to accommodate «non-Muslim natives» inhabiting both islands to protect their rights to religious and cultural freedom under Turkish

1 Map of the Aegean Sea with the national borders and location of Imbros (Gökçeada).

sovereignty and granted these communities local administrative autonomy.[4] The ancient names of both islands remained unchanged until 1970, when they received their official Turkish names Gökçeada (Imbros) and Bozcaada (Tenedos).[5]

During the peace negotiations in Lausanne, Turkey and Greece signed an additional convention on compulsory population exchange, which required the resettlement of Muslims in Greece and non-Muslims in Anatolia within the newly defined borders of the two nation-states, excluding Greeks in Istanbul, in Imbros and Tenedos, as well as Muslims in Western Thrace. This agreement testified to the mutual understanding of both nation-states that ethnic minorities—defined by their religious affiliation—were outsiders in the homogeneous identity constructions of the nation-states of the 20th century. Although the 1923 convention exempted the Greek inhabitants of Imbros and Tenedos, allowing them to remain in their homeland, the nation-building processes in Turkey (as well as Greece) did not include them. The people of Imbros have undergone long-term strategies of oppression and exclusion under national politics and were marked as «marginal» to the national order of things.[6]

Up until the 1960s, oral accounts and written records indicate a quiet rural life on the island and a rather peaceful coexistence of 8,000 Greeks and fewer than 300 Turks in administrative positions. However, the flare-up of Greek-Turkish conflicts in Cyprus was a turning point for the people of Imbros, and the island began to experience unrest in 1963. Although the Imvrii had no organic ties to the Cypriots, their Greek-Christian ethnic identity seemed to be enough for the Turkish state to classify them as allies of the Cypriots and a potential threat to the Turkish nation.[7] Beginning in 1964, the Turkish State carried out a strict restructuring program of «Turkification» on Imbros, confronting the Imvrii with various strategies of oppression and violence that eventually terrorized them into leaving their homeland.[8]

These measures began with the deployment of a gendarmerie training battalion in 1964, which defined the island as a military zone and served as physical evidence of the abrogation of the administrative autonomy granted by the Treaty of Lausanne. Discriminatory measures followed, such as the ban on Greek education, which led to the closure of Greek schools on the island, directly affecting Greek families with children and triggering the first major wave of migration. Another institution established in 1964 was the Anatolian Teachers' High School, a boarding school for the training of Turkish teachers, which aimed to create a personnel base on the island to teach Turkish, the official language of education. The children of Greek families who remained on the island had to re-attend classes with the Turkish curriculum, extending their primary school education for some more years. In 1965, the state expropriated 90 % of the arable land and olive groves owned by the Imbrian population for public use and established the State Farm, or Devlet Üretim Çiftliği (DÜÇ).[9] For the rural population, the land was a vital source of income, and the disruption of their livelihood led to a second wave of migration. In 1966, a semi-open prison with a capacity of 1,000 inmates was established to meet the demand for labor to run the state farm. The convicts had free access to the fields as well as to the villages, which led to unrest and trouble within the Imbrian community. Oral accounts record specific cases of harassment, robbery, vandalism, and murder implicitly attributable to the ultranationalist rhetoric in Turkish politics at the time.

The largest wave of immigration took place after 1974, when Turkey conducted the «Peace Operation» in Cyprus, resulting in an escalation of violence and the overnight evacuation of almost all Greek villages in Imbros. The Imvrii fled to Greece on boats and were eventually scattered across the world in a transnational diaspora. As the Greek villages were abandoned and the Greek population of Imbros drastically decreased, the island became the site of state-initiated resettlement projects. Beginning in 1980, the involuntary resettlement of hundreds of mainland Anatolians to the island not only changed the social structure, but also led to a spatial transformation of the island. In 1985, the first regulations for the protection of cultural heritage were issued by the Turkish authorities, and the entire island was designated as a protected area in the categories of nature, archaeology, and urban sites. The array of state-driven policies, such as topographical renaming and cadastral re-mapping and re-zoning of the land, disrupted the continuity of Imbrian culture by making daily life practices in the landscape unfeasible. Within a decade, the Imbrian community became a minority of about 300 people among the total population of about 8,900 inhabitants on the island.[10]

In line with the neoliberal turn in Turkish politics and the economy in the 1990s, the island's status as a military/security zone was lifted and it was declared a development area of the first degree to be promoted as a tourist attraction.[11] As a result, the semi-open prison was closed in 1992, and special visa requirements for travel to Imbros were abolished in 1993. This touristic turn specifically encouraged the second generation of the transnational diaspora community to visit the island again. In the early 2000s, the Imbrian Association in Athens launched a homecoming promotion by providing financial aid for those expatriates who chose to resettle on Imbros.[12] This financial support covered the bare minimum for living on the island and seemed to be an opportunity for a new start, especially for those who were struggling during the economic crisis in Greece at that time. In the first round, single people or divorcees whose elders lived on the island accepted the offer and returned to their old family homes on Imbros. For families with children, however, returning did not seem to be a realistic plan until Greek schools reopened on the island in 2013 and 2015. In recent years, the number of permanent returnees increased to 550,[13]

while thousands of seasonal returnees continue to visit the island during the annual celebrations of the biggest Greek Orthodox religious festival dedicated to the Virgin Mary, Panagia (Παναγία), which takes place in August. Members of the Imbrian diaspora from around the world gather on the island and take time to commemorate their past, reunite with their community, and reconnect with the island.

Summer Houses of Seasonal Returnees

In August 2018, Kosmos, a very respected member of the Imbrian community, accompanied me as my guide to some of the oldest houses on the island, which he described as representative of the traditional architecture of Imbros. Through his intercession, I met with the second-generation homeowners who visit the island seasonally and use the old family homes as summer residences during their vacation time. The greatest commonality among these seasonal returnees is that they are among the transnational elites of the Imbrian community, having had the opportunity to attain higher levels of education in cities such as Thessaloniki or Athens. Most of them have had remarkable careers as doctors, scholars, architects, etc., forming the upper middle class of the Imbrian community. Without the mediation of Kosmos, it would be impossible for an outsider like me to meet these members of the community and to visit them in their homes without an appointment. Through his advocacy, all my visits were greeted with smiling faces, and I was welcomed into one home after another.

I had done my homework and had already studied Pasadaios's detailed 1973 inventory of the vernacular architecture of the island. In his work, Pasadaios coined the term «Imbriotic House»[14] and introduced the single-room typology called the «monospito.»[15] He meticulously described the spatial organization of rural life in the villages based on a sample house, «Koutoufos,» named after its owner. Pasadaios depicted a two-floor structure, each floor consisted of a multi-functional single space, from which the typology's name (*monospito*) was derived. The ground floor (*katoe*) served as storage or an atelier for the owner's professional activities, while the upper floor (*anoe*) was the family residence, where everyday life took place. Each floor had a separate entrance, and the residential unit was limited to the exterior stone staircase called the *petraskala*.

Because the majority of the Imbrian people departed during the 1970s, most abandoned houses bore resemblance to the *monospito* typology prevalent during this period. However, the houses to which Kosmos took me were structurally and spatially much more sophisticated than the rural houses described by Pasadaios.[16] These houses were notably larger in size and different in their typology. They were affectionately referred to as «*konaki*» by their owners, as they resembled the Ottoman-era Turkish houses known as «*konak*.» Although they were much more modest compared to the sumptuous Turkish *konaks*, the architectural components of these structures unquestionably mirrored the traditional characteristics of these historic edifices. Unlike the single-roomed typology of the *monospito*, these houses were divided into rooms whose functions were based on the needs of the users. The distinctive feature of this typology was that the exterior stone staircase, the *petraskala*, was replaced by an internal wooden staircase that connected both floors. Unlike the rural house, where the two floors had separate entrances, the summer houses were only accessible from the ground floor and the platform of the first floor, previously used as an entrance, was converted to a balcony.

One year later, in 2019, I encountered this typology illustrated by the Imbrian architect Giannakis in his book detailing the vernacular architecture of Imbros. In his book, he classified local houses into three phases based on their typological development over time (fig. 2).[17] The summer houses we visited in 2018 corresponded to Phase III of Giannakis's categorization, while the rural house described by Pasadaios aligned with the Phase II. The *konaki* houses, portrayed in Phase III, particularly stood out as the most advanced structures, having undergone modernization by their owners towards the latter part of the twentieth century. These houseowners adamantly refused to abandon their homes and instead opted to stay on the island, foregoing the migration to urban areas along with their children. A significant number of them even spent their entire lives within these houses. As a result, a continuous connection between generations and with the island itself persisted over the years, leading to the regular upkeep, renovation, and revitalization of the houses by their proprietors. This unwavering commitment ensured that the structural growth and typological progression of the houses remained uninterrupted, as they were never left vacant or forsaken.

Following the passing of the elders, their offspring continued the tradition of visiting the houses each summer, specifically during the Panagia celebration in August. These second-generation homeowners, who primarily resided in big cities for the remainder of the year, would make seasonal visits to the island. The ancestral family home served as a shared summer retreat for a diverse group of family members, including siblings, cousins, and grandchildren. Together, they engaged in tasks like cleaning, maintenance, and overall upkeep of their inherited property. All these family members expressed a collective intention to preserve the houses in their original state, often stating that they aimed to maintain them «as left by the parents,» «as they once were,» or «in the manner of the past.»

Some of these houses have integrated modern features using pragmatic design solutions that do not compromise the authentic appearance of the old stone houses. In the early 1990s, the sanitary facilities attached to the houses, such as an outdoor kitchen or an outdoor shower, were manageable and bearable for summer visitors. The short

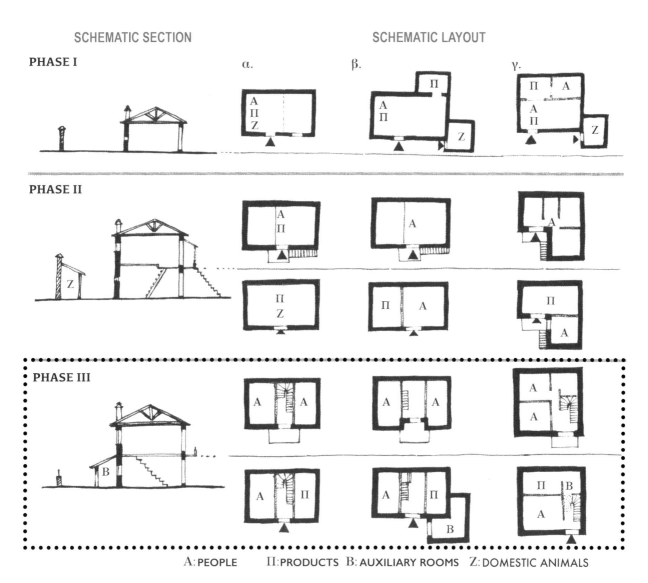

A: PEOPLE   Π: PRODUCTS   B: AUXILIARY ROOMS   Z: DOMESTIC ANIMALS

2   Giannakis's schema of the evolution of local houses in Imbros.

time spent in the houses allowed the traditional features to be retained without requiring major structural changes to meet the needs of today's users. When I pointed out to the homeowners the industrial materiality integrated into the traditional house, such as plastic mosquito nets on the windows, wood-like PVC windows and shutters, electric heaters, plastic sockets and light switches in the rooms, their response remained unchanged: all these modern features were installed once their parents had retired. Thus, the second-generation homeowners confidently declared that they maintained the houses as they inherited them. Based on the preliminary findings of my field research, the following sections highlight the social practices of second-generation returnees as they appropriate and utilize the material world of the past to create their heritage.

Exhibiting

Helena (62):

> Memories are my life. The pots of my mother, everything that my grandmother owned, everything belonged to my mother, my grandmother, I remember them all, as they used it. I said: «I will not throw them away. I will make this room into a museum.»

In one house we visited, the owner Helena introduced her house as a «museum house» and referred to it as «*müze ev*» in Turkish.[18] One crucial point to note was that Helena's house was neither an official museum nor a publicly certified touristic operation on the island. Indeed, it was her private family house where she had converted the old basement into an exhibition space for her family collection of old household items and agrarian tools. The exhibition was only accessible for community members, close friends, and invited guests—not for public visitors. Despite all the advice of her family and friends, Helena had chosen not to have a modern kitchen, but rather a «museum.» (fig. 3).

Helena had cleaned out the old cellar and sorted all the items she had found: weaving looms, an old wooden plow, kitchen utensils such as clay pots, wooden spoons, and glass bottles (fig. 4). Then she had arranged these items arbitrarily into various groups according to her own conception, such as morphological similarity or functional themes. Both the selection and arrangement of objects lacked the meticulousness of a collector or the professional methods used by a curator in an exhibition; agricultural equipment such as rakes and shovels hung from the stone walls, while long wooden

3   Helena's exhibition room, Gliki (Eski Bademli Köyü).

4　Exhibits in Helena's Museum, Gliki (Eski Bademli Köyü).

troughs called *skafes* leaned vertically against the walls. Only parts of one loom survived into the present and these could not be reassembled to provide a demonstration of the working machine. The old round wooden table, called the *sofras*, served as a platform for displaying various found artifacts, such as a wooden jack plane, a rusty hand scythe and an axe, metal pestles, wooden pestles and mortars, wooden spoons, and weaving shuttles. There was no introduction or description to the items, as it was assumed that the items were everyday tools of the rural population and familiar to the target audience. One might have considered the locally made large green bottles of hand-blown glass to be of artistic value, or the water jugs with SRD imprints used by the British Army in the 1915 Gallipoli campaign as historically valuable, but all these objects were common artifacts found in every house we visited.[19] What made it unique was «the idea of bringing them all together,» as Hera, Helena's daughter, advocated.

The exhibition did not include personal memories of the family or stories of individuals. It simply displayed a collection of rural tools commonly used in everyday activities that represented a set of daily living practices of a social group from the past. The objects on display represented a shared past among the members of this social group and provided a frame of reference and orientation for constructing their narratives and collective affiliations in the present. Following Halbwachs's model of *«cadres sociaux de la mémoire,»* this exhibition delegated the material environment relevant to a particular milieu, which enabled members of the same social group to renegotiate narratives about the past that fostered collective belonging.[20]

Our further conversation with Helena revealed a deeper emotional motivation for making her house a museum: Helena's father had been attacked and murdered in this house in 1990. She admitted that the trauma associated with this tragic incident prevented her from getting rid of objects she felt were related to her memories of her father. The objects on display were not only representative of traditional life on the island, but also the reminders of her father's life that she simply could not discard. The objects were charged with emotion and meaning because of the tragic loss of their owner. Hera (34):

> For my mother, it is like she wants to keep the stuff as it was. I don't see it [the house] as a museum myself, I see it as something more personal, let's say, [belongings] of my grandparents. But all these artifacts inside the house are common to the Imbrian for daily use. So, it is not something unique that we have. Probably, it is unique, the idea that we put them all together. But in the future, I wouldn't say no to someone who has heard of it and wants to visit it. (...) For the time being I consider it as my house...

Helena's daughter Hera was born and raised in Athens and considered herself a proud member of the Imbrian community. Hera did not recognize the house as a museum; instead, she considered it a «personal memory chest» where her grandparents' belongings were stored. Therefore, she interpreted Helena's act of establishing a «museum» as her way of dealing with their loss and fulfilling moral obligations to them. In our conversation, Hera admitted that she associated the smell of the house with the scent of her grandfather and believed that she honored his legacy by visiting the house every year. For her, the house was a «sacred place,» and there was no question of using it as a source of commercial revenue, such as renting rooms through digital platforms or charging her visitors for the exhibition visit, which she called the «Imbrian experience.» She preferred to keep the house «pure,» where she welcomed her visitors «with open doors, like her grandfather welcomed his guests.»

As the French philosopher Georges Bataille points out, sacred things are the result of an «operation of loss.»[21] The tragic incident that occurred in the house defined the house as a «sacred place» for Hera, corresponding to the intrinsic values of inheritance. Her statements revealed her emotional investment in this legacy and indicated a shared understanding with her mother in both the pathos and ethos of the past. For Hera's mother, there was a clear separation of «before» and «after,» a past and a present life on Imbros that represented a breaking point in her life. However, Hera, as a descendant born and raised in Athens, experienced only the «after» phase of the transformation as she grew up. Her emotional connection to Imbros began in childhood and was shaped by her mother's narratives about the island life of the past and her own real experiences with the place during seasonal visits. For Hera, associations from the past tended to be anchored in sensory memory intertwined with her past imaginaries, just as she associated the smell of home with the scent of her grandfather. As the future heiress of the house, Hera bore a moral obligation for the continuity of the place, for the preservation of cultural and social values and everyday rituals that represented «Imbros» for her. She was eager to preserve the humanistic values of the past, such as the hospitality of her grandparents.

The so-called «*müze ev*» was heavily laden with intrinsic values of moral and sentimental attachment to ancestors. Helena's museum was a personal phenomenon that was not intended to attract an audience; yet it resonated with many other Imvrii of Helena's generation, for all shared her pain over the loss of significant family members of the older generation, which was also intertwined with the longing for a lost pre-industrial Imbros. For the Imbrian visitors to the museum house, the exhibition resembled not only the shared past but the «collective loss» of that past. Displayed items of the rural past of Imbros evoked personal memories among the members of various social groups and furthered their narratives of collective belonging as a group; at the same time, however, they also highlighted the absence of that rural past in the present, evoking a sense of collective loss and further deepening their sense of belonging together. In addition, particular narratives about the loss of local origins were singled out and highlighted as identifying markers of the Imbrian community.

Staging

Upon entering each house, the visitor experiences an incredible time-machine effect that instantly transports them back a century. This occurred not only in Helena's so-called museum house, but in all the other houses, which also seemed like «museums.» One could find the characteristic components of the Imbriotic House, such as the ewer stand, known as the *laenoustat*, of which I had only seen the drawings in the Pasadaios study.[22] Although objects from the pre-industrial period

are no longer in everyday use, they are well preserved and decoratively integrated into the interior design of the houses.

My first impression was how clean and tidy the interior rooms were. Everything seemed to be «in its place,» «frozen in time,» «pristine», and «untouched» since the deceased owners had left them. But they also looked very fresh and immaculate. Upon a second glance, it was rather unsettling how calculated the decoration was. Photos of deceased parents were prominently situated in the rooms, and their personal belongings were aligned next to them in a dramatic display.

In the rooms, grandfather's necktie and grandmother's headscarf were hanging on each side of an old black-and-white family photograph (fig. 5); auntie's rosary was attached to the bedstead; handcrafted embroideries from the daughter's dowry, considered too precious for daily use, were

5   Personal belongings of the deceased placed next to their photo in a house in Merkez (Gökçeada).

6   Senior room, also known as the *geriko*, Gliki (Eski Bademli Köyü).

displayed on each sideboard in several rooms; an empty crib with a worn baby blanket in it stood next to a well-tucked bed; empty crystal bottles lined up on the old furnace shelf which used to hold ingredients for cooking were now only displayed as decorative elements (fig. 6). All the house interiors had a haunting atmosphere; they were decorated with highly charged personal items that represented an «absolute truth» for the owners. Moreover, each room seemed curated, even staged, as if the rooms themselves yearned for their former lives. The effort the owners put into staging the rooms seemed to be more than an unconscious act to reproduce childhood memories, and rather a powerful way to reconstruct their narratives by evoking a sense of nostalgia.

Cultural theorist and artist Svetlana Boym describes nostalgia as a sense of loss and displace-

ment, but also «a romance with one's own fantasy.»[23] For the Imvrii, the house had become a stage for remembrance in which they recomposed their own narratives about their past based on the material objects from this past. Especially for those who had lived in the houses and personally experienced the space in the past, the interiors offered tangible connotations for the reconstruction of memories. In his book *Memory and Material Culture*, Andrew Jones, a scholar of archaeology, introduces the concept of the «indexical field» to describe such a network of material media in which artifacts function as nodes in a web of relationships. He asserts that

although the material world provides a framework for remembrance, it is the social practices in which artefacts are engaged which determines how remembrance is socially experienced and mapped out. In this sense we can consider the object world as a kind of ‹distributed

7   A host describing the stories of photos on the walls, Schinoudi (Dereköy).

mind›, not only spatially distributed, but also temporally distributed.[24]

The homeowners curated the interiors with the material objects of the past in an indexical network, which provided the motifs and means relevant to their narrative reconstructions of the place in the present. Objects such as black-and-white photographs, old postcards, and decorative plates represented an absolute truth in the stories of their owners and were significant only to those who knew them. Some special objects even evoked affects and emotions in the Imvrii, who could reflect their own memories upon or through them. As a visitor, I could merely guess at the many meanings I was presented with (or allowed to see) by the storytellers. The hosts were the protagonists of their own stories, which could unlock meaning for outsiders and activate

a story-scape through their engagement with the material world inside the houses (fig. 7).

The curated interior settings, however, were not meant to replicate the memory of a past, but to remind one of it. «Nostalgia,» Boym argues, «does not always refer to the past; it can be retrospective, but also prospective.»[25] Boym points out that fantasies about the past, driven by the needs of the present, have a direct impact on the realities of the future. Nostalgic narratives about the past provide a link between individual biography and the biography of social groups, and foster the social memory of groups that lie outside the timespan of any individual life. In this regard, curated nostalgia in the homes for the Imvrii was an effective means of activating an emotional engagement with past lives to make sense of both the present and the future.

Recycling

The sense of nostalgia lasted only until one entered the modern sanitary rooms of the houses. These units contained industrial products such as toilets, sinks, and faucets; the walls and floors were covered with industrial ceramic tiles, and plastic electrical outlets and light switches were installed to meet the practical needs of their users. Although the contemporary materiality evoked a sense of familiarity, there were also some self-made objects related to the past that were deliberately inserted into the modern settings and appeared to be strange rather than nostalgic. Components or fragments of traditional tools were reassembled in a bricolage and were made into a new object with a new function; in short, they were recycled.

Recycling means taking something permanently out of an old context and putting it to a new use in another. The German architectural theorist Susanne Hauser presents two types of recycling, referring to reuse (*Wiederverwendung*) as the gentlest form of recycling, in which the object is inserted into a context different from the previous one, but retains its function: for example, roof tiles collected on site from demolished houses can find a new use in the reconstruction of a new roof.[26] The second type of recycling, upcycling (*Weiterverwendung*), erases the traditional function: an old loom stick becomes a towel rack used in the bathroom (fig. 8), or a large wine amphora becomes a barbecue grill (fig. 9).

When recycling takes place as upcycling, the object loses not only its traditional context, but

8   Towel rack made of an old loom stick, Gliki (Eski Bademli Köyü).

also its functionality, its meaning, and its history as an object. Recycling allows heirs to engage with the past in a new way. Rather than preserving traditional objects that have lost their social relevance, it offers a kind of repurposing to make them relevant to today's users by assigning them a contemporary function. It is a creative attempt to reintegrate objects from the past into everyday use in the present, which creates a tangible «before» and «after» of the material object.

In a highly selective «Frankenstein» operation, traditional objects in decay were first decomposed into fragments and later the «usable» parts were reassembled into a «new» object. In this way, the traditional objects were stripped of their original semantic expression, lost their ancestral context, and became a foreign object repurposed

for contemporary use. This technique, called «strange-making» after the concept of «defamiliarization» coined by the Russian formalist Viktor Shklovsky in his 1917 article *Art as Technique*, was introduced into architecture by scholars Alexander Tzonis and Liane Lefaivre in their article about the work of the Greek architects, Suzana and Dimitris Antonakakis, in reconstructing an ancient pathway in Greece.[27]

The technique of «strange-making» creates a moment of disruption in the order of things that triggers a surprise effect in the viewer. This surprise effect not only allows the upcycled object to serve as a reminder of a version of the past, but also demands a new engagement with that past. By mimicking a contemporary object (towel holder), the old object (loom stick) finds an operative

9   A wine amphora converted to a barbecue grill, Agridia (Tepeköy).

10   A collection of local stones, Gliki (Eski Bademli Köyü).

function in everyday tasks and continues its new social life in the present. There is no longing for a historical or traditional life, but only a fragmented «flashback» to the past as a powerful mnemonic trace in collective memory.

Collecting

Once I had made further inquiries about the backstories of artifacts in the rooms, I discovered that homeowners were not only preserving what was present but were also consciously collecting objects, artifacts, belongings, and things, not specifically items of value, but what they thought was worth preserving for the benefit of current and future generations. Objects of interest were deliberately targeted and sought out; some were found on the island or rediscovered in locked closets or in old basements of houses. They were brought to light, sorted, cleaned, refurbished, and finally displayed on shelves or walls solely dedicated to the collections. Well-educated community members who practiced notable professions in the cities also collected specific items related to their professional interests, such as an archaeologist who collected various rock samples from different zones of the island (fig. 10), or a botanist who collected samples of the local vegetation, and so on. Although their collections did not follow scientific methods, nor were they intentionally for any research projects, it was their contribution to a collective «Imbrian collection.»

Scholar of museum studies Susan Pearce describes collecting as a social practice through which individuals relate in a particular way to collective groups and their past «in order to construct their own personalities in the present.»[28] In this context, social value was ascribed to individual collections; natural stones or agricultural tools were given a community-based meaning and were referred to as «Imbrian local stones» or «Imbrian agricultural tools» and so on. These individually assembled collections on display were just the tip of the iceberg. My field research revealed that behind closed doors and in underused rooms, such as basements or attics, there was a large amount of old, unused, maybe forgotten or hidden but in any case unorganized collections of material objects. As a guest, I was kindly discouraged from entering such rooms because they were not considered representative of the traditional house. I was only allowed a brief glimpse, brief enough to record the chaotic state of the possessions before the doors were sheepishly closed and the collected items were labeled as «junk»—perhaps to discourage my interest in learning more.

In the case of the Imbrian community, the act of collecting unfolded a tendency toward the so-called «Noah complex»—a term coined by French architectural and urban historian and theorist Françoise Choay and applied to archaeology by Cornelius Holtorf and Oscar Ortman—to describe a certain type of anxiety that expresses itself in protecting and preserving artifacts from a past: a state in which one is trying to «save everything» in fear that «all will be lost.»[29] The acts of recent violence faced by members of the Imbrian community on the island were seen as a deliberate attempt to uproot the community, posing a real threat to their lives and changing

the demographic structure of the island to the detriment of the Greek population. The fact that familiar faces within the community were gradually passing away and their old homes were being sold to newcomers outside the community has raised concerns about losing control over the legacies of the past. In addition to the social transformation on the island, the natural deterioration of the material fabric of the built environment has also underscored the sense of loss associated with a cultural loss—reinforcing the sense of anxiety within the community.

As American historian and geographer David Lowenthal notes, «the heritage is most valued when it is at risk and the threat of loss spurs owners to stewardship.»[30] The actual loss of the material traces aroused an urge among the Imvrii to preserve their heritage before it disappeared. In this context, my study pinpoints that there is a correlation between the sense of loss and the desire for heritage within the community. The more the Imbrian minority experienced the loss of their homes, families, and rights, the more they became engaged in practices aimed at the formation of heritage practices to prove the mere existence of their culture. They collected and guarded any material objects they deemed relevant to their Imbrian past, which in turn was used for reconstructing the Imbrian community in the present and to be passed on to future generations.

Stacks of old books, bundles of family photos and love letters form an entropy of multiple pasts stored in wooden cabinets, patiently waiting to be unveiled. Given the limited time spent in the houses, the rediscovery of these archives is postponed until a noisy scholar revisits them or a volunteer of the younger generations decides to write their own history about the island. In the case of the Imbrian community, their commitment to the act of collecting is more prominent than the collection itself. For most of them, collecting has become an act of self-preservation as they struggle against the speed of time to gather material evidence of their past and present and future existence.

Concluding Remarks

For the Imbrian returnees, summer visits have become almost like a journey back in time away from the modern reality of the big cities they live in now, a time in which they can reunite with childhood friends, old neighbors, and other community members from their past. The whole month of August is dedicated to families and community: they visit each other in their old family houses in the villages and revive their lived memories, which are inescapably intertwined with dominant aspects of recent history. Encapsulated from the rest of the reality on the island, the summer houses define their private zones, where the owners have the freedom to decide on the management of their inheritance. My 2018 fieldwork reveals that community members actively engage with the material world of the past by collecting, staging, exhibiting, and recycling in order to create their own meanings and social values to make sense of the past in the present and for the future. In this context, this study offers insights into a people-centered understanding of heritage-making and sheds light on the heritage practices of a fragmented diaspora community.

Local architecture and its traditional components provide the functional, material, and symbolic means for Pierre Nora's notion of «*lieux de memoire*» (sites of memory) in which memory is crystallized and concealed by the second generation of Imvrii, particularly because there are no longer any «*milieux de memoire*» (social environments of memory) to represent the peasant community of the previous generation.[31] The local house provides a tangible framework for social memory through which the community reconstructs and renegotiates its past narratives in a material network of relationships based on local and historical associations. Material objects of the past instrumentalized in Imbrian narratives emphasize affect in order to bind social groups and to foster belonging on the local and collective level. The social practices highlighted in this paper represent deliberate acts of participatory heritage creation in the present. Moreover, I argue that the local house is not only used as a «site of memory» to revive the reified past; rather, it serves the minority as a mechanism of mnemonics within a larger socio-material network to enact/perform a collective act of resistance. As the heritage practices of the second-generation homeowners contribute to the reproduction of «Imbros» in today's Gökçeada, the Imbrian pasts are purposely being recollected, remembered, and recreated in the summer houses, so that they are neither erased nor forgotten.

1   The ancient name of the island was Ἴμβρος (Imbros or Imvros), which remained Imroz under Ottoman rule before the Turkish state renamed the island Gökçeada in 1970. The Greeks of the island refer to the island as Imvros and describe themselves as Imvrii, or Imvriotes. Due to respect for their self-identification practices, I will adopt the name Imbros for the island and Imvrii for its indigenous people. In this paper, all research participants are treated anonymously, and their names have been changed to pseudonyms.

2   See ACHS 2023 [2012], Smith 2006, Harrison 2013.

3   Alexanderis 1980, 5; Koutloumousians [1845] 2010, 69–90.

4   Treaty of Lausanne signed in July 24, 1923: https://jus-mundi.com/en/document/treaty/en-treaty-of-peace-treaty-of-lausanne-1923-treaty-of-peace-treaty-of-lausanne-tuesday-24th-july-1923 (20 October 2022).

5   As a result of a legislative decree (No. 5442, Decision 8479) of the Turkish Council of Ministers of 29 July 1970, all Greek toponyms were replaced by Turkish ones; the Greek villages of Άγιοι Θεόδωροι, Σχοινούδι, Παναγιά, Αγρίδια, Γλυκύ, Κάστρο have become respectively Zeytinliköy, Dereköy, Merkez Gökçeada, Tepeköy, Eski Bademliköy, Kaleköy and district names Αλίκη, Άγιος Κύρκος, Σναπίδα have changed into Tuz Gölü, Kuzu Limanı and İnce Burun.

6   Babül 2004, 3; Tsimouris, 2001, 4–5; Halstead 2019, 73–80.

7   Alexanderis 2004, 118–119.

8   In Greek literature, the discriminatory measures taken by the state were considered as a part of a long-term Turkish political project called the «*Eritme programı*» (Dissolution Project) claimed to be aiming for the absolute «De-Hellenization» of the island. For more, see Alexandris 1980 and Tsimouris 2001.

9   Aziz 1973, 93.

10 Bozbeyoğlu / Onan 2001, 1.

11 Babül 2004, 7; Babül 2006, 43–54.

12 Halstead 2019, 203–207.

13 Unofficial information received from the Imbros Association in Athens in 2021.

14 «Imbriotic House» is a term directly taken from the original text in Greek, it can also be translated as «Imbrian House.»

15 Pasadaios 1973, 11–13. For more information on the *monospito* house typology, see Dinççağ Kahveci 2022.

16 Pasadaios 1973 refers to these developed houses as *noikokyrospita*. This term is used to describe bigger houses of the wealthiest merchants or craftsmen—people of the middle class. These houses had larger rooms and their interior appearance was more representative, similar to the «Turkish House» introduced by S. H. Eldem. See Eldem 1955, 16.

17 Giannakis 2019, Table 1, 11.

18 I conducted all of my interviews with the Imbrian

homeowners in Turkish, except for those with the younger generation, which were conducted in English.

19 SRD (Social Relief of Distress) equipment, used in overseas operations by the British Army, which I encountered in every home I visited, and they were used in a decorative manner.

20 Halbwachs [1952] 1992, 52–53, 182.

21 Bataille 1971, 28. My emphasis and translation.

22 Pasadaios 1973. *Laenoustat*: A niche in the wall at the entrance to the house to put the water jug for washing hands.

23 Boym 2016, 13. The word nostalgia (nostos «to return home» + algos «pain») was coined by the Swiss doctor Johannes Hofer in his medical dissertation in 1688.

24 Jones 2007, 225.

25 Boym 2016, 16–17.

26 Hauser 2010, 45.

27 «Defamiliarization» was a term introduced by Victor Shklovsky, a member of the Russian Formalist group in Russia and influential in the emergence of avant-garde literary experiments in the 1910s and 1920s. See his *Art as Technique* (1917) in Lemon / Reis 1965. For the definition of the concepts «critical» and «defamiliarization»; see also Tzonis / Lefaivre 1986, Tzonis / Lefaivre 1991 and Tzonis / Lefaivre 1981.

28 Pearce 1995, 159.

29 Choay [1992] 2001, 141; Holtorf / Ortman 2008, 86–87.

30 Lowenthal 2014, 24.

31 Nora 1989, 7.

ACHS 2023 [2012]
Association of Critical Heritage Studies: 2012 Manifesto, 2012, https://www.criticalheritagestudies.org/history (7 August 2023).

Alexandris 1980
A. Alexandris: Imbros and Tenedos: A Study of Turkish Attitudes Toward Two Ethnic Greek Island Communities since 1923, Journal of the Hellenic Diaspora VII-1, 1980, 5–31.

Alexandris 2004
A. Alexandris: Religion or Ethnicity: The Identity Issue of the Minorities in Greece and Turkey, in: R. Hirschon (ed.): Crossing the Aegean: An Appraisal of the 1923 Compulsory Population Exchange between Greece and Turkey (New York 2004) 117–132.

Aziz 1973
A. Aziz: Gökçeada Üzerine Toplumsal Bir İnceleme [A Social Investigation on Gökçeada], Ankara Üniversitesi Siyasal Bilgiler Fakültesi Dergisi 1, No. 2, 1973, 85–119.

Babül 2004
E. Babül: Belonging to Imbros: Citizenship and Sovereignty in the Turkish Republic. Conference Nationalism, Society and

Culture in Post-Ottoman South East Europe, St. Peter's College, Oxford, 29–30 May 2004, http://www.academia.edu/6707095/Belonging_to_Imbros_Citizenship_and_Sovereignty_in_the_Turkish_Republic (Accessed 30 March 2022).

Babül 2006
E. Babül: Home or Away? On the Connotations of Homeland Imaginaries in Imbros, Thamyris / Intersecting 13, 2006: 43–54.

Bataille 1971
G. Bataille: La notion de dépense, La part maudite (Paris 1971).

Boym 2016
S. Boym: The Future of Nostalgia (New York 2016).

Bozbeyoğlu / Onan 2001
A.Ç. Bozbeyoğlu / I. Onan: Changes in the Demographic Characteristics of Gökçeada, The Turkish Journal of Population Studies 23, 2001, 79–101.

Choay [1992] 2001
F. Choay: The Invention of the Historic Monument, L. O'Connell (trans.) (Cambridge 2001). Originally published in French (Paris 1992).

Dinççağ Kahveci 2022
A. Dinççağ Kahveci: The Appropriation of Traditional Houses in Imbros/Gökçeada, in: C. Mileto et al. (eds.): HERITAGE 2022: 02. Vernacular Heritage: Culture, People and Sustainability (Valencia 2022) 663–669. https://doi.org/10.4995/HERITAGE2022.2022.15722.

Eldem 1955
S. H. Eldem: Türk evi plan tipleri [Turkish House Plan Types] (Istanbul 1955).

Giannakis 2019
G. Giannakis: Οικισμοί και σπίτια της Ίμβρου, Η προστασία και η ανάδειξή τους [Settlements and Houses of Imbro, their Protection and Promotion] (Thessaloniki 2019).

Halbwachs [1952] 1992
M. Halbwachs: On Collective Memory (Chicago 1992); L. A. Coser (trans., ed.): Les cadres sociaux de la mémoire (Paris 1952); (originally pub.) in Les Travaux de L'Année Sociologique (Paris 1925).

Halstead 2019
H. Halstead: Greeks without Greece: Homelands, Belonging, and Memory amongst the Expatriated Greeks of Turkey (Abingdon, Oxon 2019).

Harrison 2013
R. Harrison: Heritage: Critical Approaches (London and New York 2013).

Hauser 2010
S. Hauser: Recycling, ein Transformationsprozess, in: A. Wagner (ed.): Abfallmoderne. Zu den Schmutzrändern der Kultur (Wien 2010) 45–62.

Holtorf/Ortman 2008
C. Holtorf / O. Ortman: Endangerment and Conservation Ethos in Natural and Cultural Heritage: The Case of Zoos and Archaeological Sites, International Journal of Heritage Studies 14 (1), 2008, 74–90.

Jones 2007
A. Jones: Memory and Material Culture (Cambridge 2007).

Koutloumousianos et al. [1845] 2010
B. Koutloumousianos / A. Moustoxydis: A Historical Memorandum Concerning the Island of Imbros (Istanbul 2010 [1845]) 69–90.

Lemon/Reis 1965
L. T. Lemon / M. Reis (trans.): Russian Formalist Criticism: Four Essays (Lincoln NE 1965).

Lowenthal 2014
D. Lowenthal: The Heritage Crusade and the Spoils of History (Cambridge 2014).

Nora 1989
P. Nora: Between Memory and History: Les Lieux de Mémoire, in Representations No. 26 (Spring), Special Issue: Memory and Counter-Memory, 1989, 7–24.

Pasadaios 1973
A. Πασαδαιού: Η Λαϊκή Αρχιτεκτονική της Ίμβρου [The Folk Architecture of Imbro] (Athens 1973).

Pearce 1995
S. M. Pearce: On Collecting: An Investigation into Collecting in the European Tradition (London 1995).

Smith 2006
L. Smith: Uses of Heritage (London 2006).

Tsimouris 2001
G. Tsimouris: Reconstructing «Home» among the «Enemy»: The Greeks of Gökçeada (Imvros) after Lausanne, Balkanologie V 1-2, 2001, http://balkanologie.revues.org/727 (7 August 2023).

Tsimouris 2007
G. Tsimouris: Ίμβριοι: Φυγάδες απ' τον Τόπο μας Όμηροι στην Πατρίδα [Imvrioi: Fugitives from our Place, Hostages in the Homeland] (Athens 2007).

Tzonis/Lefaivre 1981
A. Tzonis / L. Lefaivre: The Grid and the Pathway. An Introduction to the Work of Dimitris and Suzana Antonakakis, Architecture in Greece 15, 1981, 164.

Tzonis/Lefaivre 1986
A. Tzonis / L. Lefaivre: Classical Architecture: The Poetics of Order (Cambridge MA 1986).

Tzonis/Lefaivre 1991
A. Tzonis / L. Lefaivre: Critical Regionalism, in: S. Amourgis (ed.): Critical Regionalism: The Pomona Meeting Proceedings (Pomona 1991) 3–28.

Image Sources

1   Drawing by Dinççağ Kahveci.
2   Giannakis 2019, Table 1, 11; with markings by the author.
3–10 Dinççağ Kahveci 2018.

Identity Policies in a Nutshell
Yeniköy Village as a Palimpsest of Contested Spaces in Turkey

Özge Sezer, Vera Egbers

The late 19th century witnessed a transformative phase in the history of Turkey, marked by the rise of new and sometimes very deliberate identity-making practices that would profoundly shape the later nation's fabric. Under the imperial authority of the Ottoman state, rural communities became designated groups in the construction of a national identity that was intended to align with the vision of a Muslim Anatolia. This narrative persisted through the transition to the republican era in the 1920s and 1930s, as the later state, despite adopting new and different ideologies, maintained a keen focus on the rural landscape, introducing interventions that sought to reshape the economic, socio-cultural, and demographic contours of the nation. These interventions, reminiscent of attempts to internally colonize the inhabitants of rural areas, manifested in the creation of top-down planned settlements during both the late Ottoman and early republican periods.

The village of Yeniköy (Turkish for «new village»), in the rural periphery of Turkey's third largest city İzmir (fig. 1), can be read as a palimpsest that encapsulates these layers of spatial identity-making policies under different political regimes. Here, the echoes of Ottoman rule, republican

1   Map of Turkey with the location of Yeniköy village.

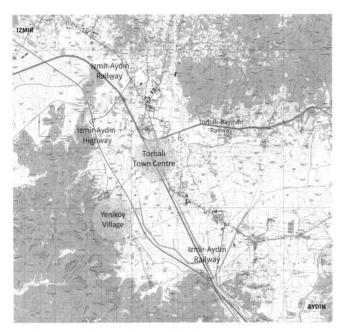

2   Map showing Torbalı district and Yeniköy.

toto site that is representative for various settlement developments across Anatolia starting from the late 19th century.

Nestled close to the railway connecting İzmir and Aydın in Western Turkey (fig. 2), the village of Yeniköy is surrounded by fertile agricultural lands and water sources, making it a hub for small-scale agriculture. The village is located close to the ancient city of Metropolis, adding an extra layer of historical significance to its landscape. With a population of around 1,500 people,[1] Yeniköy presents today a unique blend of traditional rural occupations and a younger demographic engaged in industrial sectors in the surrounding areas.

To better comprehend the selection of Yeniköy for this study, in the following section we introduce the historical context that influenced the transformation of the landscape in the late Ottoman and early republican periods.

ideologies, and post-war interventions intertwine, creating a complex narrative which presents the village as a microcosm of rural Turkey's dynamic history. For this reason, we chose Yeniköy as an exemplary case study through which we investigate the interplay of state policies trying to intervene and shape rural life on the one hand, and the adaptation, contestations, and adjustment by the rural population on the other hand. In so doing, we intend to present a balanced analysis that integrates not only a more conventional top-down view of history and change, but additionally addresses questions surrounding the impact of marginalized groups, in this case, the villagers who were subject to a variety of nation-building measures imposed first by a struggling empire and then by a newly founded republic. We do so by drawing on theories developed in the field of post-colonial human geography that foreground the agency of the rural population, providing a more holistic understanding of nation-building processes. In this context, Yeniköy can be regarded as a pars pro

Islamist Ideology and Ottoman Modernization in the Late Ottoman Period in Western Anatolia

The 19th century witnessed profound cultural and societal transformations fueled by advancements in science, technology, and industrialization in Western countries. These changes led to the expansion of territorial borders and the emergence of new national identities. The Ottoman Empire, which included territories of interest to the great powers of Europe and Russia, underwent significant adjustments in its state structure, economy, and politics to safeguard its holdings from the Balkans to the Arabian Peninsula. As a reaction to these new internal and external threats, in the latter half of the 19th century, the Ottoman state took on a more theocratic and coercive character.[2]

Upon Abdulhamid II's accession to power in 1876, the Russo-Turkish War inflicted a devastating blow to the Ottoman Empire, resulting in an influx of war refugees into Istanbul. The loss of further territories in the Balkans, through the Treaty of

Berlin in 1878, exacerbated the refugee crisis.[3] The ensuing nationalist uprisings and refugee influx created a tumultuous atmosphere, prompting the conclusion that «Ottomanism», which aimed to unite various national and religious groups under imperial rule, had become obsolete. The diminishing European territories paved the way for the emergence of a pan-Islamist ideology, portraying Abdulhamid II more as the «caliph» of Muslims worldwide than merely the Ottoman emperor.[4]

Elif Andaç, and similarly Selim Deringil, suggests that imperial states, including the Ottoman Empire, actively engaged with nationalist ideologies to legitimize their existence in the face of growing nationalism. This adaptation of Western ideas within the Ottoman state during the Hamidian period reflects a synchronization with global trends in modernization efforts.[5] According to Niyazi Berkes, pan-Islamism during the Hamidian period pursued a politically independent strategy, distancing itself from European influences by embracing traditionalist approaches.[6] The emphasis on Islamic values aimed to restore the state's reputation, with Abdulhamid II solidifying his position through a centralized bureaucratic structure. This resulted in modernization attempts such as the establishment of telegraph lines connecting the capital to distant regions, even before the construction of convenient routes for railways and roads in the imperial territory.[7]

Nevertheless, consistent with nationalist ideology, the Ottoman pursuit of modernization involved major railway projects. These large-scale infrastructure endeavors, largely dependent on foreign investments from German, British, and French companies, aimed to facilitate economic development. The construction of railways connecting European cities to Istanbul, and further into Ottoman territories, served both economic interests and the pan-Islamist agenda, contributing to the regime's political legitimacy.[8]

Railway construction, especially in Anatolia, had commenced before the Hamidian period but saw significant expansion in the late 19th century. The Berlin–Baghdad railway line, a noteworthy project, not only attracted crucial foreign capital but also intensified economic and political ties between Germany and the Ottoman Empire. However, this project heightened tensions between Germany and Britain, eventually contributing to the geopolitical conditions that led to the First World War. Despite the international ramifications, the Berlin–Baghdad railway line aimed to establish a secure military zone through Anatolia, strengthening Ottoman control over the territory.[9]

Forming Rural Identities through the Sultan's Farms in Western Anatolia

Alongside formulized strategies for the «mobilization» of state power through specific ideological channels, Abdulhamid II's initiative in procuring agricultural land and reviving farms in the rural landscapes of İzmir and Aydın in western Anatolia was of paramount importance in transforming the collective identity of communities by utilizing modernization strategies. This endeavor can be interpreted as yet another instance of «actively borrowing and adapting ideological elements from the West».[10] The reforming of rural territories and the concurrent stimulation of agricultural progress have been integral to state populist agendas since the 19th century in Europe. Particularly notable is for instance Germany's late 19th-century emphasis on regenerating rural areas, which significantly contributed to the German empire's legitimacy, particularly in the eastern regions facing political threats from beyond the Polish border. Throughout the latter part of the 19th century, a comprehensive program aimed at fostering «German» rural settlements was executed, entailing land expropriation for agricultural purposes and the establishment of new settlements where the state maneuvered to maintain its control.[11] While not an exact parallel to the German example, Abdulhamid's agricultural initiatives nonetheless align with the state's overarching presence in

3   One of the buildings in Sultan's Farm used as granary, 1899, Tepeköy, Torbalı, İzmir.

rural settings, reshaping and intervening in these environments to suit the government's interests.

The area where the sultan established his farms had already been a significant agricultural hub, with British and French companies installing economic infrastructure from the early 19th century. Torbalı and Tire, situated between the western Anatolian cities of İzmir and Aydın, occupied prime agricultural land, steeped in a tradition of cultivation dating back to antiquity. In response to the region's lucrative trade potential, the first railway line, facilitated by British companies in collaboration with the Ottoman Railway Company, was erected between 1856 and 1860. The primary aim was to connect the agricultural expanse between Aydın and İzmir with İzmir and its harbor, primarily to enable fig trading. By 1860, only the İzmir–Torbalı line had been completed, establishing Torbalı as a pivotal stopover for transporting agricultural produce and passengers between Aydın and İzmir, thereby linking the rural local market to the urban center. The construction of the railway network in the region persisted until the late 19th century, facilitating connectivity across the cultivated expanse between the lowlands of the Meander rivers.[12]

Between 1881 and 1882, the state seized properties, including eleven farms and 3,000 hectares of agricultural land spanning twenty villages, in the rural expanse between İzmir and Aydın from landowner Arisditi Bey due to his indebtedness. Abdulhamid II subsequently acquired these eleven farms, encompassing the 3,000-hectare agricultural terrain from Torbalı to Tire in the southeast, transferring them to his treasury (*Hazine-i Hassa*) for a sum of 33,000 Liras.[13] This transaction effectively vested the sultan with ownership of the land bordering the İzmir–Aydın railway line traversing the Torbalı district. During his reign from the 1890s until his dethronement in 1908, Abdulhamid initiated a development scheme for new settlements on these farms, precipitating a transformation of the built environment. This endeavor included the construction of various facilities such as an administration office, a guild, a granary, two cotton warehouses, two slaughter-houses, two gristmills, seven orchards, 89 shops, 23 gazebos within a vineyard, three bakeries, two hostelries, a hippodrome, an aviary, and a garden (fig. 3).[14]

The sultan had previously acquired private properties within and beyond Ottoman territories, including Jerusalem.[15] This tactic was employed particularly in regions where non-Muslim populations (as in western Anatolia) and non-Turkish populations (as in the Balkans and the Middle East) held sway in the social and economic spheres. By the late 19th century, the ethnic and religious makeup of the hinterlands of İzmir and Aydın was markedly diverse, comprising Orthodox Greeks, Armenians, Jews, Levantines, Turkic nomads, Muslims (predominantly Turks), and former slaves of African descent.[16] Consequently, the sultan's endeavor to procure properties and implement modernist initiatives in this specific region, predominantly inhabited by non-Turkish and non-Muslim communities, may be interpreted as a demonstration of the Ottoman state's presence, even emblematic of the caliph's influence. Yet, a certain degree of fear persisted about the delinquency of these groups that might not identify as subject to the Ottoman rural ideology. The architectural program in the new farm settlements had the intention of forming rural communities under this ideology.

In addition to administrative structures, Abdulhamid II spearheaded an architectural program across fourteen settlements housing the farms, including Yeniköy, encompassing facilities for agricultural production, commercial endeavors, and recreational activities. Each village witnessed the establishment of a standardized village center, comprising a mosque and an elementary school catering to both girls and boys. Some settlements adorned their public cores with amenities such as fountains and pools as basins.[17]

These architectural features can be understood as tangible forms of the state's authority to rule public life in the settlements and an attempt to modernize an antiquated empire from within. In this context the mosque, for example, can be read as a representation of the renewed political ideology that tried to mobilize Islam to «unify» people under the sultan's and caliph's reign, as well as generating a sense of superiority for Muslims over other religious groups. Similarly, the schools furthered modernization, but they also introduced a politically controlled education system that focused on the production of (Islamic) knowledge. In addition, water constructions such as fountains and pools served as yet another tangible element for the modernized rural landscape and carried with its monumentality the spatial organization of an authoritarian, Islamized empire at the center of each village.

Bridging the Ways of Modernization in Rural Space: The Early Republican Period

The political, social, and economic turmoil of the beginning of 20th century shook the Ottoman Empire, particularly during the reign of Abdulhamid II. The ideological pattern of forming a national identity changed with the dethroning of the sultan in 1908. From 1908 to the Turkish War of Independence between 1919 and 1923, this new pattern mostly influenced the political direction of the country by dismantling the Ottoman regime and building the nation-state on the land from eastern Thrace, bordering Greece, Romania, and Bulgaria, to Anatolia, bordering Iraq under a British mandate and Syria under a French mandate to the south, and Georgia, Armenia, and Iran to the east.[18]

From a demographic and socio-economic standpoint, early republican Turkey predominantly comprised rural areas. According to the 1927 population census, the first conducted after the Proclamation of the Republic in 1923, out of the nation's 13.6 million inhabitants, 10.3 million resided in villages and small rural towns.[19] Following the implementation of the 1923 Lausanne Peace

Treaty, which delineated the terms for the population exchange between Turkey and Greece, over one million Orthodox Greeks, primarily merchants and farmers, were compelled to depart from Anatolia and Eastern Thrace. This mass exodus significantly impacted the country's economic landscape, as the Greek population had been an integral participant in the commercial and agricultural sectors during the Ottoman Empire. Additionally, approximately 400,000 Muslim Turks, comprising mainly skilled peasants, migrated into the country from Greece.[20] These events profoundly influenced the economic scene and reshaped the rural landscape of the country in the 1920s.

In this context the Izmir Economic Congress, held from 17 February to 4 March 1923, marked a crucial milestone in the formulation of an agriculture-focused economic program. This initiative aimed to revitalize economic productivity through land reclamation and the provision of resources for agricultural and mining endeavors. Moreover, discussions at the congress centered on implementing new regulations to rejuvenate the village economy, addressing the stratification within the peasantry, which consisted of large landowners, small-scale agricultural producers, and landless peasants.[21] The outcomes of the İzmir Economic Congress led to the establishment of a novel legal framework by the state to govern the interactions among these various stakeholders.[22] This regulatory framework was further refined through the enactment of the Village Law in 1924, which formalized the village as an entity within the administrative system and delineated the economic and social activities specific to village communities.[23] Subsequently, Agricultural Credit Cooperatives (*Tarım Kredi Kooperatifleri*) were established in 1929 to provide support to villagers in both agricultural and commercial endeavors.[24] Another significant undertaking aimed at national development and agricultural enhancement was the establishment of the Ankara Higher Agriculture Institute (*Ankara Yüksek Ziraat Enstitüsü*) in Ankara in 1933, serving as the state's academic arm for

agrarian pursuits. The renowned German agriculturalist Professor Friedrich Falke (1871–1948) assumed the presidency of the institute, focusing on fostering a scientific approach to agricultural production, technologies, and methodologies. Graduates, acting as technicians, would disseminate their knowledge to peasants in villages. Following their first year of study, students underwent practical training in villages.[25] The institute collaborated with agricultural cooperatives, collectively aiding farmers in the production process, thereby facilitating the adoption of modern techniques and enhancing agricultural proficiency among peasants.

Another institutional initiative aimed at rural reconstruction and advancement was the establishment of People's Houses (*Halkevleri*) in 1932. These were centers that served as educational hubs for adults, focusing on the social and economic reforms of the new republican state and fostering national identity through cultural exchange between Turkish elites and the populace.[26] To refine this national model, Turkish elites were dispatched to European countries where similar institutions had emerged as venues for public education.[27] The «Peasantist Branch» (*Köycülük Kolu*), a division of People's Houses specializing in village affairs, launched a program comprising rural excursions and village surveys focused on rural livelihoods, traditions, and architectural conditions. This initiative also entailed collaborative economic and cultural ventures with villagers.[28]

State Regulation during the Early Republican Period

The economic and cultural reforms discussed above were associated with specific spatial interventions in rural Turkey, starting in the first years of the republic. Several factors played a significant role in forming this intervention, but the need to house incoming people after the population exchange, the war-worn inhabitants and immigrants, was the most important imperative.

The first legislative guidelines were the 1924 Village Law and the 1926 Settlement Law. The Village Law principally determined legal borders, administrative and institutional units, economic aspects of village life, self-supportive schemes in agriculture and state supplies, reconstruction methods, infrastructure, hygiene, and architectural organization via a broad building program.[29] Furthermore, the 1926 Settlement Law regulated the resettlement of people in need, and the reorganization and distribution of expropriated properties.[30]

To ease the urgent need for housing, the Ministry of Interior (General Directorate of Housing) prepared a low-cost housing type, which could be economically built and adapted to local conditions, budget, and scale. In 1925, the Ministry of Interior issued housing-type construction plans for fifteen cities and three towns. According to the plans, one house consisted of four two-room dwelling units under a single roof and was constructed out of whole timber, each dwelling separated by mud-brick walls.[31]

Rural areas around some cities—Samsun, Bursa, İzmir, Izmit, Manisa, and Adana—were better suited for this program because of their superior infrastructure and transportation compared to other regions. In addition, there were sufficient empty properties in these cities' territories to provide land for the construction of new settlements and arable fields for settlers.[32] At the beginning of the 1930s, the construction of 69 rural settlements was underway. The state gradually completed the first settlements with the housing areas and expanded the construction sites for the other components of the building program, such as mosques and schools.[33]

Here it should be emphasized that the rural settlements in the first years of the republic were designed under circumstances established after the First World War and the Turkish War of Independence. During the 1920s, the state sought

an approach to standardize construction work in the new rural settlements in an attempt to find an immediate solution for the housing and sanitation problem that the country was facing. The construction of the settlements in the first years of the republic did not strongly carry the tone of early republican ideology, which was rooted in economic welfare, social engineering, and the deliberate reconstruction of a new national identity, only gradually adding in the architectural practices of the new rural settlements during the second half of the 1930s.

At the same time, criticism of the village construction underway during the first years of the republic emerged as a critical debate among the Turkish architects, although some of them participated in the decision-making and building processes as planners and contractors.[34] The new rural settlements, which mostly consisted of housing areas established in a geometrical layout, were found to be too unfamiliar to the settlers. In the 1930s, architects claimed that the new settlements did not relate well to the traditional Turkish village and were not based on knowledge of the specific spatial organization required to meet the social needs of an «ideal» village community.[35] Architect Abdullah Ziya Kozanoğlu responded to this issue by putting forward the idea of the «village architect» as a new professional, responsible for the design and construction of the new rural settlements, concentrating on the modernist needs of the peasants and confirming their expectations in a national sense. Although Kozanoğlu insisted on this new concept of architectural practice, he did not explain in detail the duty of the village architect within this sort of operation.[36]

During the 1930s, Arkitekt, Turkey's first architecture magazine and the mouthpiece of its architectural milieu, published «ideal village» designs through which architects actively sought to be part of the economic, social, and cultural agenda of the early republican regime and to show their interpretations of village planning, underlining the modernization and nation-building goals. The common idea, architects agreed, was to design a village with a clear schematic order, include a building program for the government's new agents, and use local construction techniques and materials.[37]

The «village house» emerged as another concept along with the «ideal village» and was the most crucial architectural task in the rural settlements. On 1 May 1935, the Republican People's Party and the People's Houses announced an architectural competition for houses to be built in the rural areas of Eastern Thrace. Only Turkish architects were eligible to participate. The applicants were asked to demonstrate two types of village houses. They were invited to address issues related to local materials and construction techniques, economic, sanitary, and functional qualities, climate and local environmental conditions, and national characteristics reflecting «Turkish taste».[38] The competition potentially enabled more Turkish architects to weigh in on discussions of the Modern Turkish Village through a conceptualization of the village house, the basic spatial unit of rural settlements, as an artifact on a smaller scale.[39]

Another principle advocated by architects was the use of a spatial organization derived from the economic rationale of villages. According to the architect Zeki Sayar, a settlement principally designed on economic achievements could also assist in the development of the village's social structure. Thus, he advocated for the agricultural settlement as an adaptable form for rural Turkey. He emphasized that this form would generate a «nationalized» lifestyle better engaged with the rural environment and modernist concepts such as standardization, rational and functional aspects of building material, and the architectural usability of various building types.[40] Sayar's solution, which he described as «internal colonization», can be seen as a significant outcome of debates about village architecture, which sought to define an architecture consistent with the state's ideals and the interventions on behalf of modernization

and nation-building projects that had a significant impact on forming the new rural settlements, especially in the 1930s.

Practices of Identity Making through Rural Space in the 1930s

Within the political climate of the 1930s and the single-party regime of the Republican People's Party, rural Turkey and the village communities emerged more clearly as the core target for governmental tactics in reinforcing state power and the «Turkification» of the people. The migration of Turkish-speaking people from Balkan countries played a crucial role in legitimizing the early republican regime's attempts at population planning. Under these circumstances, new regulations were put in practice via the 1934 Settlement Law,[41] which allowed for the housing of immigrants, refugees, and those who struggled with insufficient living conditions along with organizing the settlement policies of non-Muslim and non-Turkish citizens. In other words, the law's demographic engineering aspects addressed governing the people in rural Turkey.[42]

The 1934 Settlement Law broadly facilitated the planning and construction of new rural settlements from the second half of the 1930s. It was applied in accordance with ethnic identity, which was determined by the state. Turkish-speaking immigrants would be housed in the same or neighboring settlements together with their family members, and they could choose these settlements and even establish a new village. Non-Turkish groups (meaning Kurds) would be housed in villages in which Turkish was the only official language; at least ten Turkish families would be settled between non-Turkish families' houses to prevent the speaking of any other language or the perpetuation of minority habits or traditions. In this way, it was believed that the cultural assimilation of non-Turkish people would be accomplished.[43]

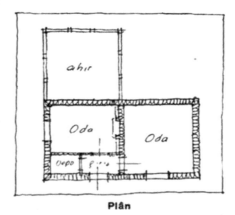

iskân umum müdürlüğü tipine göre inşa edilen bir ev

Plân

4   A Sample of the «Village House» planned and constructed by the Housing Department of Ministry of Interior.

Planning instructions in the regulation considered settlement areas in accordance with their potential in the transportation network, agricultural facilities, sanitary conditions, and the uncomplicated organization of the construction.[44] A new settlement would ideally consist of 100 houses, built on 500 m² to 1,000 m² lots, and each family would be provided with 3,000 m² of agricultural land, with settlements conveniently connected to railways, highways, or harbors. The law allowed local governorates to determine built-up areas and establish the general layout with a group of experts, consisting of a doctor, an engineer, a cadastral technician, and a housing technician.[45] The law became an effective legislative tool for housing local people and immigrants, aiming to blend them together under a united Turkishness.[46] Evidence of this endeavor was the law's enforcement in the rural outskirts of larger cities, in small towns, and in villages, where immigrant populations were in fact deported.

After enacting the 1934 Settlement Law, the newspapers announced that approximately 50,000 Turco-Romanian immigrants had been accepted into the country and granted Turkish citizenship.

The Housing Department of the Ministry of Interior directed the operation. Istanbul was the first location for settling the immigrants. Here, officers registered the immigrants and prepared them to travel to the districts where they were gradually transported and temporarily settled.[47] General inspectorates conducted the housing procedure in the provinces of Eastern Thrace and the eastern provinces of Anatolia. However, at the end of the year, the construction of houses and new settlements for these incomers had not been completed.[48]

Subsequently, the Ministry of Interior introduced another plan for a type of houses that consisted of two rooms with a small cellar-niche in the entrance and a corral attached to the house, to be built with mud bricks and timber (fig. 4). The plan allowed for adjustments made necessary by different local conditions and agricultural activities in central and western Turkey. Most of the time, settlers participated in the work on village construction sites.[49]

Parallel to the 1934 Settlement Law and its instructions, from 5 to 22 December 1936, Minister of Interior Şükrü Kaya assembled the General

5   Havuzbaşı Village, 1937.

specific «People's Houses» programs introducing Turkish culture in «non-Turkish» places.[50]

The planned rural settlements became the architectural manifestation of the practices enabled by the 1934 Settlement Law[51] to absorb non-Turkish people into a Turkified environment. In 1937, more than 18,000 rural houses were built in 24 cities.[52] At the end of the 1930s, more than 13,000 houses were under construction in Eastern Thrace alone.[53] According to official records, many Kurds were deported from Turkey's eastern provinces and housed in the new rural settlements in the western provinces together with immigrants from the Balkans. During the second half of the 1930s, the implementation of the 1934 Settlement Law around the cities of Eastern Thrace (especially Edirne, Kırklareli, and Tekirdağ) led to systematic construction works and resulted in the completion of a remarkable number of houses.[54]

Inspectors—Abidin Özmen, Kazım Dirik, Tahsin Uzer, and Abdullah Alpdoğan—in Ankara to review the settlement operation, the deportation of Kurds, conditions of state order especially in the eastern provinces, and the development program in rural Turkey in general. The committee concluded that new rural settlements should be established along the railways to settle Turkish people, and every year more Turkish immigrants should be settled in those villages according to demographic plans. New settlements should be constructed by commissions organized by the general inspectors of each region. The state would provide economic infrastructure and socio-cultural infrastructure via

In western Turkey, İzmir maintained cultivated areas and a relatively well-developed transportation network and infrastructure. From an economic perspective, the city and its hinterland were therefore aligned with the state's development program from the first years of the republic. On the other hand, the demographic situation of the city's center and rural periphery had been altered during the 1922 Greco-Turkish War when Orthodox Greeks—then the majority of the population—were deported. After the Lausanne Peace Treaty[55] and the 1923 Proclamation of the Republic, the cultural legitimation of a «Turkish İzmir» became a goal. As a result, İzmir also developed as an alternative urban scene of early republican Turkey, claiming to be as modern and as national as Ankara.[56] Moreover, the housing policies pushed through during the 1930s played a role in the demographic formation of the city.

6   Taşkesik Village, 1937.

Within the 1934 Settlement Law's scope, more than 7,000 immigrants from Romania and Bulgaria reached the city in 1936–37. The governor of İzmir and the Housing Director led the settlement operation.[57] Three new settlements—Havuzbaşı (Torbalı) with sixteen houses (fig. 5),

Taşkesik (Bayındır) with eighteen houses (fig. 6), and Yeniköy (Torbalı) with 111 houses—were constructed,[58] implementing a variation of the Ministry of Interior's 1935 housing type. One-storey village houses with two rooms and a terrace under a timber roof were located on 600 m² to 1,000 m² lots, including a barn and orchard. The state provided agricultural land, animals, and equipment, and many settlers participated in the construction works.[59]

Yeniköy as a Palimpsest: An Interpretation of Rural Space

In this section, we shift our focus away from these grand-scale historical observations to the seemingly small-scale implications of these political transformations for a village «on the ground» by examining the case of Yeniköy. Leaning on concepts developed in the field of human geography, we briefly analyze the potentially contradictory relations of these new (social) spaces, shaped not only by top-down planned state interventions but by everyone living in a specific realm. Since the so-called «spatial turn» in the 1980s, space is no longer conceptualized as a mere material backdrop, but rather as itself socially constructed.[60] This perspective means that the lived experiences of less influential or even marginalized inhabitants play a role in the production process of space, since actions and imaginations can have intended or unintended consequences for spatial knowledge, and thus, spatial realities.[61] A key figure in this new understanding of spatial relations was Henri Lefebvre whose pivotal book *The Production of Space* (1991) laid the ground for later postmodern geographer Edward Soja (1996) and his work on «Thirdspace». Lefebvre famously remarked: «new social relationships call for a new space, and vice versa.» An understanding of this recognition can be observed in the building projects of the late Ottoman Empire as well as of the early republican state. Each vision of a new

social order translates into a material reality but is transformed through mis/usage by the intended and later inhabitants. Inscribed spatial meanings changed through changing social relations, for instance decades after the advent of modernist building projects in the Turkish countryside.

It is exactly this notion of the incorporation of contradictory relations and contestations into social space and hence social reality that draws on the core of our research. It opens up the possibility of studying and valuing all actors and materials in the process of spatial production in Turkey's countryside through time: not only the planned, governmental ideas, with their strong ideological agenda (which is strongly connected to «governmentality»[62]), and the actual materiality of the villages, but also the ways in which the often marginalized subjects of the building programs grappled with the dominant dimension of their built and imagined environments («Thirdspace»). The village of Yeniköy—an exemplary case study as a village similar to many in the area—thereby presents itself as a true palimpsest with a multitude of chronological layers as well as an overlapping of differing interest groups and actors.

Ottoman Era: The Creation of Representational Spaces
According to the 1891 report in the Ottoman Annual, Yeniköy at this time already had a settlement with 26 dwellings and 116 residents. Between 1892 and 1894, pivotal public structures were erected in the village center, including a mosque, a fountain adorned with an ornamental pool, and a primary school, similar to other settlements established by the Ottoman authority in the late 19th century. The building program introduced these new elements, which represented a departure from traditional Anatolian villages.[63]

During this time, Yeniköy unveiled a centralized layout, strategically placing the new representational buildings in a square at the village's center. The mosque, school, ornamental pool, and water fountain formed a symbolic and practical

7   School and its annexes built in the late Ottoman Period, Yeniköy Village, 2021.

8   Ornamental Pool next to the mosque and school, built in the late Ottoman Period, Yeniköy Village, 2021.

9   Fountain in the square built in the Late Ottoman Period, Yeniköy Village, 2021.

core, signaling the omnipresence of Ottoman rule and an Islamic community in rural Anatolia, as well as serving as a vital social hub that aimed to unify village residents. The village's circular layout, coupled with the vertical prominence of the mosque and school, reflected a deliberate effort to manifest imperial authority as described above. Beyond their political aesthetics, the pool and fountain represented a leap into modernization, enhancing rural life while asserting control. Notably, the remaining structures demonstrated a degree of independence from the state, allowing the village to organically evolve (figs. 7, 8, and 9).

Republican Era: Imposing Uniformity

The republican era witnessed a radical departure from the more organic layout of the Ottoman village. Imposing a geometric design on both the overall settlement and individual houses, the state ideology intruded into the everyday lives of its inhabitants. Walls around house properties protected privacy but also propagated a false sense of individuality, highlighting the regulatory impact of republican governmentality. The strictly unified architecture aimed at regulating the bodies and behaviors of the people, providing stability once they adapted to the new norms (figs. 10, 11, and 12).

This development started in 1937, when construction commenced on the early republican settlement of Yeniköy, expanding from the eastern borders of the former Ottoman village. This new settlement, or rather this add-on to the late-Ottoman village, boasted a larger population and hence number of dwellings. However, with this addition, an explicit building program was implemented by the government and settlers collaboratively, with the aim of completion in the following years.[64] The main objective was housing Turkish-speaking immigrants. But using the planning strategies, the state also equipped this community with agricultural occupations and embodied a social structure aligned with the republican agenda.

The new part of the village was structured around four primary streets, each spanning

10   Street view of the village built in the early republican period, 2016.

11   Village House built in the early republican period, 2016.

12   Street view showing the additions by the settlers, Yeniköy Village, settlement built in the early republican period, 2022.

13   A view to the construction area, 1937, Yeniköy Village.

14   Construction of houses, 1937, Yeniköy Village.

10 meters in width, running along the north–south axis, intersecting with five main streets of equal width along the west–east axis. These intersections delineated building blocks of land, covering an area of nearly 10,000 m². Each building block accommodated ten dwellings situated on a 1,000 m² plot. Two blocks positioned between the second and third streets on the north–south axis, and the first and third streets on the west–east axis, were designated for public use, housing shops, a coffee house, a village office, and a gendarmerie. The school in the Ottoman settlement was used by the settlers until the early 1940s, when a new school building was completed in a spare plot in the republican settlement with financial contributions from the villagers (figs. 13 and 14).[65]

The earliest cadastral plan of the settlement dates to 1969, encompassing ten fully developed blocks and two partially developed blocks expanded with new dwellings in the north–south direction. The area constructed in 1937 comprised 111 dwellings, predominantly single houses within spacious gardens, although some parcels were divided into two for private use.[66]

By the 1940s, like other rural settlements, construction of the new settlement in Yeniköy gradually ceased, although the country's planning efforts, particularly economic development plans, remained focused on agriculture-based programs. However, the arrival of Marshall Aid, which was extended to Turkey through the European Recovery Plan in 1947, exerted a significant influence, prompting changes in state operations within rural areas,[67] subsequently impacting the spatial configuration of settlements. Marshall Aid ushered in new construction agendas centered on technical and infrastructural practices, along with addressing new welfare concerns in a nation where the majority still resided in rural areas, including Yeniköy. The village, like others in the region, became a melting pot, welcoming immigrants from eastern provinces, predominantly ethnically Kurdish origin citizens, from the 1960s.[68]

Contemporary Transformations: Negotiating Identities

The early 1970s witnessed the extension of basic infrastructure, such as running water and electricity, across the entire village. Beyond improving living conditions, these developments served as tools for the state's legitimation. Today, the core functions of both the Ottoman-era and the republican-era settlement-quarters persist, yet their meanings and tones have evolved. In the following section, we delve into the theoretical framework guiding our understanding of these transformations and re-building programs in Yeniköy and the role they played in the process of producing collective identities in these socially and politically dynamic times (figs. 15, 16, and 17).[69]

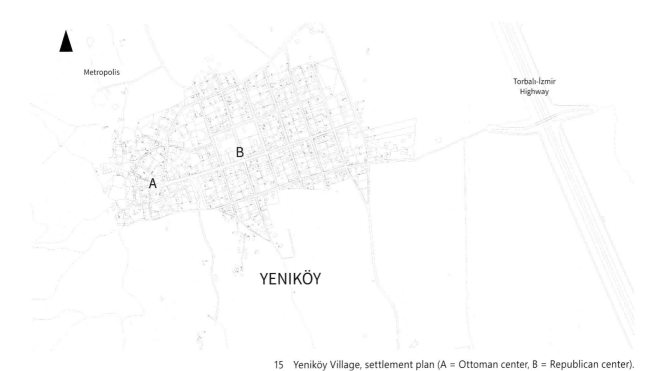

15   Yeniköy Village, settlement plan (A = Ottoman center, B = Republican center).

16   Yeniköy Village, settlement plan showing the public and commercial areas.

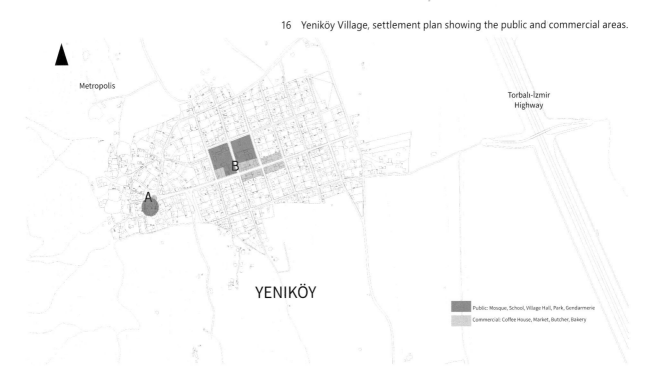

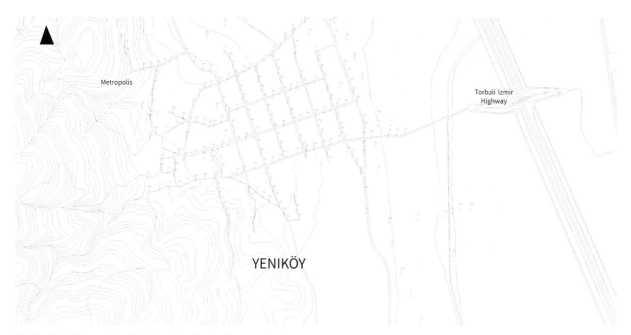

17   Yeniköy Village, electrification plan, first implemented in the early 1970s.

Present-day Yeniköy mirrors a dynamic interplay between the intended layout and locally driven changes. Unruled spaces, houses facing the street contrary to the intended layout, and varied construction methods illustrate the resilience and adaptability of the inhabitants. The appropriation of existing spaces by marginalized groups constitutes a Thirdspace—a unique version of space imposed on a location that once displayed an insatiable appetite for spaces of representation. The Ottoman ornamental pool, once a symbol of modernity, has been transformed into a communal space, now a café equipped with plastic furniture and paraphernalia.

Conclusion: A Reconceptualization of Historic and Contemporary Rural Spaces

Modernization and nation-building through rural interventions was a method for shaping the societies and people that became prevalent after the circumstances triggered by the early 20th-century agrarian crisis, particularly in the European context. Although the reasoning was different in each country, rural depopulation, agricultural depression, and uncontrolled urbanization were common to all.[70] States turned to agricultural development to reconstruct the countryside, addressing poverty, cultural and national identity, and political influence. However, «the gap between the goals and practices of governing the rural and the final results» was often striking.[71]

This «gap» resembles the case study introduced here: in the first years of the republic in Turkey, the regime set various goals to mold village communities, and their people. State agents often scrutinized rural life in economic, social, cultural, and national terms. Settlement policies were mercilessly superimposed on the rural population by relocation and housing programs that fit the new demographic agendas. Finally, the spatial practices entailed by planned rural settlements shaped early republican Turkey's rural landscape.

Although the ideals, policies, and implementation rules collided in projects to create the «Modern Turkish village», they helped to generate an architectural culture in which the Kemalist regime aimed to manufacture an idealized environment and citizens dedicated to their nation. The historiography of planned rural settlements of early republican Turkey demonstrates the manifold milieu from another angle, and it unveils the narratives of this period by reading the instrumentalized architecture in the countryside.

In conclusion, the reconfiguration of Yeniköy's space, achieved through both redesign and re-appropriation, challenges traditional notions of historical and present spatialities. Inhabitants, often relegated to subordinate roles, have played a crucial role in shaping an imperceptible Thirdspace, redefining the narrative of the village. This re-conceptualization urges a shift in our approach to the production of historic and contemporary rural spaces, emphasizing the agency of those traditionally marginalized. Yeniköy serves as a compelling example, prompting a reassessment of our conceptualization and practices in the study of rural spaces throughout history. The village's story becomes a testament to the resilience and creativity of its inhabitants in negotiating their identities within evolving spatial contexts.

1 According to the field research of the Turkish Statistical Institute in 2022, Yeniköy's population is 1533. https://data.tuik.gov.tr/Kategori/GetKategori?p=Nufus-ve-Demografi-109 (26 June 2024).
2 Mardin 1991, 94–100.
3 İpek 1994, 73; Andaç 2007.
4 Berkes 2005, 342.
5 Andaç 2007 and Deringil 2011, 67.
6 Uzer 2016, 16.
7 Berkes 2005, 343–344.
8 Berkes 2005, 364–365.
9 Berkes 2005, 365; Tekeli/Ilkin 2003, 165–167.
10 Deringil 2011, 67.
11 Sezer 2020, 27–29, 34–35.
12 Atilla 2002, 63–65, 89–91, 145; Atay 1998, 83–86.
13 Basbakanlik Osmanli Arsivi (BOA), D:30, G:10.
14 AVS 1894, 214; AVS 1896, 184; AVS 1908, 263.
15 Kayış 2012, 38.
16 Zandi-Sayek 2011.
17 According to field research conducted by Vera Egbers and Özge Sezer in 2022.
18 For a comprehensive reading of the transformation of states and territories within Turkey between 1908 and 1923, see Berkes 2005.
19 Turkish Statistical Institute 2012, 9.
20 Keyder 1987, 92; Yıldırım 2006, 91.
21 İnan 1982, 17–90; Köymen 1999, 1.
22 Keyder 1981, 57–58.
23 The Official Gazette 1924.
24 The Official Gazette 1929.
25 Falke 1935, 2–3; Çağlar 1940, 11–13.
26 Karaömerlioğlu 2006, 56–60.
27 Karaömerlioğlu 1998, 69–87; Çeçen 2000, 95.
28 Güleç 1936.
29 The Official Gazette 1924.
30 İskan Tarihçesi 1932, 76–80.
31 Cengizkan 2004, 182.
32 Arı 1995, 52–53.
33 Arı 1995, 65–66; Cengizkan 2004, 28; Kozanoğlu 1935, 203.
34 Cengizkan 2004, 84–86.
35 Çetin 2003, 101–102.
36 Kozanoğlu 1933a, 370.
37 Bozdoğan 2001, 116; Kozanoğlu 1933b, 38.
38 Arkitekt 1935, 93.
39 Sezer 2016, 57–58.
40 Sayar 1936, 47.
41 The Official Gazette 1934.
42 Öztan 2020, 83–85.
43 General Directorate of Settlement 1936, 248–249.
44 General Directorate of Settlement 1936, 259–276.
45 General Directorate of Settlement 1936, 264–268.
46 Sezer 2021.
47 Cumhuriyet 1934a.
48 Cumhuriyet 1934b.
49 Ünsal 1940, 17.
50 Varlık/Koçak 2010, 16–17.
51 The Official Gazette 1934.
52 Belediyeler Dergisi 1937, 55.
53 Eres 2008, 154–185.
54 Eres 2008, 163–248; Eres 2015.
55 League of Nations 1924.
56 Bilsel 1996.
57 Anadolu 1937a.
58 Anadolu 1937b.

59　Cumhuriyetin 1938, 133–137.
60　See e.g. Schlögel 2006, 37, 68; for a summary of the «spatial turn», see e.g. Döring / Thilmann 2008; Löw et al. 2008; Günzel 2010, 90–99 chap. II. 2; Lossau 2012; Bachmann-Medick 2014. Soja 2008, 243, on the other hand, criticizes the marginalization of the spatial turn as merely another turn in cultural studies and explicitly takes issue with the presentation in Bachmann-Medick 2014 [2006], arguing that the phenomenon would have a more profound effect.
61　This concept of the «production of space» derives especially from the French Marxist geographer Henri Lefebvre (1991; 2000 [1974]) and later his most prominent follower postmodern geographer Edward Soja (1996) and his work on «Thirdspace». See also Jazeel 2014; Egbers 2019, 93; Egbers 2023, 27–35.
62　Foucault 1991.
63　Sezer 2022, 155.
64　Sezer 2022, 156.
65　Sezer 2022, 156.
66　Sezer 2022, 156.
67　Üstün 1997.
68　Interview with the settlers by Özge Sezer, 2021
69　Interview with the settlers by Özge Sezer, 2021
70　Burchardt 2010, 147.
71　Patel 2017, 15–16.

Andaç 2007
E. Andaç: Empire-to-Nation: The Rise of Panislamism and Legitimation of Power in the Ottoman Empire, 1876–1923 (Istanbul 2007).

Arı 1995
K. Arı: Büyük Mübadele: Türkiye'ye Zorunlu Göç, 1923–1925 [The Big Population Exchange: Forced Migration to Turkey, 1923–1925] (Istanbul 1995).

Atay 1998
C. Ataz: Osmanlı'dan Cumhuriyet'e İzmir Planları (Izmir 1998).

Atilla 2002
A. N. Atilla: İzmir Demiryolları (Izmir 2002).

Bachmann-Medick 2014
D. Bachmann-Medick: Spatial Turn, in: D. Bachmann-Medick: Cultural Turns: Neuorientierungen in den Kulturwissenschaften, 5th ed. (Reinbek bei Hamburg 2014) 284–328.

Berkes 2005
N. Berkes: Türkiye'de çağdaşlaşma (Istanbul 2005).

Bilsel 1996
C. Bilsel: Ideology and Planning During the Early Republican Period: Two Master Plans for Izmir and Scenarios of Modernization. METU Journal of the Faculty of Architecture, 16 (1–2), 1996, 13–30. http://jfa.arch.metu.edu.tr/content/view/31/29/ (26 June 2024).

Bozdoğan 2001
S. Bozdoğan: Modernism and Nation Building: Turkish Architectural Culture in the Early Republic, Studies in Modernity and National Identity (Seattle 2001).

Burchardt 2010
J. Burchardt: Editorial: Rurality, Modernity and National Identity between Wars. Rural History 21, 2010, no. 2, 143–150. https://doi.org/10.1017/S0956793310000087.

Cengizkan 2004
A. Cengizkan: Mübadele Konut ve Yerleşimleri (Ankara 2004).

Çaglar 1940
K. Çaglar: Yüksek Ziraat Enstitüsü: Kanunlar, Kararnameler, Bütçe ve Talimatnameler [Higher Institute of Agriculture: Laws, Decrees, Budget, and Regulations] [report] (Ankara 1940).

Çeçen 2000
A. Çeçen: Halkevleri. Atatürk'ün Kültür Kurumu [People's Houses, Culture Institutions of Atatürk] (Istanbul 2000).

Çetin 2003
S. Çetin: Erken Cumhuriyet Döneminde Köyün Modernizasyonu: Örnek Köyler Üzerinden Okuma [Modernization of the Village in the Early Republican Period: A Reading through the Exemplary Villages]. Arredamento Mimarlık (6), 2003, 99–105.

Deringil 2011
S. Deringil: The Well-Protected Domains: Ideology and the Legitimation of Power in the Ottoman Empire 1876–1909 (London 2011).

Döring / Thilmann 2008
J. Döring / T. Thilmann (eds.): Spatial Turn: Das Raumparadigma in den Kultur- und Sozialwissenschaften (Bielefeld 2008).

Egbers 2019
V. Egbers: ‹Ein Assyrer in Urartu›: Thirdspace in der Eisenzeit in Nord-Mesopotamien, in: R. Bernbeck / V. Egbers (eds.): Subalterne Räume: Versuch einer Übersicht. Forum Kritische Archäologie 8, 92–113.

Egbers 2023
V. Egbers: Thirdspace in Assyrien und Urartu: Eine Archäologie der Sinne und Subalternität in der Eisenzeit in Nord-mesopotamien (Leiden 2023). https://doi.org/10.6105/journal.fka.2019.8.6.

Eres 2008
Z. Eres: Türkiye'de Planlı Kırsal Yerleşmelerin Tarihsel Gelişimi ve Erken Cumhuriyet Dönemi Planlı Kırsal Mimarisinin Korunması Sorunu [Survey of the History of Planned Rural Villages and Problems Related to the Protection of Planned Village Architecture of the Early Republic Era], PhD

dissertation, Istanbul Technical University, Institute of Science and Technology. https://polen.itu.edu.tr/handle/11527/4216.

Eres 2015
Z. Eres: Muratlı: Bir Cumhuriyet Köyü [Muratlı: A Republican Village]. Mimarlık [online] (386), 2015. http://www.mimarlik-dergisi.com/index.cfm?sayfa=mimarlik&DergiSayi=400&RecID=3798 (26 June 2024).

Falke 1935
F. Falke: Die landwirtschaftliche Hochschule Ankara am Schluss ihres zweiten Studienjahres [The Higher Institute of Agriculture Ankara at the End of its Second Academic Year]. La Turquie Kamâliste (9), 1935, 2–9.

Foucault 1991
M. Foucault: Governmentality. Translated by Rosi Braidotti and revised by Colin Gordon, in: G. Burchell / C. Gordon / P. Miller (eds.): The Foucault Effect: Studies in Governmentality (Chicago 1991) 87–104.

Güleç 1936
A. Güleç: Küçükyozgat Köyü: Köy Tetkiki [Küçükyozgat Village: Village Survey] (Ankara 1936).

Günzel 2010
S. Günzel (ed.): Raum: Ein interdisziplinäres Handbuch (Stuttgart, Weimar 2010).

İnan 1982
A. İnan: İktisat Esaslarımız: 17 Şubat 339 – 4 Mart 339 Tarihine Kadar İzmir'de Toplanan İlk Türk İktisat Kongresinde Kabul Olunan Esaslar ve İrat Olunan Nutuklar [Our Principles of Economy: The Principles Accepted in the First Turkish Economy Kongress Convened in Izmir Between 17 February 1923 and 4 March 1923], in: İzmir İktisat Kongresi [Izmir Economic Congress], Türk Tarih Kurumu Yayınları (Ankara 1982) 17–90.

İpek 1994
N. İpek: Rumeli'den Anadolu'ya Türk Göçleri, 1877–1890. Türk Tarih Kurumu Yayınları XVI, Dizi 73 (Ankara 1994).

Jazeel 2014
T. Jazeel: Subaltern Geographies: Geographical Knowledge and Postcolonial Strategy. Singapore Journal of Tropical Geography 35, 2014, 88–103.

Karaömerlioğlu 1998
A. Karaömerlioğlu: The People's Houses and the Cult of the Peasant in Turkey. Middle Eastern Studies 34 (4), 1998, 67–91. https://doi.org/10.1080/00263209808701244.

Karaömerlioğlu 2006
A. Karaömerlioğlu: Orada Bir Köy Var Uzakta: Erken Cumhuriyet Döneminde Köycü Söylem [There is a Village, Far Away: Discourse on Peasantry in the Early Republican Period] (Istanbul 2006).

Kayış 2012
Y. Kayış: Aydın Vilâyeti Salnâmelerinde Torbalı ve Sultan II. Abdülhamid'in Hayır Eserleri [Torbalı and Sultan II in the Aydın Province Yearbooks: Abdulhamid's Charitable Works] (İzmir 2012).

Keyder 1981
Ç. Keyder: The Definition of a Peripheral Economy: Turkey, 1923–1929 (Cambridge 1981). https://doi.org/10.1017/CBO9780511735844.

Keyder 1987
Ç. Keyder: State and Class in Turkey. A Study in Capitalist Development (London 1987).

Kozanoglu 1933a
A. Z. Kozanoglu: Köy Mimarisi [Village Architecture]. Ülkü Halkevleri Mecmuası 1 (5), 1933, 370–374.

Kozanoglu 1933b
A. Z. Kozanoglu: Köy Mimarisi [Village Architecture]. Ülkü Halkevleri Mecmuası 2 (7), 1933, 37–41.

Kozanoglu 1935
A. Z. Kozanoglu: Köy Evleri Proje ve Yapıları İçin Toplu Rapor [Report on Projects and Constructions of the Village Houses]. Arkitekt (7–8), 1935, 203–204.

Köymen 1999
O. Köymen: Cumhuriyet Döneminde Tarımsal Yapı ve Tarım Politikaları [Agricultural Structure and Agriculture Politics in the Republican Period], in: O. Baydar / O. Köymen (eds.): 75 Yılda Köylerden Şehirlere [From Villages to the Cities in Seventy-Five Years] (Istanbul 1999) 1–30.

Lefebvre 1991
H. Lefebvre: The Production of Space (Oxford 1991).

Lefebvre 2000 [1974]
H. Lefebvre: La production de l'espace, 4th ed. (Paris 2000 [1974]).

Lossau 2012
J. Lossau: Spatial Turn, in: F. Eckardt (ed.): Handbuch Stadtsoziologie (Wiesbaden 2012) 185–198.

Löw et al. 2008
M. Löw / S. Steets / S. Stoetzer: Einführung in die Stadt- und Raumsoziologie, 2nd ed. (Leverkusen 2008).

Mardin 1991
Ş. Mardin: Türk Modernleşmesi [Turkish Modernization] (Istanbul 1991).

Öztan 2020
R. H. Öztan: Settlement Law of 1934: Turkish Nationalism in the Age of Revisionism. Journal of Migration History 6 (1), 2020, 82–103. https://doi.org/10.1163/23519924-00601006.

Patel 2017
K. Patel: The Green Heart of the Governance: Rural Europe during the Interwar Years in a Global Perspective, in: L. van de Grift / A. R. Forclaz (eds.): Governing the Rural in Interwar Europe (New York 2017) 1–23.

Sayar 1936
Z. Sayar: İç Kolonizasyon: Başka Memleketlerde [Internal Colonization: In Other Countries]. Arkitekt 6 (8), 1936, 231–235.

Schlögel 2006
K. Schlögel: Im Raume lesen wir die Zeit: Über Zivilisationsgeschichte und Geopolitik, 5th ed. (Frankfurt a. M. 2006).

Sezer 2016
Ö. Sezer: The «Village House»: Planning Rural Life in Early Republican Turkey, in: L. Özgenel (ed.): Spaces, Times, Peoples: Domesticity, Dwelling and Architectural History (Ankara 2016) 51–60.

Sezer 2020
Ö. Sezer: Idealization of the Land: Forming the New Rural Settlements in the Early Republican Period of Turkey, 1923–1950. Diss. Technische Universität Berlin, 2020. http://dx.doi.org/10.14279/depositonce-9811.

Sezer 2021
Ö. Sezer: Modern Köyün İnşasi: Erken Cumhuriyet Dönemi Kirsalinda İskan Politikalari Üzerine Bir Değerlendirme – Making of the Modern Village: An Evaluation on the Settlement Policies in Rural Turkey in the Early Republican Period [article in Turkish]. TÜBA-KED Türkiye Bilimler Akademisi Kültür Envanteri Dergisi 24, 2021, 127–144, https://doi.org/10.22520/tubaked2021.24.007.

Sezer 2022
Ö. Sezer: Forming the Modern Turkish Village: Modernization and Nation Building in Rural Turkey during the Early Republic. Histoire 201 (Bielefeld 2022). https://doi.org/10.14361/9783839461556.

Soja 1996
E. Soja: Thirdspace: Journeys to Los Angeles and Other Real-and-Imagined Places (Oxford 1996).

Soja 2008
E. Soja: Vom «Zeitgeist» zum «Raumgeist»: New Twists on the Spatial Turn, in: Döring / Thilmann 2008, 241–262.

Spivak 1999
G.C. Spivak: A Critique of Postcolonial Reason: Toward a History of the Vanishing Present (Cambridge, MA 1999).

Tekeli / Ilkin 2003
İ. Tekeli / S. İlkin: Cumhuriyetin Harcı III: Modernıtenın Altyapısı Oluşurken [The Mortar of the Republic III: Forming the Infrastructure of Modernity] (Istanbul 2003).

Uzer 2016
U. Uzer: An Intellectual History of Turkish Nationalism: Between Turkish Ethnicity and Islamic Identity (Salt Lake City 2016).

Ünsal 1940
B. Ünsal: Sincan Köyü Planı, Arkitekt, 1940, no. 1–2 (109–110) 15–18.

Üstün 1997
S. Üstün: Turkey and the Marshall Plan: Strive for Aid, in: The Turkish Yearbook of International Relations 27 (Ankara 1997) 31–52.

Varlik / Kocak 2010
M. Varlik / C. Kocak: Umumi Müfettişler Konferansı'nda Görüşülen ve Dahiliye Vekâleti'ni İgilendiren İşlere Dair Toplantı Zabıtları ile Rapor ve Hulâsası, 1936 [Minutes, Report and Brief of the Issues Discussed in the Conference of General Inspectorates Related to the Interior Ministry, 1936] (Ankara 2010).

Yildirim 2006
O. Yildirim: Diplomacy and Displacement: Reconsidering the Turco-Greek Exchange of Populations, 1922–1934 (New York 2006). https://doi.org/10.4324/9780203960653.

Zandi-Sayek 2011
S. Zandi-Sayek: Ottoman Izmir: The Rise of a Cosmopolitan Port, 1840–1880 (Minneapolis 2011).

Archival Sources

Anadolu 1937a
Göçmenler Geliyor. Bu Yıl Vilayetimize 5296 Göçmen Gelecek [Immigrants Are Arriving. 5,296 Immigrants Will Arrive in Our Provinces in This Year]. Anadolu, 30 June 1937, 2.

Anadolu 1937b
Yeni Yaptırılacak Göçmen Evleri [New Immigrant Houses to Be Built]. Anadolu, 21 July 1937, 2.

Arkitekt 1935
Köy Evleri Proje Müsabakası [Project Competition Brief on Village Houses]. Arkitekt 5, no. 3, 1935, 93.

AVS 1891
Aydın Vilayeti Salnamesi, 1891, 461.

AVS 1893
Aydın Vilayet Salnamesi, 1893, 409.

AVS 1908
Aydın Vilayeti Salnamesi, 1908, 501–502.

Belediyeler Dergisi 1937
Göçmen Evleri ve Köyleri [Immigrants' Houses and Villages]. Belediyeler Dergisi 29, no. 12, 1937, 53–5.

Cumhuriyet 1934a
50.000 Muhacir Gelecek [50,000 Immigrants Will Arrive]. Cumhuriyet, 10 July 1934, 1, 4.

Cumhuriyet 1934b
Trakya'ya Yerleştirilen Muhacirler [Immigrants, Housed in (the East) Thrace]. Cumhuriyet, 16 November 1934, 2.

Cumhuriyetin 1938
Cumhuriyetin 15inci Yılında İzmir [Izmir in the Fifteenth Year of the Republic] [catalogue]. (Izmir 1938).

General Directorate of Settlement 1936
General Directorate of Settlement: İskân Mevzuatı [Settlement Regulations] (Ankara 1936).

İskan Tarihçesi 1932
İskan Tarihçesi [History of Settlement] (İstanbul 1932).

League of Nations 1924
League of Nations: N° 701: British Empire, France, Italy, Japan, Greece, &c., and Turkey. Treaty of Peace, signed at Lausanne, July 24, 1923. League of Nations Treaty Series, 28 (1-2-3-4), 1924, 11–113. https://treaties.un.org/doc/Publication/UNTS/LON/Volume%2028/v28.pdf (9 February 2023).

The Official Gazette 1924
Köy Kanunu [Village Law]. The Official Gazette (Resmî Cerîde), 68 (442), 1924, 237–60. http://www.mevzuat.gov.tr/Mevzuat?MevzuatNo=442&MevzuatTur=1&MevzuatTertip=3 (28 January 2021).

The Official Gazette 1929
Zirai Kredi Kooperatifleri Kanunu [Law for the Agricultural Credit Cooperatives]. The Official Gazette (T.C. Resmî Gazete), 1208 (1470), 1929, 7459–62. http://www.resmigazete.gov.tr/arsiv/1208.pdf (28 January 2021).

The Official Gazette 1934
İskan Kanunu [Settlement Law]. The Official Gazette (T.C.

Resmî Gazete), 2733(2510), 21 June 1934, 4003–9. http://www.resmigazete.gov.tr/arsiv/2733.pdf (28 January 2021).

Turkish Statistical Institute 2012
Turkish Statistical Institute: Statistical Indicators, 1923–2011, Ankara 2012, Turkish Statistical Institute, Printing Division. https://biruni.tuik.gov.tr/yayin/views/visitorPages/english/publicationView.zul?yayin_no=158 (20 March 2023).

Image Sources

1   harita.gov.tr/Turkey; with additions by Özge Sezer.
2   Akdeniz Harita; with additions by Özge Sezer.
3   University of Istanbul, Library of Rare Collection, no. 90485-0003.
4   Ünsal 1940, 16.
5, 6   Cumhuriyetin 15. Yılında İzmir, 1938, 137.
7–9   Photographed by Özge Sezer, 2021.
10, 11 Photographed by Özge Sezer, 2016.
12   Photographed by Özge Sezer, 2022.
13, 14 Cumhuriyetin 15. Yılında İzmir, 1938, 136.
15, 16 Municipality of Torbalı, Urban Planning Department; redrawn by Özge Sezer.

Thickening the Plot and Queering the Plantation
Queer Intimacies, Political Economies, and an Ethnography of History from A'a Teyze's Garden

Mayowa Willoughby

The first time that I went to Turkey was in 2010. I had received a scholarship and grant through the US State Department and the Department of Education as part of the National Security Language Initiative for Youth—a program that selected high school students to send to different countries around the world to learn one of six «critical» languages. At that time, these languages were Turkish, Russian, Chinese, Arabic, Persian, and Hindi. I was originally selected to travel to Egypt and learn Arabic. However, due to the fact that I had been to Israel the summer before through a program funded by the Mickey Leland Kibbutzim Youth Foundation and the Jewish Foundation of Houston, I was told that I could no longer go to Egypt, and I had to select between the two countries still available— Tajikistan and Turkey. Ultimately, I chose Turkey because a friend of mine sat down with me and discussed the illustrious history of the Ottoman Empire. I had never heard of it. However, they showed me a lot of pictures about the Ottoman Empire, specifically Turkey. And basically, they just led me to believe that Turkey would be a really cool country to visit and a really cool country to learn about via personal experience. So, I ended up going to Turkey, and I ended up choosing Turkey for a six-week summer program.

This was in 2010. I was placed in a host family that lived on the Asian side of Istanbul, one of two students on the program living in this area. The neighborhood that I lived in is a small, middle-class to working-class neighborhood, named Ümraniye. My commute from my home to school was very long. I had to walk to a bus stop, take a bus to the ferry, and then a ferry across the Boğaz (Bosporus) Straight. And then I had to take a tram. And then I had to walk some more. And during this whole time, because I was out in public space, because public space dictated so much of my relationship to and my interactions with others, I was often confronted with different kinds of interest in me or else expressed and communicated interest in my presence in the spaces that I was traversing.

I would encounter people on a train or a bus and who saw in their periphery, or who saw before them, someone or something unlike anything they had seen before, or so it seemed. That experience ended up dictating a lot of my interactions with Turkey as a country. I found that most of my experience had to do with the element of surprise, or how surprised others were to encounter me or how surprised others were, other Turkish people in particular, by my presence in that space, and the sounds emerging from me being Turkish or sounds with which they were familiar. Perhaps it wasn't so much my presence, but my body and my being in that space, as opposed to it being me. And so, I ended up receiving a lot of sound, or a lot of acoustic information while I was in these spaces, and this acoustic information taught me a lot about the Turkish language, and it taught me a lot about what the introduction of my presence into a space incited in others who were around me, or who noticed me, or noticed my presence in that space as well.

At that time, I heard this kind of a sound of «*maymun*» being cast in my direction. I recall that I heard that often and I recall that I didn't know what «*maymun*» meant in the beginning when I first started learning the Turkish language. And so one day I approached my Turkish teacher at my language school in Taksim on Istiklal Street in Istanbul—TÖMER, Türkçe ve Yabancı Dil Uygulama ve Araştırma Merkezi—and asked her what «*maymun*» meant, and she let me know that «*maymun*» was the Turkish word for «monkey.» And so suddenly I began to learn at that point, that there was something «sonic acoustic» so to speak, or «graphic acoustic,» that emerged in these kinds of everyday ordinary pedestrian spaces that my body interacted with. Moreover, as I entered into those spaces, and I encountered different Turkish people, and different Turkish people encountered me, I was catalyzing a certain kind of reaction and response that I had not anticipated. My lack of expectation around this frame of «call» (where the call is the introduction of my body into a space) and «response» (where the response is the verbalized feedback directed toward me, communicated by others, regarding their feelings about having noticed me) led me to wonder whether different people who were not related to each other, who did not live in the same places in Turkey, who did not live in the same places in Istanbul, were responding in a similar way. For example, it was not intuitive to me to assume that everyone in Istanbul would see me and want to utter the word «*maymun*,» or monkey. Still, even if it wasn't everyone, it was not intuitive to me that a body would be in a place and that from it would emerge a response that was shared by different people. That was really curious to me. Further, it was curious that there was so much friction, because the ways in which I was attempting to articulate myself and translate myself in space were not the ways that others in space were rendering me visible, or ways in which they were able to see my «me» and able to engage and interact with my «me.» Though this was not a general experience, though

everyone I encountered was not like that, the prevalence and frequency of this kind of incident really led me to question what it was that was present in the historical milieu, in the historical imagination of this nation-state called Turkey, that would or could allow for this kind of friction to emerge within the realm and context of my own everyday ordinary experience. Further still, how did my own experience in that place allow me to illuminate a particular approach, a particular corner or space of history and of a contemporary moment, that did not prevail in the general discourse around identity, nationhood, nationality, citizenship, Turkey, and demographics in the Turkish context?

I continued to learn Turkish and as I learned more Turkish, I was able to speak with more people and the more surprise people had around my level of fluency added to my curiosity about how I was being figured as a subject in this national context. And the level of surprise at my end also came as I was an American, who did have certain levels of mistranslation, mischaracterization and misunderstanding that I could anticipate and expect from a stranger (strange, other). I had been groomed and primed to expect certain levels of mischaracterization, given that as an American there is already a logistic and a grammar by which you must be regarded and by which you must be apprehended as an American, as an American who is read as African, and as an American who is read as woman and who is read as black. And these particular registers are part of the linguistic framework that you come to know to be true. When I went to Turkey at such a young age, I was immediately just left speechless. It rendered me speechless. Not even so much just because I could not speak the language in the beginning, but also because the grammar that I knew to translate myself, to articulate myself, to make myself visible to another was now incorrect or it had no purchase, no currency. It had no mobility, it had no utility in this other context. And so I embarked on a journey to understand what kind of grammar could render a subject such as myself visible.

The issue then with my research is that my research now takes up subjects like myself who are unlike myself. So now I must be certain and firm about how I direct history. I am African, I am American, and my American mobility allowed me to recognize this level of untranslatability. It allowed me to recognize a level of impossibility of transference that could not be regarded by a Turkish person who is of African descent, who would be in Turkey, or an African American, in America. Yet my mobility gave me the vantage point and perspective to recognize the level at which discourse allows and also prevents certain kinds of visibility, and allows them to prevent certain kinds of language and speakability, particularly self-speak ability.

Therefore, this project asks: What are these acoustics that emerge for African-descended subjects in contexts that do not give the hermeneutics of self-nomenclature easily and readily? What then is the capacity for an African-descended subject to name self? Given that there are communities of African descent in Turkey, my impetus and motivation then became to learn and observe how subjects «be» and «are» in space. Moreover, how subjects «be» and «are» survived, and how subjects «be» and «are» thrived in space. Given the historical similarities and parallels between the laborability of African-descended subjects in American contexts and the laborability of African-descended subjects in Middle Eastern contexts, there are parallels that we can draw. However, the differences and the nuances between the historical experiences lend themselves to the nuances of the sociological experiences, which lend themselves to the nuances of the psychological experiences, all of which reveal endlessly the differences in nation-state emergence. These differences require attendance to the specificity. Labor then emerges in these spaces and racialized subjects called «black» or «arap» or called a name do emerge in these spaces. Therefore, how can we then speak to the specificity of the subjects in these different places? And my research questions, and my approach to thinking about village life,

and thinking about survival and village life, and thriving and growth and life and village life, allow me to observe how a blackness, an Africanness, has reproduced itself over time in space, in intimate spaces and personal spaces, in spaces that can be belonged to.

Emergent Care and Blackness through the Freedom in A'a Teyze's Garden

Sitting inside A'a Teyze's home, on her couch, in the village of Tulumköy, a plate of crackers resting on the tray next to me, I make out hundreds of thousands of tiny flowers embroidered in the

1   A'a Teyze's garden and house, 2019.

carpet and on the rug in front of me. «The stove is hot,» A'a Teyze tells me, gesturing to the center of the room where there is a large iron stove connected to the ground and by way of one singular, thick, grey metal pipe, also connected to the ceiling above us. «Be careful.» A'a Teyze hands me a small sprig of fresh *nane* and three bulbs of *hayit tohumu*.[2] «These are from my garden,» she tells me. She points outside (fig. 1). I look in the direction of her hand and take in the assortment of *yemyeşil* (very green) things immediately surrounding us—small potted plants, large potted plants, medium plants rooted directly into the ground, shrubs, trees—all surrounded by A'a Teyze's small brown fence and single blue door. I think I can see exactly where the *nane* is, but I have never seen a *hayit tohumu* plant before. «What are these for?» I ask A'a Teyze, looking back into the palm of my hand. A'a Teyze shrugs, «for tea, for women's pains, for cramps.» «Oh. Cool.» I responded. It occurs to me to ask her if she goes to the doctor often. She shakes her head no saying «*güvenmiyorum onlara*», (I don't trust them). «But you trust yourself,» I ask. She laughs saying, «of course.»

Hakan Erdem notes that the resettlement program initiated by Sultan Abdulhamid II in 1890 was driven by a desire to provide care for manumitted Africans.[3] This care—defined through manumitted Africans' legally mandated relocation to western Anatolia, marriage to one another, resettlement on empty Ottoman lands, and encouragement to invest in the agricultural productivity of those lands—was the remedy for two gubernatorial anxieties. The first anxiety was a fear of European imperial powers—specifically British imperial power—encroaching upon Ottoman territory. In July 1890 Sultan Abdulhamid II joined the United Kingdom, France, the Congo Free State, the Kingdoms of Portugal, Italy, and Spain, the Netherlands, Belgium, the Russian and German Empires, Austria-Hungary, Sweden-Norway, Denmark, the United States, Zanzibar, and Persia in signing the General Act of the Brussels Conference, which stipulated that all signatory

powers could «extend their protection» to missionary bodies without «distinction for creed» and establish foundations of refuge and education for liberated women and children. Given European imperial history in Ottoman territories, Sultan Abdulhamid II considered the General Act nothing more than grounds for Christian European powers to legitimize infiltrating populations that were under Ottoman rule, all under the banner of providing them with necessary forms of care. Therefore, resettling manumitted Africans by the Ottoman state could be seen as a means to provide enough sustenance and protections to keep Christian European intervention at bay. The second anxiety animating the sultan's resettlement project was the rising economic pressure facing the Ottoman government in the wake of the newly non-housed, non-jobbed population into which these Africans had been transformed upon their manumission. The care of manumitted Africans through their resettlement in Izmir was, thus, meant to relieve the Ottoman state by providing it with long-term economic potential through manumitted Africans' agricultural labor.[4]

The historical processes that led to the formation of agricultural, Afro-Turkish communities in the provinces of Izmir and Aydın thus expose one layer of Afro-Turkish peoples' relationships to the plant life in their environments. That is, that of a productive logic circumscribing rural, Aegean, Afro-Turkish communities' relationships to growing and caring for the plants around them—specifically in their homes, and on farms in their communities. As Y. Hakan Erdem points out, today, descendants of these manumitted Africans resettled in Izmir and Aydın provinces—along with Kurdish, Turkish, and some Afro-Turkish people who migrated to western Anatolia for agricultural work following their service in the Ottoman military during World War I—constitute familial and kinship networks in rural and mountainous villages of the provinces of Izmir and Aydın today.[5]

As a consequence of the ambiguity that comes with border establishment, the provinces of Izmir and Aydın have been connected as one autonomous region, then divided into two distinct provinces, and back again several times over the past century. Today they remain as two distinct provinces. Each is located in the Aegean region of the modern republic of Turkey. As Ehud Toledano points out, the individuals of these communities were incorporated—albeit unevenly— into the Turkish state as Turks through the establishment of the modern republic of Turkey. Afro-Turkish people within this region reside in the villages of Yeniçiftlik, Hasköy, and Subaşı as well as in the towns of Balıkesir, Bayındır, and Ayvalık.[6] Over the years, some Afro-Turkish people have migrated from these small towns and villages into Izmir proper for educational and work opportunities, but by and large the vast majority remain in Izmir and Aydın's rural towns and villages.[7] Roberts et al. describe the ways in which the province of Aydın was built in the Little Menderes basin.[8] It is surrounded by mountains in the south and the north; its central and western regions are purely fertile plains. Today, the most important economic activity in the provinces of Aydın and Izmir is agriculture and the most well-to-do Afro-Turkish families are those of paid agricultural workers or of those that manage their own lands.[9] Over the course of the past century, agriculture and agricultural labor have come to characterize the livelihoods of Afro-Turkish people living in the provinces of Aydın and Izmir where the only black agricultural community in Turkey exists.[10]

A conventional historical paradigm considers it presumptuous to argue that there must be a direct connection between the settlement of emancipated Africans by Sultan Abdulhamid II in the fertile plains of Izmir and Aydın provinces for the express purpose of land cultivation and the contemporary interdependence of Afro-Turkish people in rural Izmir and Aydın provinces with plants—for food, for farming, for health. However, it is similarly problematic to ignore what can be insinuated by the analogous location of African-descended communities in the

Little Menderes Valley, precisely where manumitted Africans were said to have been resettled by Sultan Abdulhamid II in the 19th century.[11]

Ethnography therefore presents itself as a unique frame through which to analyze the rhizomatic connections and emergences occluded by conventional historical paradigms. It can avoid the traps of rationalizing traditional archives as the paradigmatic representation of history by emphasizing that the recognition of what is happening in dialectical relationship directly insinuates the accumulation of events that have made such relationships possible. Moreover, the analysis contained within this chapter does not assume that communities of Afro-Turkish people in the villages of Izmir and Aydın are the same as the ones that were settled by the sultan at the end of the 19th century. Given the nearly 130-year gap, the biological requirements necessary for this to hold true would be insurmountable.

Manumitted Africans were expected to labor upon the land upon which they had been settled to produce crops for the Ottoman-turned-Turkish state. Manumitted Africans' labor with the land, their attendance to the seeds they were given to harvest, and the crops they harvested after planting, were intended to be productive, generative, and oriented towards the proliferation and expansion of the Ottoman-turned-Turkish state. This I call a form of domestication. The contemporary ways that Afro-Turkish people, descendants of those emancipated Africans, as well as others who emigrated to the rural and mountainous villages to join the agricultural labor force of the region, have come to be with plot and production are direct examples of how agricultural space, or else plant production and humans, can come to remake space and in so doing fashion their own orientations to futurity and by extension to notions of freedom.

The preoccupations contained within this chapter lie squarely at the intersections of land, labor, the steady insistence of life, and the unsettling ways people and plants can come to inhabit

2   A'a Teyze and her plants in her garden, 2019.

space together. This paper is a reflection on the capacity for organic plant–human relationships to emerge and in so doing transform predetermined plant–human grammars of extraction, production, and order. The anecdote which opens this chapter indicates A'a Teyze's casual imperative to trust herself, her *nane*, and her *hayit tohumu* to regulate her pains and to mediate her wellness over the state agents assigned to intervene at that juncture, thus providing a counter to a historical expectation of agricultural production solely for economic return. Moreover, the temporally transferrable nature of A'a Teyze's plant knowledge—from A'a Teyze's grandmothers to A'a Teyze

to me—demonstrates how relationships to land and environment are constantly shifting across time and space (fig. 2).

Finally, this chapter stakes at the center of its analysis the grammars that govern relationships between rural Afro-Turkish people and the plants in their environments. This analysis reveals that everyday relationships between people and plants not only subvert inherited arrangements but produce an emergent relationship to both blackness and freedom. And, further, this analysis reveals what is to be gained in reading those inherited arrangements together with those arrangements newly formed.

Rigid Gender Expectations in A'a Teyze's Home Juxtaposed with the Freedom of A'a Teyze's Garden Space

The gender dynamics in this community are really overwhelming for me. I find that I don't really understand the ways in which I am supposed to behave, particularly as someone who is neither a man nor a woman a boy or a girl, but who is read in this context as a girl and who is expected to meet certain sorts of care obligations. Yesterday, when A'a Teyze's family came over with guests, I was expected to treat the children with a certain sort of care and attention that sort of met the requirements of giving myself over to them but not necessarily in a fun and joyful way. Or in the ways I have observed that the men are allowed to and expected to. I don't really understand how the men are allowed to parade the children as if they did any sort of labor to provide or bring them into the world—they are able to just hold them and play them and be «monsters» but not actually put energy or attention into caring for them. Yes, I had a conversation with A'a Teyze in which I expressed that I felt that the village was like a prison, and she responded, «but an open prison», and I tried to get her to understand that her telling me what to do actually violates the idea of being able to live whatever life I want to live because my life belongs to me. But she didn't understand and she kept saying, «but this is our village and this is how we do things in our village,» as if there is no other way to live. As if there is no other way to experience yourself in the world. I also see that A'a Teyze watches the exact same television station every single night and I thought for the longest time there were no other television stations. But there are other television stations and she just watches the exact same traditional *halk müziği* (folk music) station every single day. It has the same walnut commercials running on it constantly and continuously.

Someone with a survey came over the other day and was asking political questions to see how A'a felt about the political climate and to what she was going to give her vote. And I thought it was really interesting that the other women in the house, Nuray Abla and her daughter Olcay, were helping her answer the questions and she would look to them to ask them for clarification and they would help her answer and then they would turn to her ... or they would even answer on her behalf. Or say that is not really a question that someone asks during a study or someone asks during a survey when they go to someone's house.

I think I was really taken aback by how there are certain expectations regarding food and there are certain expectations regarding what kind of energy I am supposed to give over to food. I feel like the only kind of control that I can have is if I decide to eat or not to eat, which is really strange because I generally like to eat. I generally like to be someone who ... right now she [A'a Teyze] is telling me to hurry up and I am like I am already ready. I don't know what you want me to do.

As I was leaving today, A'a Teyze told me to watch out because in Torbalı there are a lot of «refugees» and they steal a lot. It's really interesting to me that she was promoting a certain fear-mongering and sort of promulgating and reinscribing and recirculating, trying to get me to be fearful. And so I think it's interesting that they want to further the notion that there's something particularly scary or dubious about refugees, which is really strange to me because I don't believe that to be true.

Yesterday I asked A'a Teyze what she does, and what people in the village do, for fun because things felt like a prison. The sort of expectations that are placed upon women feel like a prison. And so I told her actually that where I grew up, and how I grew up, no one told me what to do. It was more of a cultivation of a life without obstacles because if you want people to live a life in which they feel big and free then you don't actually put obstacles in every part of their world. You figure out ways to make them feel big. And she started to distract herself from hearing what I was talking about by turning on the television and raising the volume and things like that. I think she was trying to adjust her world and make herself feel like something more of what she was used to. Like I was rocking the boat and she was trying to make it more of what she was used to. I think it was interesting when I asked her what are the things people are bound here to do for fun and she said «weddings.» People go to weddings to have fun. Which is just so interesting to me.

Something I really appreciate about A'a Teyze is how her «no» means «no» and how her «yes» means «yes.» And how she is not embarrassed or ashamed of any parts of herself. Whatsoever. She just lives in accordance with what she wants and what she desires. And expected that others will do the same (fig. 3). The only thing she does work hard at is pushing her desires onto me. And that is just something I can't stand and that I find is really hard to deal with and maneuver as a researcher who is coming into a community. And who is trying to find my own way and deal with the things I want and need.

I find that men find me very interesting and try in different ways to get my attention. Try in different ways to get my time and energy. I wish

3   A'a Teyze's neighbor visits her in her garden.

I had my skateboard. I wish I had something that allowed me to move faster through the space. I do appreciate the ways that moving at a different speed within a landscape and a geography allows me a certain sort of autonomy and a certain sort of relationship with myself that is denied me when I move or when I appear to move at the same pace as others. I do recognize there is a certain sort of time. Like time parallels—I am moving at a pace, they are moving at a pace, and due to certain sorts of cultural concessions or ways in which I try and forgo my own autonomy and forgo my own boundaries in order to concede culturally, I find that I am being groomed for myself to slow down and I am being groomed for entry into a world that would normally be denied. Or that is denied people for not actually meeting me where I am at. Which is quickly, which is slowly sometimes, which is strangely upwards, downwards, and I find myself stopping constantly or moving fast or just changing my pace. For the sole purpose and reason of attempting to meet people where they are at—or to be courteous or kind or demonstrate some sort of understanding of myself as someone who does see and believe that there are cultural norms and cultural values that supersede or that overturn my own personal autonomy or my own personal endeavors or desires to sit and be with myself.

I think there's a certain way in Turkey, which doesn't really happen in other parts of the world. There is a posturing and signification that deals greatly with optics and the ways things seem, and the way things appear has a lot to do with how people interact with it. And I think that is scary, and I think that has a lot to do with the pathologization of women's bodies and the ways that people attempt to draw your attention or attempt to pull you in, which is very strange and weird because it is as if it's a given that your attention should be drawn or your attention should be pulled for the sole purpose or reason that someone does feel like you have something too. Because someone feels like they should get your attention or draw your attention away from what you are doing, which is very weird. My attention is very hard to acquire and I feel like I am cheaply bartering it. And I am cheaply doing it out by foregoing my own boundaries and autonomy under the guise of cultural concessions.

In *Life Beside Itself*, an account of how Canadian bureaucratic care may be understood as biopolitical, anthropologist Lisa Stevenson juxtaposes the Canadian state's response to Inuit deaths during the tuberculosis epidemic of the 1940s with the contemporary response of the Canadian state to Inuit suicide.[12] The juxtaposition of the archival record with Stevenson's contemporary ethnographic investigation allows «signature forms of care to come into relief»[13]. Through this juxtaposition, Stevenson reveals that Canadian bureaucratic care can ultimately be understood as «murderous» despite the ostensibly recuperative intentions of the Canadian state programs developed to address Inuit deaths.[14] Ottoman bureaucratic care of emancipated Africans prioritized the economic well-being of the Ottoman state and in so doing maintained Africans' laborial investment in the maintenance of Ottoman lands, economy, and production, an investment that mirrored the condition of Africans' enslavement.

In relocating emancipated Africans to the province of Aydın in the west of Ottoman Anatolia for the express purpose of land cultivation, the Ottoman government affixed emancipated African bureaucratic care to an Ottoman-turned-Turkish—in the disintegration of the Empire and precipitation of the Turkish state—productivist logic. Production was the arrangement of expected associations between emancipated Africans and the natural world around them. In their care, they were expected to work the land and produce crops for the state from it.

In this chapter, I argue that an attendance to the «otherwise» arrangements of plants and people— quotidian, personal, intimate—necessarily exposes the shape of prevailing grammars of governance and that in their exposure there is an implied admission about what is important, useful, and transformative in those otherwise arrangements—namely freedom. By exploring moments found in the home of 91-year-old Afro-Turkish woman, A'a Teyze, as well as from within A'a Teyze's garden, and in the commute between Izmir and this space, this combined ethnographic and discourse analysis demonstrates that everyday, intimate encounters between plants and Afro-Turkish people, in the form of their gardens, for example—as opposed to their labors within agricultural farming—challenge the grammars that have governed the daily lives of rural, Afro-Turkish communities in the small villages of the provinces of Izmir and Aydın. Despite the various grammars rendered through governance regarding the expected and allowable ways plants and shrubs and rocks and humans can interact with each other within a given space, there are otherwise grammars that can and have emerged. These otherwise grammars are of new languages and new associations. New languages and associations that not only subvert those arbitrated through governance but also produce emergent grammars of freedom in everyday life. Archival records of this program, intended to resettle manumitted Africans into «empty state lands»[15] by Sultan Abdulhamid II in an effort to compensate for a newly, non-housed, non-jobbed population demonstrating a need to resolve grounds for British intervention in alignment with the General Act of the Brussels Conference, cannot be located in either the Hansard debates of the UK Parliament, or in The National Archives in Kew, or the Ottoman archives in Istanbul. However, traces of «otherwise» ruins mediated through the use of ethnography argue for agrarian modes of relating within Turkish communities in western Turkey, where African-descendants of assumed resettled populations are observably in existence and effectively produce the conditions for a «black» or else «Afro-Turkish» ontology.

1   To be candid, I have been to Palestine under occupation by Israel.
2   Mint and vitex.
3   Erdem 1996, 179.
4   Erdem 1996, 179–181.
5   Erdem 1996.
6   Toledano 2007, 12.
7   Erdem 1996.
8   Roberts et al. 1970, 27.
9   Roberts et al. 1970.
10 Erdem 1996.
11 Erdem 1996.
12 Stevenson 2014, 3.
13 Stevenson 2014, 3.
14 Stevenson 2014, 3.
15 Erdem 1996, 183.

Image Sources

1–3 Photographs from Author's Personal Archive.

Erdem 1996
Y. H. Erdem: Slavery in the Ottoman Empire and Its Demise, 1800–1909 (New York 1996).

Kayacan / Karaer 2008
G. Kayacan / M. Karaer: Sessiz Bir Geçmişten Sesler: Afrika Kökenli ‹Türk› Olmanın Dünü ve Bugünü [Voices from a Silent Past: The Past and Present of Being a «Turk» of African Origin] (Istanbul 2008).

Roberts et al. 1970
T. D. Roberts et al.: Area Handbook for the Republic of Turkey (Washington 1970).

Stevenson 2014
L. Stevenson: Life beside Itself: Imagining Care in the Canadian Arctic (Oakland, CA 2014).

Toledano 1982
E. R. Toledano: The Ottoman Slave Trade and its Suppression, 1840–1890 (Princeton 1982).

Toledano 2007
E. R. Toledano: As if Silent and Absent: Bonds of Enslavement in the Islamic Middle East (New Haven, CT 2007).

Ayşegül Dinççağ Kahveci, born in Istanbul, is an architect and urban planner based in Berlin. After completing her Abitur at the German Private High School (Deutsche Schule Istanbul) in 2004, she graduated with a Master Engineer Architect (Dipl.-Ing. Architektin) degree from the University of the Arts Berlin (Universität der Künste Berlin) in 2010. Throughout and after her studies, she worked in architecture and design studios in Istanbul, Berlin, and New York, contributing to urban renewal projects in Turkey from 2010 to 2012, with a focus on strategic and participatory planning. In 2014, she became a member of the Berlin Chamber of Architects (Architektenkammer Berlin) and started working as an independent architect. From 2015 to 2016 she furthered her expertise by completing the Design Thinking programme at Hasso Plattner Institute, later co-founding a human-centred design collective. From 2019 to 2023, she was a research assistant in the DFG-Research Training Group «Identity and Heritage» at TU Berlin. She is currently pursuing her PhD at Universität der Künste Berlin, focusing on «Reclaiming Localities on Imbros.» Her research interests include interdisciplinary methodologies in intersection of architecture, material culture and critical heritage studies.

Vera Egbers is an archaeologist specialized in ancient Western Asia with research interests in subjectivation processes, sensory archaeology, architecture, feminist approaches, and archaeology of modernity. After studying in Berlin, Istanbul, and Paris, she later held fellowships at the Department of Anthropology in Harvard as well as at the Research Center for Anatolian Studies of Koç University Istanbul. She received her PhD from the Institute of Near Eastern Archaeology at Freie Universität Berlin – published 2023 in Sidestone Press Leiden («Thirdspace in Assyria and Urartu»). Vera participated in various field projects in Turkmenistan, Iraqi-Kurdistan, Turkey, and Germany. From 2020 to 2023 she was a Postdoc at the Brandenburg University of Technology Cottbus-Senftenberg, where she worked with architect Özge Sezer on the meaning and impact of rural space in times of political and social change in 20th century (CE) Turkey. After traveling for one year with the *Reisestipendium* of the German Archaeological Institute, she now works as Junior Professional Officer at the Living Heritage Entity of UNESCO.

Eva Maria Froschauer studied architecture at the Art University Linz as well as postgraduate studies at the ETH Zürich. Since 1998 she has pursued freelance work as an author and specialist journalist. From 2001 to 2007 she was research assistant at the Bauhaus University Weimar; in 2008 she received her PhD in Architectural History from that institution. From 2009 to 2011 she was research assistant at the Brandenburg University of Technology Cottbus, at the Department of Theory of Architecture; she founded and was until 2017 board member of the Netzwerk Architekturwissenschaft. 2011/12 she was a Research Fellow at the IKKM-Weimar; from 2013 to 2017 academic assistant in art history at BTU Cottbus-Senftenberg, where she received her habilitation in 2017 and became Assistant Professor of Art History until 2019. Since 2020 she has been Professor of Architectural History and Theory at Berliner Hochschule für Technik. University of Applied Sciences in Berlin (BHT). Her main research interests are: (historical) media of architecture, criticism and mediation; collecting as a «tool of design» and the term and methods «reflective design research».

Paolo Gruppuso is a social anthropologist working as a research fellow within the Horizon Europe research project «BioTraCes: Biodiversity and Transformative Change for plural and nature positive societies» at the University of Catania, Italy. His research interests focus on societal relations with wetlands and rivers in Europe. He has published articles in journals such as Conservation & Society, Social Anthropology/Anthropologie Sociale, Theory, Culture & Society. From November 2024 he will conduct a research project on European wetlands funded by the German Research Council and based at the Rachel Carson Center for Environment and Society, at LMU, Munich, Germany.

Aleksa Korolija is an architect graduated from the Politecnico di Milano in 2012 with a thesis in urban-design and landscape. Since 2017, he holds a PhD in Architecture, Urban Design and Conservation of Housing and Landscape. His PhD research has focused on Yugoslav post-WWII architecture and urbanism, in particular the memorial landscape as a multidisciplinary field of architectural design embedding symbolical and figurative meanings. His research on the memorials by Bogdan Bogdanovic has been published in 2023 as a monograph entitled *Di pietra e di piuma: Bogdan Bogdanovic e lo spazio memoriale*. From 2017 to 2020, he held a post-doc position as member of the European-funded project *MODSCAPES – Modernist reinventions of the rural landscape in Politecnico di Milano* (Polimi). His research has focused on the Italian inner colonisation and mapping the formal and the social impact of technical and infrastructural networks in the rural realm. Currently he is an adjunct professor at the School of Architecture Urban Planning Construction Engineering at Politecnico di Milano (Polimi) teaching Architectural Design.

Cristina Pallini is an architect (Politecnico di Milano, 1990) and holds a PhD from IUAV (2001). Associate Professor at the Department of Architecture Built Environment and Construction Engineering, Politecnico di Milano, where she teaches Architectural Design Studio at AUIC School. PI in PUMAH (Planning Urban Management and Heritage, 2012-2016) and MODSCAPES (Modernists reinventions of the rural landscape, 2016–2019). PL in UpGranT (Updating the Grand Tour, 2023–2026). Her research on the relationship between architectural design, settlement dynamics, and urban change has been funded by Italian and foreign institutions, including AKPIA@MIT (2004), the Onassis Foundation (2006), and Newcastle University (SALP, 2016).

Marta Prista holds a PhD in Anthropology. She is a researcher at CRIA – Center for Research in Anthropology, having integrated its Executive Board in 2015–2018 and 2021–2024, and at In2Past – Associate Laboratory for Research and Innovation in Heritage, Arts, Sustainability and Territory, where she co-coordinates the research line Museums, Monuments and its Collections. She has also been an Invited Assistant Professor at NOVA University School of Social Sciences and Humanities and co-coordinator of training courses on heritage. Her research delves into the uses of culture with special focus on the memory of the 20th century and its objectification in the fields of heritage and tourism. Among others, she was a researcher in the projects *MODSCAPES – Modernist Reinvention of the Rural Landscapes* (HERA 3rd JPR 2016–2019) and *#ECOS – Exiles, Countering Silence: Memories, Objects and*

Narratives of Uncertain Times (Europe for Citizens 2019–2022), currently being the Co-PI of the project *Building Salazar's people: Architecture in the making of Portugueseness (1932–1945)* (FCT 2023–2025). She also co-curated exhibitions like *Out of Monument. Memories of the 1940 Exhibition* (EGEAC 2016), *Are You a Tourist?* (EGEAC 2019) and *Countering Silence* (#ECOS 2020), and published and co-organized scientific events within these fields of interests, like the book *Vila Medieval* (FFMS 2019) or the *Congress of Public History in Portugal* (2023; 2024).

Özge Sezer received her bachelor's degree in architecture from Izmir Institute of Technology and her master's degree in architectural history from Istanbul Technical University. In 2019 she received her PhD with her dissertation «Idealization of the Land: Forming the New Rural Settlements in the Early Republican Period of Turkey» from TU Berlin. Her first monograph *Forming the Modern Turkish Village: Nation Building and Modernization in Rural Turkey during the Early Republic*, published by Transcript Verlag in 2022, was fully funded by Zeit Stiftung Ebelin und Gerd Bucerius. Özge Sezer worked as an architect in restoration and conservation projects of historic buildings and archeological sites in Turkey and as an adjunct lecturer in Art and Architectural History in Izmir and Berlin. From 2020 to early 2024 she was a post-doctoral member and associated researcher in the DFG Research Training Group 1913 «Cultural and Technological Significance of Historic Buildings» at Brandenburg University of Technology Cottbus-Senftenberg. Currently she is an independent researcher in architectural history based in Berlin, Germany.

Mayowa Anjolaoluwa Willoughby is a literary theorist who graduated from the Africana Studies & Research Center at Cornell University in 2018 with a thesis in Africana Studies. Their PhD research has focused on Afro-Turkish identity formation in Turkey, in particular the intimacy of the General Act of Brussels 1890 with the semiotics of blackness in contemporary Turkey. From 2018 to 2019, they held a visiting researcher appointment at Koc University as a recipient of the Koc-Holding Fellowship through the Institute for Turkish Studies. Their research focused on the role of land resettlement in the formation of minoritarian identities in contemporary Turkey. Currently they are an independent researcher based in Ithaca, New York.